THE CHANGI BROWNLOW

'Given our reputation in war, which is strong, and our reputation in sport, which is also strong, Changi Brownlow is a fascinating combination.'
Australian Rules football legend, Ron Barassi

Also by Roland Perry

The Australian Light Horse
Monash: The Outsider Who Won a War
Last of the Cold War Spies
The Fifth Man
The Programming of the President
Mel Gibson, Actor, Director, Producer
The Exile: Wilfred Burchett, Reporter of Conflict
Lethal Hero
Sailing to the Moon
Elections Sur Ordinateur
Programme for a Puppet (fiction)
Blood is a Stranger (fiction)
Faces in the Rain (fiction)
Bradman's Invincibles
The Ashes: A Celebration
Miller's Luck: The Life and Loves of Keith Miller,
Australia's Greatest All-Rounder
Bradman's Best
Bradman's Best Ashes Teams
The Don
Captain Australia:
A History of the Celebrated Captains of Australian Test Cricket
Bold Warnie
Waugh's Way
Shane Warne, Master Spinner

Documentary Films

The Programming of the President
The Raising of a Galleon's Ghost
Strike Swiftly
Ted Kennedy & the Pollsters
The Force

THE CHANGI BROWNLOW

ROLAND PERRY

This book is dedicated to the memory of
Peter Chitty's wife, Lilian

Published in Australia and New Zealand in 2010
by Hachette Australia
(an imprint of Hachette Australia Pty Limited)
Level 17, 207 Kent Street, Sydney NSW 2000
www.hachette.com.au

10 9 8 7 6 5 4 3 2 1

Copyright © Roland Perry 2010

National Library of Australia
Cataloguing-in-Publication data

Perry, Roland.
The Changi Brownlow / Roland Perry.

978 0 7336 2464 3 (pbk.)

Changi POW Camp (Changi, Singapore)
Australian football—Singapore—Changi.
World War, 1939–1945—Prisoners and prisons, Japanese.
Prisoners of war—Australia.

940.547252

Cover design by Luke Causby/Blue Cork
Cover photographs: portrait and medal courtesy of Australian War Memorial (AWM P04441.001/AWM REL32808); other photographs from author's collection
Maps by Raylee Sloane/Kinart
Text Design by Post Pre-Press Group
Typeset in 12/17pt Sabon by Post Pre-Press Group
Printed in Australia by Griffin Press, Adelaide, an accredited ISO AS/NZS 14001:2004 Environmental Management System printer

The paper this book is printed on is certified by the Programme for the Endorsement of Forest Certification scheme. Griffin Press holds PEFC chain of custody SGS-PEFC/0594. PEFC promotes environmentally responsible, socially beneficial and economically viable management of the world's forests.

PEFC/COC-0594

Contents

SINGAPORE: THE JAPANESE TAKEOVER, FEBRUARY 1942

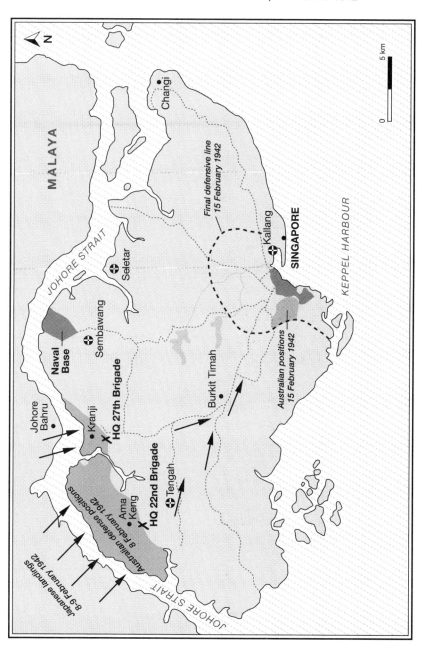

THAI-BURMA RAILWAY 1942-1945

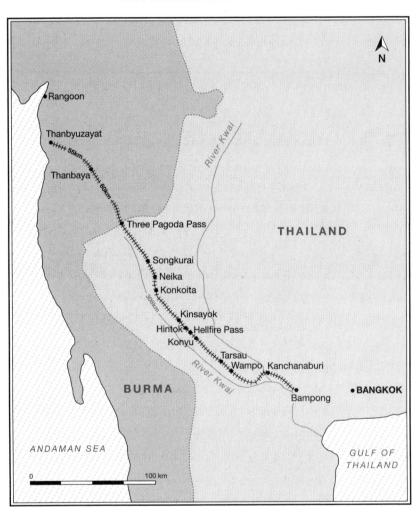

Changi Rules

The Japanese guards at Changi prison in Singapore's north-east filed out of their barracks, some with rifles slung over their shoulders, others carrying machine-guns. There was growing concern among the captors about the huge number of Australian POWs sauntering past guards from their quarters. They were heading for the Australian Rules football match on the brown padang (field) carved out of the jungle between the two main barracks: Selarang and Roberts. The date was Sunday 24 January 1943. More than 70,000 British prisoners, including Australians, Gurkhas and Indians had been in Changi for nearly a year. This 'event', the final game of the season, promised to draw the largest crowd ever assembled in the prison for any event except a mandatory musical concert put on in the square at Selarang prison early in 1942.

The day had begun fine, with no wind. Now it was a typically cloyingly hot afternoon when the humidity sapped energy and slowed minds. At 2 p.m., the crowd had built to more than 10,000. POWs were packed into the viewing area, some spilling on to the hard arena. Japanese guards were moving discreetly beyond the crowd, positioning themselves and their weapons in the thick jungle surrounds.

There was no reason to expect a mass break-out or uprising. Their moves were precautionary. The captors had never really understood the ferocity of the footballers or indeed the spectators, but they had learned that there was more exuberance than malice in any on or off-field demonstrations. Six months of competition had proved that. The Australian organisers of the matches had formed a 'tribunal' with guidelines for dealing with players who transgressed on the field. The umpires were strict, aware that an on-field fracas could see some of the more trigger-happy guards using their machine-guns to break it up. The captors had become used to the games played on Wednesdays and the weekend. The crowds ranged up to 7,000 during the 'season' and there had not been one major incident. But the build-up today was worrying for the captors. There was more excitement. Even the sight of 200 cheering amputees in open-carriages of a train chugging along the embankment by the side of the padang raised tensions as they and the fans greeted each other. This was a special occasion. Anything could happen. Japanese officers had given the orders: all those off duty were reassigned for the afternoon just in case this encounter between 'Victoria' and 'The Rest of Australia' got out of hand. The atmosphere in the growing crowd was festive. A band played on the arena. A buzz of anticipation ran through the spectators.

They were in for a treat—a hard-fought encounter between two talented teams. Many of the players had performed at the highest level in their states. The two teams had been chosen from a pool of more than 200 registered footballers, most of whom had performed during the season for one of the six teams.

Sports had been allowed in Changi in the first year. Cricket, rugby, basketball, soccer, athletics and others kept the prisoners occupied while the Japanese decided what to do with the massive numbers of men in their charge. The building of a railway to the north through Thailand to Burma, where the Japanese had taken control from the British, was already secretly underway. POWs were being treated as slave labour. Many were dying of malnutrition and because of the brutality.

Oblivious of this, in 1942, sports went on in the Singapore prisons. The Australians played the English at cricket in games called the 'Changi Ashes'. They were hit and giggle one-day matches, with everyone having a bat and a bowl. Rugby League and Union games were played hard and attracted modest crowds. They were willing affairs, with broken collar bones, ribs and limbs too common for the Japanese officers' comfort. They spoke to the British and Australian officers in an attempt to get the players to tone down the vigour. The Japanese could see the bigger, stronger POWs being unfit for later work on the railway.

A basketball competition was more to the captors' liking. It was competitive, but without the body contact. The British had a soccer competition that, while also without body contact, was a further concern for the officers. Players were receiving too many injuries to legs and necks. A year of malnutrition and diseases in captivity had weakened bones, sapped muscles and caused alarming weight loss.

The Japanese now viewed every activity at Changi through the prism of the ongoing and proposed railway, which they planned to run for 415 kilometres and well into Burma. Their aim was to go overland to avoid the sea-lanes, where Allied submarines were wreaking havoc, and to prepare for an attack on India, the 'Jewel in the British Crown'. It seemed feasible to the Imperial Army commanders given the relative ease with which they had taken Singapore.

Sporting games had continued through 1942, but at the end of the year, the Japanese had shut down all physical contact sports. They wanted as many men as possible fit for the fast building of the railway. This final game of Australian Rules had been a special dispensation. When it was over, all such competition would cease. (Within months, thousands more of the POWs would be taken by train from Singapore to Bangkok, and then marched to the railway, where work had been going on for half a year.) All POWs sent to Thailand would find the deprivations and hardships at Changi mild by comparison as the Japanese moved with manic haste towards completion of the road and rail routes to Burma.

The football competition was a tribute to the durability, determination and common sense of the organisers and players.

Victorian ambulance driver Sergeant Leslie Allan 'Peter' Chitty led out the Victorians in their traditional navy blue guernsey with the big white 'V' on the front, and white shorts. He had a compact build and seemed extremely fit. There was determination and pride in his expression as he turned to his players, clapping hands and encouraging them.

'No game for the Saints or any other club meant more to me,' Chitty said. 'It was a great honour to lead out those players wearing the "Big V" in front of the cheering crowd. They were packed into the padang and the Japs had stopped them coming from Selarang [the prison]. I could see the amputees in the train, waving and yelling. I loved those blokes. They had suffered more than most, some losing not one but two limbs. But they were the most cheerful patients I ever dealt with. I especially wanted them to be at the game, and they loved it.'[1]

Tall, powerfully built Lou Daley, formerly an outstanding ruckman for Geelong and Subiaco, led out The Rest of Australia in white singlets and a red 'V', and black shorts. The big crowd, estimated 10 minutes before the scheduled 3.30 p.m. commencement at about 12,500, roared their approval with hardly a boo for either side. Soon afterwards, Chitty led the warm-up, and then his players bunched and headed for 'the Selarang end' goals. After a few minutes, the diminutive umpire 'Chicken' Smallhorn (a former champion) signalled for the teams to approach a bench on one side of the ground. 'Chick' was the brain and inspiration behind the competition and its organisation. It was his idea to create the 'Changi Brownlow', a replica of the top award in Australia's number one football competition, the Victorian Football League. It was named after a prominent Geelong player, official and Victorian Football League (VFL) administrator Charles Brownlow. From 1924, the medal was given each year to the 'Best and Fairest' player.

Short and at just 61 kilograms, Smallhorn had shown exceptional courage for his size as a football star for inner city (Melbourne) Fitzroy, where he was born and bred. He knew a lot about the Brownlow, having won the medal himself as an agile winger in 1933, aged just 22. Smallhorn's win was all the more meritorious given the champions at Fitzroy, such as Haydn Bunton, an 'import' from Western Australia. Smallhorn would have loved playing in this game, but a broken leg and a nagging knee injury to his other leg ended his playing days in the 1940 season. It caused him to join the army. But while he could no longer twist, turn and baulk like a wizard, he could run backwards and forwards in straight lines, like an umpire. That was his role throughout the season and on this final, special occasion.

Japanese guards in towers set in the jungle eased their machine-guns into place. About 50 armed guards at all points beyond the crowd and padang watched, not alarmed but still alert.

Smallhorn climbed onto the bench. He called for quiet, his voice reedy and frail after a recent illness. He waved to Ben Barnett (an organiser of the Changi competition and a former Australian Test cricketer), who moved forward and handed him a small velvet purse. He passed it to the popular Captain John Frew of the Australian General Hospital. Frew pulled out the Changi Brownlow medal, hung on a silver chain. The 'Brownlow' was the most prized medallion in Australian football. At Changi, this unofficial award meant more than any 'real' Brownlow to every player and spectator alike. It was a symbol of things excellent, fair and courageous in Australian sporting life. These characteristics were even more important in Changi to survive the ordeal of imprisonment.

Frew held the small medal up to the crowd and said: 'During our season the umpires have cast votes 3, 2 and 1 for this medal—the Changi Brownlow.' The spectators cheered and clapped. 'It is my great honour to announce the winner by a clear margin: Sergeant L. A. "Peter" Chitty.' The big crowd voiced appreciation. Smallhorn motioned to Chitty, who was standing in the tight group of Victorians. He appeared shocked.

'Peter Chitty had a truly magnificent season,' Smallhorn said later, 'I saw almost every game he played. He copped plenty because he was so good. But he was tough. Really tough. And fit. In all my playing days and afterwards as a commentator, I never saw a player with more stamina. He had skill and was a born leader.'[2]

'I really couldn't believe it,' Chitty remarked. 'No-one had warned me. I knew I'd had a good, even season, and I did captain the best team, so we were bound to score more [umpire] votes. But this was an unreal moment. I was floating.'[3]

He emerged from the middle of his players and strode to the bench. Frew placed the medal around Chitty's neck, and gave him a firm handshake.

'Well done, Peter,' Frew said. 'You were the best player of the competition.' He made sure Chitty examined the coin-size silver piece. On the front was a small gold piece embedded near the top. At the bottom, it read: 'Geelong FC'—which was the team for which Chitty played in Changi.[4]

Already engraved on the back was:

'1943 Changi POW Brownlow Medal Won by Sgt L. A. Chitty.'

Chitty was overwhelmed, but had the presence of mind to take off the medal, kiss it and hand it back to Frew for safe-keeping while he played. He tried hard to focus on his next assignment of winning this game. Yet while it was a surreal moment, Chitty collected himself to make a quick speech.

'I would not trade that medal for Haydn Bunton's three Brownlows,' Chitty commented. The crowd applauded and cheered. He turned to Smallhorn and Ben Barnett and thanked them for their efforts in running the competition. He concluded by saying that the two teams should show the 'gentlemen of Japan's Imperial Army' what they 'were all about!'[5]

The crowd roared. The two teams were ready to go.

Umpire Smallhorn tossed the coin. Daley won and elected to kick into the breeze. The ball was bounced by Smallhorn at precisely 3.30 p.m. in front of the fans, who would be transported, in their minds at least, back to any given Saturday in their cities and home towns around the vast expanse of Australia. Observers likened the atmosphere to that of a big league final. The padang area could not have contained another spectator. Hundreds now had spilled onto the arena but just outside the white marked boundary line. Guards began closing off the barracks, keeping all other POWs behind the barbed wire. Their attention would be on the massed group of prisoners for the next two and a half hours.

Players threw their bodies in as if they were in a final on a grander stage at home in what quickly became a willing affair. Chitty, as the 'Vics' skipper and best player, came in for undue attention from the opposition intent on pressuring him out of the game. But this running machine from country Victoria could not be contained. He moved as if it were the most important sporting performance in his life. At times, he was a player possessed, always dashing, chasing, tackling, inspiring, very much in the mode of a modern-day Gary Ablett Junior. Chitty relied on his exceptional stamina, which had seen him dominate the season for 'Geelong'. Smallhorn had told him he gained Brownlow votes (best, second best and third best on ground) in every match he played. In this game, he wished more than in any other to excel. He had played a couple of games of league football (for the St Kilda club) in 1936 before a workplace injury ended his career at the elite level. He never dreamt he would one day captain his state—Victoria—even if it were an unofficial representation as a POW in a foreign land ruled by an uncompromising enemy. Chitty wore the 'Big V' and led ably on the field, as he did in his job as sergeant on the motor ambulance convoy. As ever, he led by example. In the war, as an ambulance driver working in hazardous conditions, he never asked his men to do something he would not do himself. All his subordinates knew of his mental and physical courage, whether taking a risk to save a fallen soldier from the battlefield or in dodging enemy fire in getting a man to hospital. On the field, he paved the way by doing the team things: shepherding, tackling, bumping, diving into packs, backing into packs. Chitty never stopped. He was a rover, which in Australian Rules meant he followed the ball up and down the ground. He rarely rested to give the second rover a go on the ball; not because he was selfish, but because he was rarely fatigued. His stamina was legendary, running an estimated half-marathon every match. Even with the starvation rations doled out by the Japanese in Changi, Chitty was one of the few men who could claim his weight had not changed. His metabolism seemed to adapt despite his labouring in the camp and exertion on the football field. When others dropped a third, even half their bodyweight, his frame remained static, the same lean, muscular machine all the time. There were reasons for this. He was a 'bushie' who could scrounge extra food and digest what others would find unpalatable. The upshot was a durability that few in the camp possessed. On top of this, he had always been a fitness fanatic, decades before it was fashionable or even believed as something worthwhile. These things combined made him a formidable, unstoppable competitor on the field.

His leadership this day was the difference between the two teams in a tight, spectacular match that had the crowd roaring constantly. At half-time, the Vics led by only 9 points. At three-quarter-time, it was 10 points. At the final break, Chitty's address to his team-mates highlighted that they had to keep moving and run their opponents ragged. It had been a consistent refrain all year. He wanted his players not just to tackle their opponents but to 'thump' them into the ground. It meant, he said, that every time one of The Rest took possession they would get rid of the ball in a hurry. He urged his men to bump hard and often. Chitty warned it would be tough but reminded them that in 25 minutes they could take it easy and have a well-earned drink. He added, as he always did, that there would no second chances. He believed in the survival of the fittest. The most durable would win.[6]

And he was right. The game was in the balance in the last half of the last quarter, when all participants were almost out on their feet. At the most critical moment, Chitty spun from a pack, baulked past two opponents and let go an awesome torpedo punt, which spiralled up and through the upright bamboo goalposts. And with it went a huge roar crescendo from the spectators that lingered. Everyone knew it could be the 'sealing' goal.

Chitty's endeavour, drive and captaincy proved the most telling factors when his team broke clear at the finish.

He was elated.

'Next to my wedding [day],' he said later, 'that experience with the medal and victory, was the most memorable day of my life.'[7]

It was a brilliant moment in a dark experience that was about to get worse when he would be sent with 'F Force'—7,000 British and Australians POWs—to slave on the Burma–Thai railway. This would test even his freakishly high mental and physical strengths, and will.

To understand the development of Peter Chitty's capacities and character, we must go back to his roots and background in the remote north-east of Victoria at the foot of the Snowy Mountain Range.

2

The Long-Distance Runner

Young Peter Chitty left the family farm running in the half-light of dawn. The schoolbag on his back was an extra burden, but it did not impede him as he loped along barefoot. Peter headed up the first hill, stepping up the pace to meet the challenge. He was in Victoria's remote north-east Mitta Range of mountains and hills—grey, blue then green—as an unconvincing sun rose and changed the hue in the hour's run. It was August and mid-winter. A white mist to his left had settled on the peaks like a white crochet blanket as he headed north-east. To his immediate right was the flat country of a sheep and cattle property. In the distance to the right was the range including Mount Kosciuszko, Australia's highest mountain at 2,228 metres.

There was dew on the bush track over several hills that he pounded up and down as he crossed or passed landmarks: to his left was a waterfall, then 'The Bluff', a hefty escarpment; in front of him was Stony Creek, which he would cross twice; and the bush by the side of hills. Along the way he set 120 rabbit traps camouflaged by dirt among the myriad burrows between 5 and 6 kilometres into the run.

The end of his 8 kilometre run was the local state school of North Cudgewa, not far from the one-pub town of Cudgewa, a few kilometres from the Murray River, which formed the border between New South Wales and Victoria.

Peter would arrive at school at about 8.30 a.m. He would sit for a while, regain his composure and join in any sports before first class: in the winter, football; in summer, cricket; in spring, athletics.

School finished at 3.30 p.m. He set out again for the 8 kilometre run home, stopping at the traps to see if he had any catches, which would be placed in his bag. This went on five days a week.

He was 13 years of age and covering 80 kilometres a week, equivalent to two marathons. Considering he had no running shoes and the undulating, sometimes steep hills he covered, these runs needed endurance and stamina.

*

Peter had been making this run for two years. It had built tremendous strength in his body and lungs. His legs were strong. This 'training' was more to put meat on the table for his parents (Allan and Hannah) and 11 siblings than a deliberate, organised effort to be fit for some form of sport. On the football field, he was a rover—someone who followed the ball—all over the big paddocks for Australian Rules, which was *the* sport in the upper Murray region. The games lasted about 100 minutes. He literally did not stop moving. In last quarters, when games were often won or lost, he would dominate. No-one could stay with him.

Peter Chitty as a teenager had the 'motor' of a hardened athlete a decade older.

He was a sturdy lad to begin with, inheriting good physical genes from both parents. Most of the men in the family were of similar physique. The oldest brother Phil (aged 16) was the strongest. Already Peter's sinewy limbs were growing faster than his chest and shoulders, which would fill out later.

The weekend was not a rest from physical activity. There might be sport to play—tennis and athletics in the summer, football in the winter. There was also boxing all year round, and big brother Phil would be looking for one of the brothers to go a few rounds with him. In the mid-1920s, few of the youths in the district would take on Phil. Peter would more often than not have to be the sparring partner. He would never beat Phil in a real fight. Age, weight and height would tell against him. But the consolation was Peter's capacity as a pugilist. He was not the type to seek a fight or to bully. It was not in his nature. Yet he was known from then on to be very 'handy with his fists', if the need arose, as it often did in country Australia.

Saturday and Sunday were still work days in the bush. There were always cows to milk (at 4.30 a.m.), fences to build or mend, cattle to herd, crops to tend to. Chitty Sr. also kept an abundant orchard, growing grape vines, peaches, figs, apples, nectarines, oranges, carrots, cabbages, tomatoes, beans and peas. This precious patch had to be tended with care. In the Depression years, it kept the family self-sufficient in food, along with meat from sheep, cattle and the ubiquitous rabbit.

Bush-tracking was another outlet, as much occupation as pastime. The boys would hunt often. Just about everything of size that flew or ran in the animal kingdom was 'fair game' in the Depression years. Fishing in the river streams and Murray was bountiful with cod, red fin, and fresh-water crayfish. All the Chittys were proficient with a rifle. Rabbits, birds, wallabies, kangaroos and even wombats were on the menu. The women could shoot too. Peter's son Lindsay recalled his uncle Phil's wife Jean being useful with a 'little 22 pee rifle'.

'No rosella was safe with aunty Jean around,' he said, 'she would cook them and they were beautiful! Conservationists and environmental bureaucrats had not been invented in the 1930s and 1940s.'[1]

The Depression years of 1930s Australia were an apprenticeship in survival. Bush life was the master-class.

By 1935, Peter, at 22, was a compact build, standing 170 cm and weighing 76 kg. He had thrown off his boyish looks and had the typical Chitty facial features of compact nose, strong jaw and prominent ears. Football had developed as his favourite sport. He was biggish for a rover for Cudgewa, but could play centre or forward. He was a prodigious kick and a determined overhead mark for his size. He had balance and poise either side of his body, and was an outstanding stab-kick pass. Peter also had pace. He displayed it to advantage playing in the centre for the Border United club, and in 1935 missed out by one vote in winning the Ovens and Murray League's Best and Fairest. It was a fearsome competition and included another five teams—Albury, Wangaratta, Rutherglen, Yarrawonga and Corowa. Despite a brilliant performance by Chitty, Border United, after a nine-game winning streak, lost the grand final to Rutherglen.

1936 was a year of change for him. Scouts from the big league in Melbourne, trawling the Ovens and Murray competition in the border region, had spotted Peter in scintillating form during 1935. The Melbourne bayside club of St Kilda invited him down for the 1936 season. Peter accepted. He would be paid a pittance. A job was found for him in a local wooden box making factory. In October 1935, soon after arriving in Melbourne, he met the attractive Lilian May Prowse, 19 (the only daughter of George and Annie Prowse in a family of seven children). Peter escorted her home to Brunswick, using up all his money. He proceeded to walk the 13 kilometres to St Kilda, where he was lodging. It was an instant mutual appeal. She liked his quiet strength. He had 'friendly, warm eyes'.

'He was a strong character,' she recalled, 'yet a gentleman. The thing that attracted me most was that he was a good "family man".'[2]

This was code for a bloke who would work hard, not

stray, and be more interested in being at home with the wife and children than drinking with the boys at the pub, despite mythology about the 'average' 1930s Australian male. He was not a rare breed in 1930s Australia. Nor was this type in abundance. In keeping with the times of deep economic depression, the steady 'family man' was more attractive than the footloose, irresponsible 'player'. In some ways, Lilian was in the same position as Chitty's mother Hannah. Her father George, a man of some means, had wanted her to marry a rich squatter. She had defied him in favour of a capable, solid, hard-working farm worker. Hannah never regretted a moment of her life with Allan. Similarly, Lilian decided on a partner determined to raise and provide for a family in tough times.

Peter and Lilian were married on 8 February 1936 at the Wesley Church, Melbourne, a few months before the football season. After a patient apprenticeship in the seconds, he was selected in Round 11 on the wing for the senior side for his first league match. It was against Fitzroy at the Brunswick Street oval, Fitzroy's home ground. A fair crowd of 10,000 attended on Saturday 18 July. Peter was 'toey'—keen to perform—in this debut game, rather than nervous. The 'Saints' (St Kilda) were 6th on the table of 12 teams with 5 wins and 5 losses. The 'Roys' (Fitzroy) were having a shocking season for such a star-studded side. Their captain-coach was Haydn Bunton, a triple winner of the Brownlow Medal. Doug Nicholls (one of the few Aboriginal players in the era, who represented Victoria and would later be Governor of South Australia) was a champion winger. Fitzroy's 'Chicken' Smallhorn, the diminutive winner of the 1933 Brownlow was present but did not play in the game. (He would later loom large in Chitty's life.) St Kilda, captained by Jack Perkins and coached by Dan Minogue, had a star full forward in Bill Mohr, who was top of the goal-kicking table.

The morning began in fog, but it lifted to reveal a fine mid-winter's day, with little wind—perfect for football. The Brunswick Street Oval was hard, dry and fast. The scoring was high. Chitty, wearing number 36, ran out for his first game in the seniors.

'I was 5 foot 7 inches and felt 6 foot tall,' he remarked. He was ready for the challenge. 'I was a fitness fanatic, worse than Tommy Hafey [the teetotalling successful Rules coach, who thrived on a super-physical condition well into his maturity]. My training included boxing, foot-running and wrestling.'[3]

He acquitted himself well in the game, using his speed and staying power to gather possessions against the talented Nicholls, who took the honours in a good battle. Chitty found himself often competing for the ball with the amazing Bunton, who was playing in the centre. St Kilda came from behind in a brilliant last quarter to win 19 goals 15 behinds (129), to 16 goals 9 behinds (105). Chitty was not in his side's top six performers but his effort would have secured him an immediate second game. A minor leg injury kept him out of Round 12.

He returned to the St Kilda firsts for Round 13 on 1 August against South Melbourne (the Swans)—at the Lakeside Oval, Albert Park. The crowd was bigger at 16,000. The Swans, second on the ladder, were one of the top crowd-pullers of the era, mainly because of their so-called 'Foreign Legion' of magnificent footballers, including Herbie Matthews (who would later win the Brownlow in 1940) and two of the finest forwards of all time—Laurie Nash and Bob Pratt. The Swans won a close, tough game, which had its free-flowing moments on another fine Saturday afternoon. The score was South Melbourne 14.19 (103) to St Kilda 13.11 (89). Best-on-ground Bill Mohr was magnificent, kicking eight goals. Bob Pratt was the Swans' best.[4]

Chitty had a useful match and had played well enough in his two appearances to be confident that if he persevered he would earn a permanent spot by the end of the season. Soon afterwards a workplace accident curtailed his career at the top level. A log for cutting rolled onto his leg, damaging a knee. He had no immediate future in the game and was forced to sit out the year.

'It was devastating for him,' Lilian recalled. 'All those hopes and dreams [of a career at St Kilda] were dashed.'[5]

Peter, in typical style, put the mishap behind him. Work prospects were better in the country. He brought his new bride home to the bush in far north-east Victoria where he took up farm-work once more.

The Chitty name was to run on in top football. Peter's younger brother Bob, 21, started the 1936 season with Sunshine in the next level down of Australian Rules in Victoria, the VFA (Victorian Football Association). Within a few games, the VFL's Carlton had recruited him. Bob was 177 centimetres and solid at 84 kilograms. Like Peter, he was talented. There was also the added dimension of the 'mongrel' in him. Even at his age, he had the reputation of being exceptionally tough. There were never 'beg-pardons' in his performances. He preferred the half-back flank, where he could slice his way through the oncoming opposition and deliver accurate long drop kicks to position. Carlton placed him in the centre in the second XVIII for the rest for 1936, an obvious grooming for advance in following years. He made his debut in the firsts in Round 7 of the 1937 game against Footscray and retained his spot for the season.

In the same year, on 23 February, Lilian gave birth to a brown-eyed, fair-haired daughter, Norma. Peter was further committed to the security of family life in the bush.

3

In the Name of the Emperor

During the tranquil Australian winter of 1937, Japan began a war against China with the aim of securing its vast raw material reserves and other resources. The Chinese put up strong resistance in the opening stanza in Shanghai, which surprised the Japanese, who bragged they would overrun their enemy quickly. The conflict dragged on until November. The two countries had fought on and off in smaller skirmishes since they clashed in Manchuria in 1931, and the invasion six years later was the result of a decade-long policy of Japanese imperialism to dominate China.

In tandem over that time, Japan's military took almost complete control of the Japanese Government. Political enemies were assassinated. Communists were persecuted. Indoctrination and censorship in education and media intensified. Naval and army officers took over key government posts, including the prime ministership.

After taking Shanghai, 50,000 Japanese soldiers of the Kwantung Army (which had been in Manchuria) marched on to the capital, Nanking. The Chinese defenders had the numbers and the ammunition but they were poorly trained and organised. The fierce Japanese forced their way into the city on 13 December. Their orders were chilling in their simplicity. They were to 'kill all captives'. This, in effect, was a directive and licence to slaughter anyone they wished. Ninety thousand Chinese soldiers were captured. The Japanese found surrender dishonourable in the extreme. It was a violation of their rigid code of military honour handed on down the centuries from a warrior past and drilled into every male from childhood. A soldier should either die fighting for the emperor or commit suicide rather than be taken by an enemy. This culture developed contempt for anyone (or any nation) who did not hold the same 'values'. Hence their Chinese captives were looked upon as less than human, and unworthy of life. This attitude was reinforced in propaganda and aided and abetted the order to liquidate them.

The Chinese POWs were trucked to the outskirts of Nanking. Then the butchery began, with Japanese officers encouraging their men to inflict maximum pain and suffering on the defenceless prisoners. This was meant to toughen the young 'warriors' for future battles. They were to become accustomed to showing no mercy. The Japanese had film units and scores of photographers taking stills to document the atrocities. The footage and shots would be used later for propaganda purposes and to frighten future enemies. Japanese soldiers conducted bayonet 'practice', decapitation and dismemberment. Cameramen moved in close for this 'action'. They directed the slaughterers to move among the mutilated and dead for this grisly documentation. Wide-angle camera pans and stills also caught the mowing down of rows of Chinese. Many were soaked with fuel and set alight.

With the men disposed of, the soldiers of the Imperial Army turned their attention to the women. More than 50,000 females, with hardly any discrimination for age, were gang-raped, then murdered by bayonet or bullet. Their blood lust up, the Japanese rampaged in the city, killing randomly and looting. They bundled people into buildings and set them on fire. Anyone who tried to escape by climbing on rooftops or leaping into the street was picked off by the Japanese, as if in some sadistic sport.

The carnage continued for six weeks until early February 1938. Then the Japanese settled in for a long occupation, having secured control of the entire China coast. Yet the Chinese nationalist government never surrendered completely.

After the shock of the blitz, the Japanese decided to pacify Nanking residents by distributing addictive narcotics such as opium and heroin. More than 50,000 people, including children, became addicted. The city's opium dens became a haven for lost minds that would not challenge the brutal and cunning conquerors. The Japanese soldiers had to be catered for too, not with drugs, which were banned to them, but women. After the initial depravity, Chinese 'comfort women' were organised, forcing females from 13 to 40 years of age into prostitution.

Japanese military correspondents dutifully reported many of the atrocities. The government wished to fuel Japan's militaristic mood towards so-called 'inferior peoples', the Chinese being at the top of the list in 1937 and 1938. Leading Australian papers carried page-one reports of the events in Nanking. But the public was sceptical or unconcerned. Like most Western nations, Australia, in general, was not bothered about happenings in Asia, despite it being in the same region.

Japan had been considered as a threat to Australia by only a few in the early 20th century. It was viewed until 1938 as a benign Asian neighbour. It had been an ally in World War I. Its navy had escorted the Australian armada carrying troops to the Western and Eastern Fronts. The Japanese had helped remove the enemy German boats from the South Seas and off the coast of Western Australia where they were a formidable presence. The British in the late 19th century had helped develop Japan's fleet. By the early 20th century it was a sea power to be reckoned with, as the Russians discovered in losing the Russo-Japanese War of 1904–05.

There had been minor-level Australian–Japan exchanges, especially concerning trade and people, since the 1850s. Thousands of Japanese came to Australia as traders and workers from the 1850s. The grand exhibitions in Sydney and Melbourne in the 1870s and 1880s increased those numbers, and they kept coming over the decades. The 'White Australia Policy' instituted by the new federal government in 1901, curtailed Asian immigration, and to a degree thwarted the Japanese connection. But there were soon concessions. Amendments in 1904 to the *Immigration Restriction Act*

1901 allowed Japanese merchants, tourists and students to enter the country on passports.

Until after World War I, Australia was dependent on British foreign policy for its alliances, which did not include the Japanese. But matters developed after the war. Cordiality was at its peak in 1928, when Vice Admiral Kobayashi became the first person to lay a wreath at the new memorial in King's Park, Sydney. It commemorated those servicemen and women lost by Australia in World War I. He mentioned in his speech the admiration his navy had for the Anzacs on Gallipoli and those who died on the beaches there. Sydney's archbishop replied with equal enthusiasm, suggesting that the relatives of the fallen would be grateful to the vice-admiral for his wreath-laying. Then the former head of Australia's Fifth Division during World War I, Lieutenant-General Talbot Hobbs recognised Japan's support.

'Had Japan stood aside,' he claimed in a pitch of high diplomacy and hyperbole, 'it is difficult to say what would have happened, especially to Australia.'

Relations slipped an almost indiscernible notch in 1931, when the Japanese invaded Manchuria and began their direct hostility towards the Chinese. Considering the bloody nose it had given China, it was wondered in Australian Government circles if it had aggressive intent elsewhere. The Australian Navy welcomed the visiting Japanese fleet into Sydney Harbour as it had done for many years. But in the greeting party this time was an intelligence officer (unbeknown to the foreign guests) liaising with them. Australian officers kept an eye on the onshore activities of their Japanese counterparts and sailors. If they used a camera near dockyards, it was reported. A note was made if they wandered around the Heads taking shots. Visitors to the Japanese ships were also recorded, including the representative of Mitsui & Co., which had arranged ships' provisions since 1907.

Then came Nanking in 1937. It was such a blatant and horrific act of aggression that the Australian Government was now far more alert to Japanese activity on its shores. The several thousand Japanese residents were put under surveillance. Some had been known as foreign spies for a few years. They were now shadowed and reported on. A laundryman who had arrived in 1901 and married an Australian was of particular interest. He dealt in espionage for the Japanese. His dirty linen in the demi-monde of spying would not be aired or exposed. He was too important to Australian intelligence. Its operatives kept watching. (In 1940, he was noted driving Japanese spies around Sydney, Newcastle and the Blue Mountains.)

Yet still in 1938, Japan was not viewed as a priority in terms of a threat to the British Commonwealth and its dominion, Australia. The main foreign developments capturing attention centred on Europe. The German chancellor, an 'odd', feisty Austrian, former World War I lance-corporal, Adolf Hitler, was busy rearming Germany and expanding the borders of the Nazi Third Reich through devious political moves.

Australian citizens with German background and connections were put under wide surveillance and scrutiny, as they had in the lead-up to World War I.

4

Fire-Storm

And Clancy of the Overflow came down to lend a hand,
No better horseman ever held the reins;
For never horse could throw him while the saddle-girths would
    stand,
He learnt to ride while droving on the plains.

From 'The Man from Snowy River' by Banjo Paterson

Peter Chitty honed his experience as a bushman in the late 1930s. Droving cattle was part of it in the tradition of 'The Man from Snowy River', in the territory that inspired the legendary verse by Banjo Paterson. Peter broke horses, and did all the usual jobs that made up work on the farm. There were also always those long runs to set rabbit traps that kept him super-fit, despite his knee injury. In 1938, he had recovered well enough to play football again at Cudgewa. At 25, he was bursting to return to the game. But he demanded conditions. He would be captain-coach and sole selector. This way, he could prevent wealthy locals from 'buying' selection for their less-than-skilled sons. His dictatorial approach upset a few. But it worked. Peter led the team to two successive premierships.

His younger brother 'Toxa' was playing in the team. He was the best looking of the Chitty clan and the finest all-round athlete.

'I put Toxa on the half-forward flank in a grand final [called the graveyard position because no-one went there],' he told Australian Rules legend Ron Barassi in a radio interview. 'He wanted to be rover [on the ball, therefore much more in the play].'

Toxa was annoyed. But Peter knew what he was doing.

'We beat Corryong 22.12 (144) to 2.2 (14),' Peter noted, 'Toxa kicked 14 goals from half-forward.'

Peter believed that Toxa was the best footballer in the family.[1]

Despite that assessment, Bob in Melbourne was the only one among the talented Chittys to beat injury and circumstance and sustain a career in the big-time. He was making a name for himself as a dashing, vigorous half-back flanker for the Carlton club. Bob was adept at the 'shirt-front'—the legitimate hip-and-shoulder bump that often left an opponent concussed. He was in the 1938 premiership team that defeated Collingwood. Back in the bush, Peter and his brothers were playing football for four different teams in the local Australian Rules competition.

Nancy Chitty, 15 in 1938, recalls animated, often heated discussions among her brothers around the dinner table on Saturday nights after the games.

'I used to ride to the games and watch sitting on horseback,' she said, 'but I'd have to leave before the matches ended. The boys were occupied playing. Someone had to help dad bring the cows in and milk them. Later we'd have a big dinner. No-one would take a backward step about which was the best team, and why.'[2]

*

In August 1938, Peter and Lilian's daughter Norma, just 18 months, contracted meningitis (where a viral or bacterial infection inflames the membrane covering the brain). Melbourne doctors were contacted. They sent a serum to Corryong but it was found to be the wrong one. Little Norma died and was buried on Lilian's 22nd birthday, 22 August.

Nothing could assuage a mother's sense of loss for an infant.

'She was a very strong, happy child,' Lilian said. 'I cried for six months.'[3]

It was a particularly stressful and emotional time for Lilian. She was three months pregnant.

A few months later at Christmas 1938, Peter was cutting wood in the hills above his home at Walwa. It was a hot day, with the temperature soaring over 39°C. A withering northerly wind had been blowing for several hours and Chitty was wary of the dangers from fires. Victoria was tinder dry. A year of severe drought had left plenty of fuel on the floor of forests.

A flame shot up less than a kilometre away. Within minutes the thickly wooded bush in the Mitta Range was aglow.

'It could have been lightning,' Chitty told Lilian, 'or something else.'

There was not time to worry about the cause. Fire was soon raging across the hills threatening Walwa, Cudgewa and Corryong in the valley below. Chitty rode his horse to a neighbour with the only car in the district. They drove to the face of the fire to tackle it with what they could—buckets of water, brushes and blankets. They were soon joined by bushies and townsfolk who attempted to prevent the fire sweeping down to the valley. Exhausted, Chitty and the others, black from the ash and with burns from 'ember attacks', wandered back to their homes in the early hours of the next morning having done all they could. There was no local fire brigade or any authority to assist. It was left to the community and their bushcraft. All the locals had experienced fire before. Yet it didn't make it easier to cope. They were all now praying that the fire would dissipate with a change in the weather or just burn itself out.

A recent heatwave had sapped the vegetation's moisture, making perfect fuel for the roaring beast as it soared through properties, devouring sheds, livestock and anything else in its path. Mercifully for the few hundred people in the valley's towns, it did not spread to them. Spot fires defeated any chance of the local bushmen controlling it. Parts of the front then fragmented, creating fingers and tongues of fires that spread up the Mitta Range's spurs and gullies.

'It was nasty,' Lilian recalled, 'and at night after fighting it we could only watch the glowing rocks of the [Mitta] Range. As strange as it sounds, it had a terrible, awesome beauty.'

Winds grew in strength. The fires began to spread and join up. Chitty and all the able-bodied men and women in the area fought the blaze into the early days of 1939. Chitty, the local footy coach, was the natural leader in the area. He mustered the manpower, allocated the fires to be tackled and led on the front.

By Sunday 8 January, a fire burning over 40 kilometres was out of control in the Kiewa Valley. The firefighters could not rest easy as they daily tackled the blaze and, while not bringing it under control, kept it from their towns and properties.

They could do no more. The main inferno would soon be the problem of other areas in the bush, where there were few cars and no fire trucks. Most farmers still travelled on horseback. Bikes were more the mode of transport than vehicles. This lack of speedy transport limited ways to avoid or escape the wind-driven mobile hell.

The country between the Mitta Range and Omeo was uninhabited but for a crew working on the State Electricity Commission's Kiewa hydro-electric scheme. One of the crew was pessimistic. He estimated the heat generated as it spread could have supplied Victoria with electricity for several months. By 10 January, the Dargo High Plains were ablaze.

As the days went by, fires reached the top of the ranges above Omeo and started to 'spot' around the town. On Friday 13 January 1939, spot fires developed 15 kilometres in front of the main blaze and further built its ferocity.

Prevailing winds, with blistering gusts reaching hurricane-force levels, kept the front moving. It had become a monster of its own physics, literally exploding here and there.

The cauldron was pushed hard by the harsh northerly into Omeo, which was not as fortunate as Walwa and the other alpine villages. Omeo was almost razed to the ground. The local pub—the Golden Age Hotel—was burnt out, its walls left standing. A hospital, 20 houses and 11 shops were destroyed. The local vet, chemist and dentist, Francis John Perry, managed to flee his home, which held one of the best and biggest private libraries in the state. It was demolished. His surgeries were also burnt out.[4]

The blaze continued its rampage towards Gippsland. At Swifts Creek, the local fire brigade spent 28 days on end fighting it.

In all, an area of almost 2 million hectares was burnt. Seventy-one people officially lost their lives, but other estimates put the number at more like 200. Logging was a thriving industry in country Victoria. Many sawmills were lost. Scores of millers, swaggies and itinerants in the region perished, some without any official record, or evidence. The massive heat had vaporised them.

Three weeks after the bushfires, a royal commission was convened by Judge Leonard E. B. Sutton. He concluded that '. . . these fires were lit by the hand of man.'

Reading this remark in the paper, Peter Chitty's mind went back to that day around Christmas 1938 when he saw the flash as the fire began. He wondered if it had been deliberately lit.

On 25 February 1939, Lilian gave birth to a second daughter, dark-haired, blue-eyed Dawn. No-one could make up for the loss of little Norma. But the advent of this ever-smiling new baby did much to salve feelings and renew hopes.

5

Fights Big and Small

‘Who'll take a glove?’ lean Jimmy Sharman called, from the elevated stage of his bright red and yellow tent. The gravel-voiced growl was repeated with each beat of a bass drum as the crowd of young men at the autumn 1939 Corryong Show grew. Four Aboriginal boxers and one 190 centimetre African American prize fighter, all wearing different coloured dressing-gowns, were on the stage next to Sharman and the drummer. The adrenaline of several onlooking youths pumped. Would they dare go up there and show what they had? The spectators included a group of the Chitty family: Peter, Phil, Frank, Ron and ‘Toxa’. Toxa was 19, and recognised in the area as someone special in the ring. Where Phil was a fighter, who packed a punch with his Popeye forearms, Toxa had developed into a brilliant boxer.

‘He was like [world champion] Johnny Famechon,’ Peter's son Lindsay noted. ‘[Brother] Phil was closer to Mike Tyson.’[1]

Toxa's training was to fight his older brothers from a young age, especially Phil, who according to younger brother Ken had ‘a reach on him like a sick dog. Both of them [Phil and Toxa] could fight. If you were going to cop a hiding, Phil could give you the worse one.’[2]

There was another dimension to Toxa. He was an outstanding athlete with a will to succeed against all comers. He had once gone 52 rounds against several opponents, one after another, which also demonstrated exceptional endurance. He was said to have the sharpest left jab ever seen in Australian boxing. He would follow up with a speared, classic, 'elbows in' straight right. No opponent in an official fight had ever avoided a knockout when young Toxa released that combination. He had modelled his capacity to beat opponents either hand on the silky skills and power of US world heavyweight champion Joe Louis.

'Go on, Toxa,' several in the crowd urged, 'have a go!'

Unaware of Toxa's skills, this was music to Sharman's ears. The drum beat continued.

'C'mon, who'll take a glove?' the troupe man repeated, 'three rounds. Five quid if you go three rounds with licorice [Aborigines]. Ten pounds if you take on our American Negro. C'mon!'[3]

Toxa remained silent, looking up at the five fighters. None of the young men in the audience wanted to be first. Then a tallish, scrawny youth put up his hand. He said he would have a go.

Sharman beckoned him up eight steps to the boxing ring, asked his name ('Dasher'), and motioned for him to make a choice among the five. Dasher pointed to an Aborigine wearing a yellow and brown check gown, and slipped into the ring. The crowd grew as the two slugged it out. The Aborigine went down in the second round.

Peter caught Toxa's eye and shook his head, indicating the fight was a set-up to entice a 'sucker'. Sharman, himself a top-line boxer of three decades earlier, made great play of flicking off a fiver from a large wad of notes.

Toxa put up his hand. A big cheer went up. He climbed up the eight steps. Toxa nodded to the American. Toxa was giving away height, reach and weight. There was a drum-roll as he put on the gloves. The two men touched gloves. Toxa boxed. The American lunged. Sharman refereed. Toxa dipped and surged around the ring, the bigger man following and displaying good footwork himself. The Chittys urged their talented brother to avoid the clinches. He did for one round. In round two, he came in closer, taking a couple of blows on the body that pushed him back. But he landed one jarring right, followed by a hard left jab. It shook the big man. In round three, Toxa moved in and out jabbing, scoring often with the bigger man unable to lay a glove on him. Then he did what no-one expected; he knocked out the American with a sharp, whipping right hand. He went down for a count of 10. The 200 or so onlookers roared.

A bucket of water was thrown over the American. He struggled to his feet. Toxa shook his hand and then collected the £10 from Sharman. The crowd applauded and cheered. No-one had told the troupe owner what 28-year-old (Footscray footballer) Ambrose Palmer, an Australian boxing champion in three divisions, had said about young Toxa that year:

'He is the best boxer I have ever seen. He could be the lightweight champion of Australia.'[4]

6

On Again

It was Prime Minister Robert Menzies' 'melancholy duty' on 3 September 1939 to tell the nation that it was at war with Germany. Germany's invasion of Poland was the reason that Great Britain had declared war. 'As a result,' the PM informed the country, 'Australia is also at war.' There was not quite the sense that there was a conflict. Europe was 20,000 kilometres away. Japan was looking increasingly predatory but Menzies had not mentioned it. It was barely 21 years since General Sir John Monash and his digger army on the Western Front, on 8 and 9 August 1918, had smashed two enemy armies and ended the Germans' chances of winning World War I. To revisit the horrors of the Great War—the one to end all wars—seemed like a bad dream more than reality to many, especially the older generations. But there it was. Britain, as Menzies pointed out, had 'a quite perceptible disposition to treat Australia as a colony.' The British wished all their former colonies to help out again. The big difference, which promised a dilemma for any Australian leader, was that this time around Japan was not an ally. It could even be an enemy. This changed everything from an Australian perspective. If the Japanese had expansionist aims now that the conflagration was on again in Europe and the Middle East, what should a leader do? Help out the 'Mother Country' or defend the 'homeland'?

Menzies hoped to mollify Japan by sending an ambassador to Tokyo. This would be quite a step. Australia had only one other independent (of the UK) overseas mission. That was in Washington, DC.

The machinations of high office aside, Australians once more flocked to enlistment offices around the country. The number who joined up in World War I (415,000) looked likely in 1939 to be overtaken in this conflict. Nearly every unit in the entire new armed force included men entitled to wear the ribbons of the Great War. Two men in the 2nd AIF 3rd Reserve Motor Transport bluffed recruiting officers about their ages. They were both aged 60 and had served in the Boer War at the turn of the century. Many were under age but hirsute enough to fool the recruiters. One of them was Private Frank 'Titch' Lemin from Albury. He was 14 years old. (He would later have Peter Chitty as his Sergeant in the 2/2nd Motor Ambulance Convoy.)[1]

Most recruits were not naive. They had relatives and friends from the Great War. But they wanted to prove themselves on the battlefields of the Western Front and the Middle East. There was much to live up to. Monash's 208,000 men in France had been the dominant army corps (of 20 on the Allies' side) in the last six months of the Great War. General Sir Harry Chauvel's 34,000 horsemen had been the strike force that had done more than any other entity to defeat three Turkish armies and finish the Ottoman Empire in the Middle East. Every child, youth and man knew of those fighting performances that did much to change the course of the 20th century.

The average age of those joining up in 1939 was 22 years. Some, particularly among the teenagers, were out for adventure, travel and far away exotic places, with the emphasis on thoughts about Europe. The 'older' volunteers, ranging in age from their late twenties on, were enlisting for different reasons. They were closer in age, knowledge and comprehension to events in World War I. They were aware how serious the current war in Europe was. They wished to do something about it knowing that their fathers' generation had been there and had had an enormous impact when it counted.

The fall of France to Nazi Germany in June 1940 saw a huge boost in recruitment. General Monash's genius as a battle commander and planner had stopped the Germans in August 1918 at Amiens, just 100 kilometres from Paris. Now in this war the Germans had taken it. Hitler was strutting down the Champs Elysees. All the achievement of 1914–1918 and sacrifice (with more than 60,000 Australians killed, double that number injured and countless more mentally scarred for life) was in danger of being wiped out.

It was enough for tens of thousands of men, including Peter Chitty. Until then, he had felt bound by his responsibility to a young wife and family. But when the owner of the share property decided to return to work there (in an 'essential' war industry producing milk), Peter was suddenly out of work. He could have found other employment, but he was pushed off the property just days after Paris fell. Both events influenced him to volunteer to serve. He was also touched by the government push urging enlistment. This featured billboard advertising which depicted a civilian in a suit among several diggers with slouch hats and bayoneted rifles. The caption read: 'One in—all in . . . Join the AIF today'.

The catch-word in the country pubs and football grounds around the country was 'to do your duty'.

The Chitty family was typical of those with a sense of national pride. Seven of the family's men and women volunteered to serve.

First up were Phil, 32 and married, and Ron, 18. They joined the 22nd Field Ambulance as drivers. They would be later attached to the 2/7th Battalion, part of the 17th Brigade of the 6th Australian Division, which opened its headquarters at the Royal Melbourne Showgrounds on 25 October 1939. Nine days later it relocated to the new camp at Puckapunyal. Basic training began. They coped well. They were bushmen used to all sorts of rigours and self-discipline. Yet it was rushed and hectic. They expected to be shipped to places as yet unknown after completing basic training, which would be in about five months time.

Peter was already in the local Light Horse. He had wanted to join his brothers but they thought it better to split up the siblings. This would increase the odds that some of the serving members of the family would survive. Peter decided to switch to the 2nd Battalion Motor Ambulance Convoy attached to the 9th Field Ambulance.

This sudden promise of family upheaval came at a particularly tough time for Lilian. She was pregnant and Dawn was 18 months old. She was experiencing the emotions that hundreds of thousands of women would face over two generations: her man was going to war. Doubts and worries emerged. How long would he be away? Would he come back? And then, the third concern: would she and the family survive while he was away? Yes, the Chittys and the farming community would form a network, a safety net. But it would still be hard going without the primary breadwinner.

Peter joined up on 27 June 1940. A son, Lindsay, was born on 22 November.

'He took one look at me,' Lindsay joked, 'and took off!'[1]

Peter would be sailing on the *Queen Mary* a few months later.

Toxa felt the pressure to join. At 21, he was a reluctant starter. He had a serious future as a world-class professional boxer. Ambrose Palmer's endorsement was supported by everyone who knew the sport. If he joined up, he had a sense that it would end his chances for stardom in the ring. He was super-fit, at his peak and ready to take on the world.

There was more at stake. Toxa had attracted plenty of VFL talent scouts, even to the remote town of Cudgewa, more than 100 kilometres from the Victorian border town of Wodonga. Any interested parties had to negotiate rough bush tracks by horse. Footballers rode horses to the matches at Cudgewa, Walwa, Tintaldra, Towong, Corryong, Shelley and other small 'villages' in the valleys and the foothills near the Murray River. Many an outstanding sportsman in the bush never came under scrutiny from the 'big smoke' of Melbourne and Sydney because of the isolation. Yet still league clubs became aware of Toxa and made offers. For the moment, his boxing took precedence.

'He was also the most versatile and fastest [of the Chitty clan],' Peter would always say, 'and he had ingredient "X"— "the mongrel"—in him, even more than Bob did.' Brother Ken agreed with this assessment.[2]

He didn't mean in the sense of the wild dog of mixed breed. He was speaking in the vernacular. This extra factor was viewed as the essential characteristic for prominence in the Australian game at the highest level. The connation for 'mongrel' in this sense meant 'wildness', 'determination', 'courage', and a touch of the devil in his play.

Toxa, his brothers all noted, was the stylish boxer on every occasion. Quick on his feet; fleet of hand; agile of body. But he also had a killer instinct. He wanted to win every contest by a knock-out. It was the same with his footy. He and his team were never beaten until the final siren.

Apart from Toxa's older brothers, many of his mates intended to join up as the recruiting offices reached into the bush. The 2/23rd Infantry Battalion was raised at the nearby Albury Showgrounds as part of the 26th Brigade in June 1940. (It would start with the 7th Division but end up with the 9th.) The battalion trained at Bonegilla. It was all too close for comfort and Toxa's conscience. He too enlisted.

Bob Chitty was staying in Melbourne playing football with Carlton. To a degree he was insulated from similar pressures. Like Toxa, he wanted to continue a sporting career that was already beyond promising. He had cemented a place on the half-back flank for the Blues. After three years in the seniors, the rugged defender was a team leader and a favourite son at the club. He was just 23 at the beginning of the 1940 season, but already was known as the team's 'enforcer'. It was another word for 'tough guy'. They were needed in the big league if a team had aspirations to win premierships. Such players, in the minds of parochial supporters, were nearly indispensable.

Bob would be offered all sorts of enticements not to join his brothers-in-arms. Carlton wanted more grand final wins.

Younger brothers Dick 14, Pat 12, and Ken 10, were too young to volunteer. Frank, 16, who had been accidentally blinded in one eye as a youngster, was judged unfit for service. He had to stay at Cudgewa to help out Allan and Hannah. That left the girls among the 12 siblings. 'Nellie' (Ellen) 34, joined the Women's Auxiliary Australian Air Force (WAAAF) and was promoted to sergeant. She worked as a cook at Wagga and Tocumwal air bases. Nancy, 17, planned to follow her elder sister into the WAAAF as a wireless and radar operator. Third sister, Agnes, 30, was also needed for Chitty family duties at Cudgewa.

The Chitty clan was exceptional, with seven about to serve their country. It was a microcosm of the impact on Australian families as a million people would eventually find their way into enlistment buildings in every state and territory.

Life in countless villages, towns and cities around the nation was in for upheaval.

In September 1940, Japan occupied French Indochina (Vietnam) against the fervent wishes of the Indochinese themselves. The indigenous interests were ignored by the (Vichy) French, who did the bidding of their new masters, the Nazis. The Japanese had now joined the Axis powers of Germany and Italy.

The Japanese stride into South-East Asia rang alarm bells in Canberra. They were already a few steps ahead of the British in the region. A year earlier, the British commander in Malaya, Lieutenant-General A. E. Percival, at the request of the British High Command had prepared a 'war game' scenario. The directive was to 'Plan the invasion of Malaya and Singapore and how best to prevent such an event happening'. The plan predicted that the unnamed enemy would attack the west coast of Malaya from a neutral country—Thailand—simultaneously as a seaborne attack was launched against the east coast. Percival and his staff worked out the force and equipment requirements to prevent an enemy invasion succeeding. The British hypothesis also suggested an enemy would have to occupy a portion of southern Thailand. This would be feasible for an adversary such as Japan, which could take it by force. But Percival's report concluded that it would be not advisable for the British to do this. It would not be appreciated by the Thais—an ally at the time, and such a British 'occupation' would be a diplomatic disaster. On top of this, Percival's impressive scenario-sketching was shelved for another more pertinent reason: the British were not prepared to fund it. They were already stretched too far with men, supplies and armaments in Western Europe and the Middle East.[3]

Not so the Japanese. By coincidence, they devised a near-identical 'war game'. Except for them it was not a paper scenario. They prepared to go through with it. In effect, the plan was underway by 1935 when the entire stock of C56 class locomotives built in that year and the next were adapted to run on the narrower one-metre gauge railways found in most South-East Asian countries, including Malaya, Thailand and Burma. (The rims could be moved inwards on the wheels to accommodate the different gauge.)

The Japanese kept secret their intention also to invade Burma. The rugged country on the border with Thailand, which had only tracks and no railway, was not considered an obstacle, despite it preventing the movement of heavy armaments. The British had only light-armed forces with which to defend Burma. The Japanese were confident that once they had captured Rangoon, heavy equipment could later be shipped there by sea via Singapore and the Straits of Malacca.

Burma would be an important Japanese acquisition for many reasons. First, it was rich in food supplies and natural resources: oil, tungsten ('wolfram', used as a steel alloy), and other minerals. Second, it would cut the Allied supply line to China on the 'Burma Road', a highway in south-western China. It ran 720 kilometres from Kunming, capital of Yunnan Province to the railhead at Lashio, in Burma. This was the only route for transporting vital supplies to the Chinese. And third, once Burma was held, it would provide a springboard for invading India.

7

Destination Unknown

Peter Chitty had no idea where he was going when the lumbering converted ocean liner, the *Queen Mary*, left Sydney carrying 5,750 troops of the 22nd Brigade on 2 February 1941. It was part of a four-ship convoy carrying the 8th Division. The other three were trans-Atlantic liners: *Mauritania*, *Aquitania* and *Nieuw Amsterdam*. There were plenty of rumours about the location of the battlefields they were heading for. West Africa was a long shot. The troop train that had carried Chitty to Sydney had been decorated with chalked slogans, such as 'Berlin or bust' and 'Look out Adolf', which suggested perhaps they would end up closer to Europe, possibly the coast of France.

The main betting was on the Middle East, especially when all on board were given lectures on malaria, the disease transmitted by mosquitoes—in particular the blood parasite *Plasmodium*. The men were back at school taking notes on symptoms such as fever, anaemia and an enlarged spleen. It also hit the brain and kidneys. If it infected the liver it could reside there and break out from time to time causing relapses. Hadn't the troopers suffered with this in Jordan in World War I?

Late plunges were on Malaya after further lectures concerned tropical hygiene.

'We'd have lectures about diseases such as malaria and the precautions we had to take,' Len Lemke, another member of the 2/2nd Motor Ambulance Convoy (2/2 MAC), said, 'and of course, the women. The way they talked you'd think that if you looked at a woman, you'd catch a disease!'[1]

Chitty believed the 8th would follow the 9th Division and the 6th Division into North Africa. He hoped to meet up with Phil and Ron, and learn firsthand of their experiences in Bardia and Tobruk.

Joe Jameson was also in 2/2 MAC made up of Victorians as part of the 22nd Brigade. He recalled the trip.

'We were on lowly F deck, just above the water line,' he

said. 'There was a wind sock which drew in the cool air. Every now and again a wave would shoot a jet of water and thirty men would get drenched.'

If it was hot at night, the men would sleep on deck.

Len Lemke recalled: 'We didn't worry about the wind, but the rain made it miserable, especially for those of us who were seasick and on deck.' One night, he and his mate 'Jack' were on deck and feeling 'really crook'.

'The moon's coming up Jack,' Lemke said.

'It bloody well feels like it too,' an anguished Jack replied.[2]

Jameson remembered being dressed in a heavy khaki uniform, which was unsuitable for any tropical or desert destination.

'The shirt was outside the trousers and buttoned to the neck like a collar.'[3]

Off Fremantle, Chitty learned of the destination: Malaya. It was a disappointment for him. He would not be united with his brothers after all. For others, dreams of conquering the Nazis and frolicking in a regained Paris evaporated. Instead, there was a collective disappointment. No-one knew much about Asia. Defensive garrisons in Malaya and Singapore did not have the same appeal as attacking the Germans or Italians. But before any disgruntlement could become endemic there was a manoeuvre at sea that decided a new route. The Queen Mary pulled out of the convoy and circled.

Gerard Veitch of the 2/9th Field Ambulance was there when the speculation ended on 16 February. He noted in a dairy: 'Queen Mary swung out of the port helm and opened up her engines to full speed. Excitement was at full pitch.'

It eased round behind the other three liners, making waves which broke over the other ships. Its siren sounded three times and it moved to the north-east. 'The remainder of the convoy continued on their course never having altered speed. In half an hour, they were only a smudge on the horizon.'[4] The *Queen Mary* continued on at an increased pace. Bands started up. Cheers followed. The men were mollified for the moment as their Anzac comrades on the other ships continued west across the Indian Ocean on the way to Egypt and the Middle East.

The Australians would join English, Scottish and Indian troops in the garrisoning of Singapore island and defending Malaya. The *Queen Mary* sailed through to the Johore Straits separating Malaya from Singapore, then on to the island's naval base at Keppel Harbour. Many on board were having breakfast. The sun was shining in a bright blue sky. An emerald sea was dotted with Malayan fishing boats. All were excited to see the pretty white bungalows set against the striking green hill-side on the north-eastern corner of Singapore where Changi was located. Changi Prison, named after the Chengai tree that was used as landmark for passing ships, had been built in 1931 to hold 600 prisoners. A British regiment began playing 'Roll out the Barrel'. Many on board soon formed a chorus. It was 18 February 1941 and war seemed unlikely to visit this sleepy Asian hollow.

'We were fascinated with this new place,' Lemke said, 'especially the kids. We threw money into the water. They would dive down and retrieve it.' It reminded him of his days as a kid growing up in Albury in the 1920s. He was taught in school that 'the British Empire had two of the greatest strongholds in the world: the Rock of Gibraltar, and Singapore . . . I remember a saying then: "as strong as the fort of Singapore".'[5]

All seemed well and attractive in this quaint, far-flung British outpost.

Part of its appeal for colonisers was its location. Stamford Raffles saw the possibilities of Singapore being 137 kilometres north of the equator and on the busy sea routes connecting east and west. In 1819, he claimed it for the British East India Company. In 1826, it became part of the Straits settlement with Penang and Malacca. They became crown colonies in 1867.

Singapore expanded rapidly as a free port, drawing immigrants from China, India, Indonesia, Malaya and other neighbouring states. It was a key link in Britain's network of overseas ports, especially after the development of Malay Peninsula trade in tin and rubber.

Singapore took on strategic significance as a vital defence base in the Far East, particularly after the Great War of 1914–1918. The German naval threat had been overcome, but Japan emerged as a potential rival and menace. Britain was prepared to send its navy to tackle any Eastern crisis. Singapore was the chosen base from 1923. As Japanese ambitions became apparent, naval facilities were expanded. New airfields were built on the island. It was viewed by the British and Australians as an 'impregnable fortress'.[6] Experts claimed it could only be assaulted from the South China Sea.

Early after arrival, the 22nd Brigade had the additional task of manning Mersing on Malaya's south-east coast, which was 160 kilometres from the Johore Causeway to Singapore Island. Chitty, Jameson and the rest of 2/2 MAC were stationed at Kajang, 25 kilometres south of Kuala Lumpur in south-west Malaya. The 2/10th Australian General Hospital was situated on an existing local hospital location 95 kilometres further south on the east coast at the historic city of Malacca. Within months it would have 600 beds.

The main illness to begin with was malaria. The climate led to heat exhaustion, skin lesions, sores, dermatitis and tinea. Any skin problems in the conditions if not treated could lead to blood poisoning and infections that were life-threatening.

The heat and the aromas of South-East Asia were foreign to the new arrivals. Chitty was interested in the different rural lifestyle, especially the use of water buffaloes, which were common in South-East Asia. The Malays used them to pull single furrow ploughs in paddy fields.

The Australian motor ambulance men were accommodated at Kajang in 'attap' weatherboard huts with palm-thatched roofs. They were built on stilts high off the ground. These houses were hot but waterproof from the frequent tropical downpours. Only a few degrees separated the coolest and warmest part of each day. Temperatures hovered between 30 and 37°C, but were higher in the mountains and hills. The humidity was huge. A short walk to an outside latrine would cause perspiration.

'We were a bit of a disgrace on arrival in the heat,' Jameson noted, 'we refused to button our shirts. We bought cooling Tiger beer at 26 cents and it wasn't long before we were drunk.'

The motor ambulance drivers did their job, taking supplies in their canvas-covered, Chevrolet trucks.

'They were the conventional three-speed Mark 6s,' Jameson said. 'Pretty mechanically reliable. In times of conflict they could carry nine stretcher cases, with four sitting.'[7]

Their longest trips were about 300 kilometres north to Ipoh. The roads were ungraded and dangerous. Accidents were frequent. Trucks would have to dodge locals, who seemed careless of traffic, cows, bullocks, bikes, rickshaws, motorcycles and other vehicles. There was no break from the restless mass of humanity and animals on the move. Vehicles, including the trucks and ambulances, could be forced off the path into roadside gullies.

Chitty drove an ambulance truck that the people of Corryong donated to the army. A small plaque on the back noted the country town's generosity.

In this 'peace-time' period, often the worst problems were from recreational injuries. Broken bones were top of the list in football matches, particularly rugby. Sexual disease issues arose, as they had in Europe and the Middle East in World War I. Gonorrhoea was a frequent pick-up. The men thought their urges would be met by the sexy Asian girls, especially on Singapore's Lavender Street, while on leave. But seduced by hip-swinging, over made-up, perfumed prostitutes, they often received more than they bargained for. Penicillin—dubbed 'the antibiotic for the man who has everything'—was still being experimented with in laboratories. Most would recover and return to their units, perhaps wiser. A minority were designated B2, which saw them sent home with a secret that might be with them for life.[8]

Joe Jameson recalled going with a mate for a swim in a river near Kajang. There were local young women swimming naked. He did not engage with them. The ambulance units, like all the others, had been lectured about not having sexual dalliances. Perhaps they knew too much, especially ferrying 'casualties' to the Malacca hospital. But Jameson said they avoided contact in every sense beyond a smile and a wave.

The medical unit members themselves were determined to keep fit, fitter perhaps than others. When and if the time came for battle, everyone would be flat out.

In the meantime, there had to be retraining. Earlier programs in Australia had desert warfare in mind. Now jungle tactics had to be absorbed. Platoons would begin by marching in single file either side of the road. The instructor would choose an area that included a rubber plantation, some open terrain and then the jungle, where the trainees would learn to camouflage themselves.

Chitty the 'bushie' revelled in the conditions of the route marches. Where most struggled, he was invigorated by the exercise, inspiring others to carry on.

The jungle was a huge challenge. It was dense and thickest where it had been cleared and allowed to grow wild again in deserted kampongs and villages. This 'bush' was like nothing most Australians had encountered, except in northern Queensland. Malaya was dark, damp and steamy. Tangled vines and undergrowth tied together giant trees, which fought to stretch towards the sky's light obscured by the abundant growth.

Chitty's background was advantageous. He was cheerful in the conditions whereas many of his companions, who had not experienced the bush, were unhinged by the silence except for the chilling 'drip-drip' from the foliage above. There would the snap of a twig or the footfall of a scurrying animal—a tiger perhaps. There might be the depression of leaves under slithering pythons, cobras, or the krait, whose

poisonous bite killed a human in seconds. All the sounds that broke the eeriness were perpetual worries for most. But not Chitty. He kept the code of not speaking during training exercises. The relaxed look on his face was just a little reassuring for those raised in Australian cities. The bushies knew to be alert and watch where they trod. Less reassuring was to be told that reptiles only attacked when disturbed.

The unnerving sound-free zone was split by the chatter of monkeys swinging through the trees high above them. Yet there was one thing that bothered even Chitty: tropical rainstorms. Again, they were heavier than anything experienced except in Queensland's deep north. They further limited the thin light squeezing through the growth. Storms caused water to torrent down tree trunks, turning the ground into a bog, which was bad for footwear and feet. Soon the trekkers would be dragging through deep, leafy mould. Steam would rise, giving off pungent odours that one of the men called 'rotten egg' gas—hydrogen sulphide. If this gathered and men lingered too long it could cause a quick asphyxiating death. The bucketing rain formed deep, fast flowing rivers. Mangroves were thick and close on the banks. Some of the men, such as Jameson and his mate, were brave enough to swim, especially if they saw locals in the water. But not where there were water snakes or where cumbersome tin mining dredges formed toxic sludge.

Only water buffaloes would inhabit the slush.

Everyone abhorred the blood-sucking leeches that latched onto bare-skinned extremities and had to be torn off. Only a vampire could have affection for the endless mosquitoes, particularly those that carried malaria.

Sladangs—the vicious wild boars—were a menace on

another scale. They gave warning with their willingness to charge humans. The only way to avoid them was to scramble up one of the mighty, statuesque trees that were never more welcome.

The perpetual horrors and threats were so terrifying that few on the jungle exercises could always appreciate the beauty of rare orchids bred in the natural hothouse, every imaginable species of bird, and butterflies with 30 centimetre wingspans. Despite noxious smells, every so often something fragrant such as a tropical flower would dominate the air.

The rubber tree plantations reached on the exercises were the only relief in the incessant jungle. They had been carved out by British traders. The rubber trees were imported from Brazil to London's Kew Gardens then taken to Malaya. British scientists developed a pest-resistant plant that produced big amounts of latex. The plantations were visible to the marchers when they reached the road. These 'estates' were privately controlled by British, Australian, Japanese and Chinese. The labour was carried out by Tamils and Indians from Ceylon (now Sri Lanka). Each estate had its own viable community with schools, stores and bungalow accommodation.

Chitty was fascinated with the way Malayan indigenous people lived, especially with their obsession with bamboo. Thick poles of it were strapped together to make light rafts. It made a fine, flexible bed if slit in two and flattened out. This was then laid out over the bamboo that kept sleepers off the ground and clear of snakes, scorpions and hornets. When sectioned off, bamboo was used as a drinking vessel. The natives also made music with it, but for practical purposes rather than cultural. If tops were lopped off and different lengths cut, the varying whistle from the breeze would inform tribesmen of their exact location.

The bamboo was also a weapon when shaped into 3 metre blowpipes for poisoned darts, or swung like a baseball bat.

Chitty and the other footballers in 8th Division had one other use that was just as important to them as any of the locals' inventions. Poles could be shaped easily into goalposts, which avoided makeshift arrangements.

For players of all codes, a field of contest was only complete when authentic looking 'goals' were erected. For Chitty, the sight of four bamboo uprights at each end was a little touch of home as meaningful as the information in a letter, the taste of Vegemite (in all World War II military rations) or the newspapers.

The familiarity comforted him and his mates, and perhaps led to the belief that they might be home experiencing the real things sooner rather than later.

8

Mad Dogs and Englishmen

The eight-month siege of Tobruk, Libya in 1941, in which Toxa Chitty took part, was in contrast to the so-called 'phoney' war of inaction in Malaya and Singapore. The British, perhaps living up to the song 'Mad dogs and Englishmen go out in the midday sun', believed that the way to beat the boredom of this lull and the heat in Malaya and Singapore was to keep active and in good condition. Everything from golf and squash to croquet and cricket was encouraged. In time off, Peter Chitty enjoyed the chance to play football on tropical fields. He became acquainted with some elite footballers. Among them were Wilfred 'Chicken' Smallhorn and big Harold 'Hal' Ball.

Wilfred 'Chicken' Smallhorn, born in 1911, was as 'small as a chicken' according to his mother. The name stuck. For those close to him, he was simply 'Chick'. He played his first league game at 19 on 24 May 1930 against St Kilda. It was tough going in the Depression. Fitzroy promised him a job but did not quite follow through to his satisfaction, preferring to give more support to star 'imports' from interstate, such as Western Australia's brilliant Haydn Bunton. When a Fitzroy player returned to the country, Smallhorn was offered his tea 'round'—a job in which he had to sell packets of the beverage door-to-door using a pushbike. His familiarity with the suburb helped. Many footy fans bought from him. Smallhorn's developing form as a rover and winger coincided with success in his work. He did so well flogging tea that he bought a motorbike with a side car. Later he graduated to a horse-drawn piano-box buggy. He had room for more selling items including coffee, cocoa, flour, honey and jellies. 'W. SMALLHORN' adorned the side of the buggy, a moveable mini-delicatessen. Goods were wrapped in Fitzroy colours.

In 1932, Smallhorn was starring on the wing. He finished in the top 10 votes for the most coveted award in Australian football, the Brownlow Medal, which was won by his team-mate Bunton, who had also won in 1931.

In 1933, aged just 22, Smallhorn's career reached a zenith when he won the medal. He gave drive to Fitzroy, which had been the VFL's 'easybeats' in recent years. In 1933, it just missed out on the finals.

Smallhorn had gained serious respect at his chosen club after tension between himself and officials. The next year he fell only three votes short of taking the Brownlow again.

In 1936, an injured knee needed a cartilage operation, which finished his horse and buggy selling and jeopardised his football career. He sold his door-to-door business. Once more, Fitzroy failed to find him satisfactory work, offering a job at a motor wrecker's garage, on a bread cart and in a factory. Still the club seemed more intent on helping 'imports' from interstate. Smallhorn threatened to leave for rival neighbouring suburb, Collingwood, which offered him employment. Fitzroy blocked the move, as it also did later when he tried to switch to Melbourne. In 1938, despite his knee problems, he was third to Bunton in the Brownlow (Bunton's third).

Smallhorn more or less maintained his form in 1939 when he finished in the top 10 votes, as he had in 1932.

Smallhorn broke his leg in the fourth game of the 1940 season. It was in plaster for six weeks. He decided to retire and join the army.

On the *Queen Mary* in February 1941, he became acquainted with the young, 189 centimetre Harold Ball, who was just beginning what promised to be an outstanding career with the Melbourne club. Ball had been a star through the 1940s finals with a best-on-ground preliminary final performance in which he took 15 marks on a wet day. That effort did much to catapult Melbourne into the grand final against Richmond. Once more his fine marking helped Melbourne win its second successive premiership. Ball had been in both of them. Smallhorn had played 150 games for Fitzroy without performing in one final. He envied Ball his luck in already being in five, with two flags.

Ball was born in Mildura in 1920 and joined Melbourne from Merbein. He was instantly at home in the big league, playing 20 games for the 1939 season and being named Best First Year Player. He was 19. He had a job as a groundsman at the MCG. Then war intervened. The fall of Paris stimulated him to enlist in mid-1940. He was posted to the 2/9th Field Ambulance as a driver. He became acquainted with Chitty.

The three men played in a scratch match in Singapore, with Ball and Smallhorn captaining the teams. Smallhorn struggled in the game. His legs would not stand the twists and turns anymore. Ball, a most popular character, went on to captain the 2/9th Field Ambulance football team, which was formed when the unit began in Victoria. It played in several fierce games against other 8th Division units. The matches were of a high standard, estimated at one level below the top league. Ball, like Chitty, was outstanding in every encounter.

Chitty had plenty of time to correspond with Lilian. He learned that her father, a widower, had come to live with her at Cudgewa. He thought they would be better off living in his Melbourne home. The family made the move in the middle of 1941.

'I was happy to be anywhere Peter was,' she said, 'but I preferred Melbourne over country life. It was less difficult with two little ones.'[1]

It was not easy for Lilian. She had to bring up the children and keep house for her father. He was good with the children and helpful, but when she tried working he could not cope being left alone with them. She had to give up the job. War brought other social upheavals. Lilian had a brother (Horace Auber Prowse) in the army also with the 2/23rd Battalion, who was in the Middle East, and another (Stewart Harvey Prowse) in the air force. When on leave, they and their friends would stay in Melbourne with the family. This added to Lilian's stresses and work in the home.

She was comforted by Peter's upbeat letters, but always in the back of her mind was the worry that he too would be involved in the fighting.

'It seemed inevitable,' she said, 'with Ron, Phil, Toxa and Horace [her brother] all in [Middle East] battle zones, and the Japanese rampant in this part of the world, it just seemed like a matter of time before they would be challenging the British [in Malaya and Singapore].'[2]

*

Most men in the 8th Division were kept active during this waiting period, where the intentions of the Japanese were not clear. All sports were played. Athletics meetings were organised by the 8th Division Signal's Doug Lush (whom Chitty taught to drive a truck). Lush was an accomplished runner and hurdler. He arranged for an event at Port Dickson, on the west coast, 50 kilometres south of Kuala Lumpur. His main rival was another champion, Dr John Park, who like Harold Ball was with 2/9th Field Ambulance. Park had shown such promise that former Olympic hurdler Wilfrid Kent Hughes decided to coach him when he was running for the Melbourne athletic team Powerhouse. Park was in his second year as a doctor at Melbourne's Alfred Hospital when he too decided to serve. He also loved his football. He played in Ball's 2/9th Field Ambulance team.

If Chitty and his mates were in Malacca (about 100 kilometres south on the coast) at night they went to the cinema. If in Singapore they rode in a rickshaw to the Lulu café or the Happy World and New World fun parks.

'They were great places for entertainment,' Lemke said, 'particularly dancing. They called the women "taxi dancers". You bought a ticket and gave it to a girl to dance with you. They were very attractive, Chinese and Eurasian, and very good dancers. The music was good too.'

The more the soldiers turned up, the more the women were there to greet them.

'We used to look forward to getting leave at night,' Lemke recalled.[3]

*

The entertainment at the fun parks included boxing matches. They always brought talk of Toxa Chitty's ability, and thoughts on how he was faring in Tobruk.

Peter and his mates even sat in cane chairs and sampled Singapore Slings at the famous Raffles Hotel while roof fans whirred overhead, and myriad of servants scurried around British, Scottish and Indian army officers. Gin and tonic and treating native servants with contempt was not to their liking. The Australians preferred the beer and bars.

There was always something to do in Singapore town with Robinson's department store, the Fullerton Building, the city hall, the post office, banks and the ornate, gabled Victoriana of the cricket club. Chitty more than once stopped to watch a game of cricket in progress on the level, green field, surrounded by flame trees and a quaint view of the sea.

Servicemen were often seen with cameras slung around their necks. They snapped shots like relaxed tourists. There was even entertainment from home. Attractive singer Betty Bryant visited and performed for the troops. Malaya and Singapore were not home, but more like a modest couple of foreign holiday countries, which would have been enjoyable if the troops had stayed three weeks. But as the months dragged on boredom set in.

Chitty read the *Bulletin* and the *Sporting Globe*. The latter gave him results of Australian Rules games, and reports on Carlton's matches. Bob Chitty started the 1941 season with panache and was listed in the 'best' for his team in the early rounds. There was even speculation that he was a good bet to win the Brownlow Medal. Peter was surprised but pleased with Bob's progress. The Blues' hard-man must have tucked in his elbows and put away his shirt-front bump.

From reports, he seemed to be the 'umpire's friend' early in the season.

There were newspaper reports too on the battles going on the Middle East. Chitty wondered about the progress of his brothers Ron and Phil, who had fought a rearguard action in 6th Division in Crete. In June 1941, Phil had been taken prisoner and was in Stalag XVIIIA at Wolfsberg, Austria. But Ron was free, living rough in the hills of Crete.

9

Confusion at the Top

Complacency emerged in Malaya and Singapore in the middle months of 1941 with more virulence than malaria and would be more dangerous if the Japanese attacked. It infected the leadership, politicians in the UK and Australia, and the commanders in their safe, distant offices and in the field. This caused it to trickle down to every member of the force. The fates of the Chitty brothers and the rest of the British expeditionary force in Greece then Crete, along with reverses in the North African desert and the bottling up of Toxa and 23,000 other Australian, British and Indian troops in Tobruk, was enough for British Prime Minister Churchill. He determined to concentrate the war effort in the West. The Far East was now way down the list of his priorities in fighting against the Axis powers. The slender forces in Malaya were to be kept that way. Under the cover of strict censorship, the propaganda put out to the world was the opposite. British newspapers reported that the forces were being built all the time. Emphasis was on the size of the 'magnificent' air force. 'Clouds of bombers and fighters are hidden in the jungle' ready to come out of camouflaged tarmacs and 'roar into action at the first move of the Japanese towards this part of the world'. But this did not fool the enemy. It had a strong intelligence service in Malaya and Singapore.[1]

Deception corroded into self-delusion.

Behind the scenes, the astute commander of the 8th Division, Major-General Gordon Bennett, 54, fought hard for reinforcements.

One problem in the reaction to the requests was the man himself. He was one of the most controversial figures in Australian military history. Bald, lean Bennett had been at odds with General Sir Thomas Blamey, Australia 2nd AIF commander-in-chief, for 30 years since Blamey had been thrown in a horse trough by some soldiers in 1912. Blamey for a time claimed Bennett was behind it. The two men hated each other from then on. Another factor was Bennett's ambition, which at times caused him to overreach. While Blamey was his superior, Bennett's fervent desires for advancement and opportunities would be checked. He also had a distrust of regular army officers.

At 21, in 1908, he was commissioned in the 5th Australian Infantry Regiment, based in Victoria. Bennett was an actuarial clerk with the AMP Society. He believed in the citizens' forces and the officers they produced. If men had lives away from the military—other professions and serious interests—then they would be more effective leaders in wartime. His model as ever was Monash, the brilliant lawyer, engineer and arts lover, the very embodiment of the Renaissance Man, who was regarded by most British observers as the finest battle commander of World War I. Bennett felt that those who stayed full-time in the military were dulled by the experience and not equipped to handle pressures in battle. This antagonism spilled over here and there. Regular officers, especially on Blamey's staff, were aware of and sensitive about his attitudes.

Bennett was one of the original Anzacs who hit the Gallipoli beaches on 25 April 1915 as a 28-year-old major in the 6th Infantry Battalion. His capacities were in evidence that fateful morning. He showed exceptional courage and initiative when he gathered his scattered men above the beach at Anzac Cove and then led from the front. Bennett, under intense fire, reached a point 200 metres on, more than a 'touchdown', in the tight encounters that were to come on Gallipoli. In the afternoon, he wanted to press on, but he stood to direct fire at Pine Ridge and was shot down by Turkish snipers. Hit in the shoulder and wrist, he had the presence of mind to hand over battalion command to another officer before he was stretchered off to a hospital ship for medical attention. He was expected to recuperate, perhaps for the rest of the war, but Bennett would have none of it. Defying doctors' orders the next day, he took the chance to 'desert' the hospital ship so that he could go back to Anzac Cove to lead his men. He was wounded again on Gallipoli but returned to the front once more. He repeated this act after being wounded again on the Western Front in France. Inside a year, Bennett, who turned 29 on 15 April 1916, had a reputation as a fearless front-line operator. He earned promotion to brigadier-general, and was one of the youngest men ever in the British Army to be so rewarded.

Some detractors suggested that his need for challenges on the front-line led to his frustrations in the current war. This desire to be involved in the heat of action was not always advisable activity for a divisional commander in modern warfare. Journalist A. B. Lodge thought that his time out of the armed forces between the wars had been a drawback, not the asset he himself thought it was. Lodge suggested he was out of touch with modern warfare and tactics.

Perhaps a greater problem for Bennett was his lack of diplomacy in the Allied force. His background made him intolerant of poor soldiering. He was critical of Indian and British infantry in the campaign. Bennett tended to judge others by his own exceptional guts. Anything short of his standard was dismissed out of hand.

The *London Times* war correspondent Ian Morrison covered the entire Malayan conflict, and was known for his 'fair and balanced' assessments of the leading officers. He had a low regard for the British leadership. But he made an exception with Bennett, whom he judged as 'the best of the senior military officers', which included all the commanders in the British, Australian and Indian forces.

'He was a rasping, bitter, sarcastic person, given to expressing his views with great freedom,' Morrison wrote. 'As a result, he quarrelled with a good number of people. But he did have a forceful personality. He was imbued with a tough, ruthless, aggressive spirit. As a soldier he was unconventional, but one wanted an unconventional soldier to deal with what was an unconventional situation. He was passionately proud of his men and devoted to their interests. His men knew it and had confidence in him.'[2]

Despite any alleged or real shortcomings, Bennett still had pull. After some pleading he was sent the Division's 27th Brigade in August 1941. He believed he still was one brigade—5,000 men and armaments—short. He enthusiastically used his new acquisition to defend Johore, setting up his own HQ at Johor Bahru, across the causeway from Singapore Island. The Sultan of Johore, 68, was most appreciative. Bennett saw him every day and they got on well. The sultan was aware of the importance of the Australian force to his own survival. He responded by letting it use building sites, camps and even his polo field for sporting activity. Bennett also paid a deal of attention to the sultana, in her mid-thirties and amenable to his flirtatious overtures. This relationship provided tittle-tattle ammunition to Bennett's numerous enemies and rivals within and outside the force.

Undeterred, he set about setting up defence posts at the east coast beaches of Endau and Mersing where the Japanese might land. Near these beaches was the important junction at Jemaluang, where a road from the west coast met the main thoroughfare to Singapore Island, which was just 95 kilometres south. Bennett directed the 22nd Brigade to build up the beach defences. The newly arrived lads of the 27th were placed around Jemaluang and sent for tough jungle training.

Meanwhile, the phoney war dragged on. It was a test of another kind, a war of attrition of morale. In the Boer and Great Wars, Australians had volunteered with the desire, aim and hope of going straight into action. The men of the 8th Division were all aware of the traditions built in the previous two conflicts. They were reading about their brother divisions in the Middle East and North Africa in this one. In all these instances, Australians had been fighting formations. There was little experience of base or garrison duties that prevailed in Malaya and Singapore. The tropical weather did nothing to appease the growing frustration and strain.

The aggravation and dissatisfaction was not confined to the lower ranks. British Air Chief Marshal Brooke-Popham, overall commander in Singapore, became concerned about new intelligence he was receiving about Japanese intentions and movements in the region. He sent spies in plain clothes to Singora on the east coast of Thailand north of Malaya. It had the only sizeable port on that side of the neck of land, which was thought probable and appropriate for invasion. The British agents were bemused to find Japanese spies, also allegedly 'incognito' in civvies, doing what they were doing.

This further alarmed the British commanders. The London war office was asked for 48 battalions (about 50,000 soldiers). They received three. They were poorly trained and equipped Indians. This thin offering was effectively next to nothing in the light of the size of the force the Japanese might send. The British commanders in the Far East became agitated, then nervous.

In late August 1941, the Japanese held an Imperial Conference at which they decided that their war preparation for attacks in the Pacific and the Far East had to be completed by the end of October. If their diplomatic efforts to gain concessions (effectively to kick the British and Dutch out of those regions) were not attained by early October, then they would go to war. In 1940, US President Franklin D. Roosevelt moved the US Pacific Fleet to Pearl Harbor as a further deterrent to Japanese expansionism. The Western powers tried to curb their aggression by cutting off their oil supply. By 1941, all trade had been blocked. Japan then looked to oil in the Dutch East Indies (Indonesia) and mineral-rich South-East Asia as an alternative source of essential resources.

Early in September 1941, the Japanese military began moving some of its stock of C56 class locomotives towards docks for imminent loading onto ships. This was done in secret. It was the first clear sign of Japanese plans for invasion somewhere in South-East Asia.

In September 1941, a gaggle of British and Australian ministers and top military brass gathered in Singapore for a round of further self-delusion. The conference 'decided' that Japan was grouping for an attack on Russia, not Malaya-Singapore. They also came to the conclusion that the Japanese must be fully aware of the dangers of becoming embroiled in a war against the British Commonwealth, the US and the Dutch. It was as if the meeting would somehow divine what the Japanese would do. If they were foolhardy enough to invade any nation under the control of this colonial power triumvirate, surely they would not attack next month (October 1941) during the north-east monsoon season. This logic was staggering in its blindness. Yes, the Japanese would not attack in the rainy

season. But after that—from late November on—they might.
If the British were using this precious time to really prepare for
invasion, it would be one thing; wishing it away was another.

The conference further decided on the 'propaganda' value
of sending a couple of battleships to Singapore. This flimsy
show of strength was meant to scare off the potential invaders.
The US's General MacArthur in Manila added to the fantasy
by telling Australia's minister for commerce, Sir Earle Page,
that after five years of war in China since the rape of Nanking
in 1937, the Japanese had 'over-extended' themselves.

'They needed a long period of recuperation before they
could undertake another major struggle,' Page was told.
'Japan had gone to the limit of its southward expansion.'[3]

Bennett did not agree. He was on the spot. He knew the Japanese had been landing spies and disguised military officers in
Thailand for months. They were not there on holiday. Nor
were they making themselves conspicuous as a diversion-
ary tactic. In October, Bennett requested that he be sent the
Darwin-based 13th Brigade, the third brigade of three in his
division. But the tyranny of distance was against him. The
Australian Military Board, in Sleepy Hollow Land, denied
him his full divisional complement. He asked for permission
to fly to Darwin to inspect the 13th. Then the truth came
out. It soon would be broken up and sent to the Northern
Territory, New Britain and the Dutch East Indies. Bennett
was shocked. He was informed that he himself might be
going to the Middle East. Confused, he receiving a clarifying
blow when Australia's commander-in-chief, General Blamey,
turned up at his HQ to tell him that he would be pressing the

Australian Government to send the 8th Division to the Middle East. Blamey's secret aim was to unite the entire 2nd AIF under his command there. Bennett had never trusted Blamey since working with him under Monash in World War I and was never convinced of his competency or suitability for the top job. Now Blamey's ignorance (of Japanese intentions) was added to his perceived list of shortcomings.

Bennett tried to explain his beliefs based on his intelligence on the ground. Blamey, putting his own ambitions ahead of everything, including Australia's interests, refused to accept there was an imminent threat. He was buying what Bennett saw as misinformation and wrong-headed analysis from observers far from Malaya.

Chitty learnt of brother Toxa's movements in 1941 from newspaper reports on his battalion and letters from home. Toxa had spent eight months as a Rat of Tobruk and had been in the heaviest fighting in August, September and into October against the Germans when Rommel's tanks and infantry attacked and failed to break through. At last report, Toxa's 23rd Battalion had been evacuated to Alexandria, Egypt. Ron Chitty was finally rounded up on Crete early in November 1941 after five months on the loose. He was taken to Stalag VIIA, at Moorsberg, north of Munich, Germany.

At least the family would soon know he was 'safe' like Phil and out of a combat zone.[4]

The disgruntled and uneasy Bennett made an urgent trip to Egypt in late November. He was sent to 'observe' in the

Middle East. He spent 48 hours in Cairo and then visited the battlegrounds in the desert. On 3 December, he boarded a Qantas flying boat for the return trip to Malaya. He wrote in his diary that he feared the Japanese would soon make their big push from Indo-China into Thailand, Malaya and Dutch East Indies (Indonesia).

It was a long, slow trip. At each stop, he received news from his Malaya HQ that all was quiet on the Thai–Malaya 'Front'. Nothing to worry about. He should relax and enjoy the flight home. In Calcutta, he called at Government House on Field Marshal Earl Wavell, the Supreme British Commander of Far East Force—covering South-East Asia and South Pacific regions. Blamey, still with his aspirations for uniting the AIF under his own control, was there too, en route to the Middle East again.

Wavell was only interested in events in the Western Desert. Blamey would not listen to Bennett's views about the 8th staying in Malaya to fight the Japanese. He wanted it in the Middle East. Bennett repeated the intelligence he had gathered in Thailand about Japanese activity. Blamey dismissed it. He was adamant: the Japanese would not extend the war that far.

It was 6 December 1941. Gordon Bennett felt frustrated and annoyed. He cut a solitary figure as his plane touched down in Rangoon, Burma a day later.

Despite his serious concerns, things appeared normal in 8th Division camps all over Malaya. The troops received their mail, which was late, bringing news and clippings a couple of months out of date. But still, as ever, letters were a warm touch from home that brought nostalgic twinges. Chitty had been away a year. He longed for his family, friends and the smell of the bush in late spring before the summer heat dried up all the moisture. He thought daily about his wife and children. How were his beautiful daughter Dawn and tiny Lindsay, the son he had known just a few months? How was Lilian coping?

Letters from home brought the mixed news about Ron and Phil being alive but incarcerated. Knowing the aggressive spirit of all his male siblings, he would have been relieved. There was a nagging worry about Toxa. He had seen more action than anyone in the family. But for the moment he was doing garrison duty. Recently his 23rd Battalion had been shifted from Palestine to Syria. This meant that Toxa had not been fighting for two months, and from limited correspondence he did not know when he would be in a battle again. Chitty knew that Toxa, no matter what he had been through, would be itching to be in the action once more.

On the lighter side, he learned that Bob had had another excellent year for Carlton. He had come fourth in the Brownlow Medal count for 1941, which indicated he must have behaved himself on field for the entire season, which was out of character. Carlton had slipped. It didn't even make the finals. Harold Ball's team Melbourne had won its third successive premiership, this time without him. Chitty's team St Kilda was languishing on the bottom the table. He also said that because of the war, the Brownlow Medal would be suspended for the 1942 season.[5]

He went to bed early on 6 December. There was a very early morning call for a convoy exercise that would run all day. He would have slept at least content that all seemed well at home, and that none of his brothers had been harmed in their various battle zones.

10

Japan Attacks

A low drone of aircraft flying in formation caused churchgoers on a lazy early Sunday morning at Hawaii's Pearl Harbor US naval base to look up. It was 7 December 1941. There was not much concern when bombs were dropped. Most people thought it was a US flight command training run. The last thing expected was an attack by the Japanese. But when battleships began to go up in flames, stunned onlookers forgot about church. This was real. 353 planes from six Japanese aircraft carriers in two waves let their loads go in a two-hour bombardment.

They sank 18 US warships, destroyed 188 aircraft and killed 2,403 service personnel.

US President Roosevelt responded with an address to the nation. He spoke of a 'day that would live in infamy'. War was declared on Japan, but the attackers at that moment had pulled off a well-planned, cunning and audacious blow, which set the Americans and the West back on their heels. Admiral Isoruka Yamamoto, who masterminded the move, feared Japan would not be able to win a protracted war with the US.

His aim had been to wipe out the US fleet with one smashing attack.

The night of 7 December was hot, even for Rangoon. Bennett, oblivious of the chilling news from Hawaii, used binoculars to spy through a window at a bedroom across from him. He was no peeping Tom. Four Japanese spent six hours poring over maps of Malaya. Bennett advised British military HQ in Burma. But nothing was done.

In the early hours of 8 December, Peter Chitty, Joe Jameson and other 2/2nd Motor Ambulance drivers were travelling south in a convoy training run in Johor in Malaya's south when a wave of planes swept low over them. The trucks were moving with 100 metre distances between them just in case there was an air attack. At first, in the dark Chitty and other drivers had no idea which side—theirs or the enemy's—the planes belonged to.

'We were not sure if they were Japanese,' Jameson recalled. 'The red dot markings under the wings would later be discernible in day-light raids. From then on we called them "flying arseholes".'

The Japanese pilots were at that moment unconcerned about attempting to bomb the trucks. Their mission was to hit Singapore, after a fellow squadron had earlier attacked Kota Bharu and Patani near the Thai border on the east and west coasts respectively.

There was no defence ready to counter them, either in the air or on the ground. The causeway and Singapore, lit up and an easy target, did not receive a proper alert. Sixty people, mainly civilians, were killed by the bombs. The defence was also hamstrung by an order to anti-aircraft gunners, who could not fire until a bomb landed. Japan was not officially at war with Britain and Australia. Authorities feared provoking war if the fly-over of 60 heavy bombers was just a token demonstration.

The 13th Australian General Hospital at Tampoi Hill 6 kilometres from Johor Bahru was the destination for Chitty's convoy drill. It was also one of the targets for the Japanese bombers. Observers thought they were friendly aircraft in a similar reaction to those at the naval base at Pearl Harbor. Everyone was used to a bit of anti-aircraft fire 'practice'. The surprise element by the cunning enemy, which had not declared war on the nations they were attacking, had worked again.

The raids continued.

Ambulance worker Stan Young was standing on the highest hill (Bukit Timah—'Silver Mountain') with a full view of Singapore when 123 Japanese bombers came over low in formation.

'All the planes dropped them [bombs] at once,' he said. 'It shook the island. They had to block half the city off because of the devastation.'[1]

The initial raid on Singapore followed those on Pearl Harbor and Manila. The Japanese had also bombed bases in Thailand. The aim was to take control of airports and then move south in a three-pronged thrust on Malaya's west and east coasts, and through the middle from Patani (moving about 100 kilometres from the Japanese western force).

Not everyone reacted with fear. Many of the diggers were pleased that the war was on.

'The boys had been restless and unhappy for some time,' Sister Betty Pump at the 2/10th Australian General Hospital noted in her diary. 'They spoke with irritation at being "Garrison Troops". At last we were to do a job for which we had prepared and waited.'[1]

Chitty and Co. responded to the code word 'Raffles', the signal from the Malaya command that the war had begun. All ranks had to stand to arms ready for action. The Australian brigades were directed to defend Singapore and Johor in Malaya's south, the last bastion before the causeway to the island.

Many ambulance drivers had rifles and revolvers in their cabins, for self-defence on the battlefield. But they did not expect to use them in anger. They would be busy ferrying the wounded from dressing stations—makeshift forward hospitals—and then to the properly equipped hospitals.

It was the end of the lazy days of the past 10 months in the poor man's holiday camp that was Malaya and Singapore in the Phoney War.

The Japanese had stunned the world by attacking the American possessions of Hawaii and the Philippines, along with Malaya, Thailand and Hong Kong in separate blitzes. American troops in the Philippines, primarily composed of local Philippines troops, were pushed back into a tiny enclave on the Bataan Peninsula. In Malaya and Hong Kong, untrained British troops were no match for the battle-hardened Japanese soldiers, who had toughened up for years in China.

Thailand was invaded by land from Battambang, Cambodia, by air at Don Muang airfield and by sea in seven amphibious landings from Hua Hin and Pattani on the coast of the Gulf of Thailand. Despite savage fighting at several points in the south, organised resistance was brief.

Thai field marshal Phibin Songkhram ordered a ceasefire, believing his troops had no hope. (He signed a 'peace treaty of alliance' with the Japanese on 21 December, which effectively handed Thailand to the invaders.)

Japanese daring, brutality and military precision were a shock to the Allies. The war in Europe, North Africa and the Middle East had expanded worldwide, and clear 'sides' had been taken. The Japanese had joined the German and Italian fascists. Now the US would come in beside the British. German invasion of Russia in 1941 had pitted the British, Americans and Soviet Union in conflict with the fascist powers.

The British Navy sent two of its great warships, HMS *Prince of Wales* and HMS *Repulse,* to bolster Singapore's defence and morale. They chased a Japanese invasion flotilla off Kuantan, on Malaya's east coast. The Japanese countered with 50 planes with torpedo bombs. Once more, they carried out a surprise attack without any opposition in the air. The two warships fired back, but were too cumbersome in their desperate manoeuvres to avoid being struck. In a two-hour afternoon battle, the warships were sunk. Admiral Sir Tom Phillips, the British Navy's chief of staff for the Far East, was a casualty. The loss of the ships that were meant to boost the spirits of the beleaguered troops instead lowered morale at a critical time. The dual sinking following the destruction of the American Pacific Fleet at Pearl Harbor left the waters between India and the West Coast of the US almost without Allied battleships.

All remaining Allied warships were combined into a single fleet under the command of a Dutch admiral in an effort to defend the Dutch East Indies. The Japanese destroyed this fleet in a series of engagements. The last two Allied cruisers, USS *Houston* and HMAS *Perth*, made a run for Australia but were sunk between Sumatra and Java in Sunda Strait.

Australia sent troops north to several major islands of the Dutch East Indies (including Timor and Ambon). Troops later recalled from North Africa and the Middle East were to be sent to Java.

Singapore and Malaya seemed more vulnerable than ever.

These shocks accentuated the main initial problem facing the defenders. They provided no opposition to speak of in the air. Japan's fighters and bombers could attack with impunity anywhere they wished. Sortie after sortie was sent to hammer the ground defences of the British, Indian and Australian troops. The impact lowered resistance. Added to this was the more subtle, but no less effective, Japanese fifth column activity on the ground ahead of its troops moving south. Locals were paid to help the advancing invaders learn where the defences were ahead of them. Japanese troops, disguised as Malayan natives, infiltrated Australian positions as the diggers waited for the inevitable clashes.

There were about 3,000 Japanese in Malaya, but the information gathering for the Imperial Army could have come from 10 times that number. Espionage material of every kind was gathered, from assessments of British military size and commentary about morale to photographs of installations and the troop locations. Companies in Malaya such as Nissan pushed Japan's political goals through the Japanese Chamber of Commerce and Commercial Museum. Brothels were a source of espionage. Officers and soldiers alike blabbed more than they should, especially with a few drinks in them and a lovely girl attending to every whim. Japanese fishermen used their boats to patrol rivers and coastlines. Journalists at the *Eastern News Agency* and the *Singapore Herald* were active in creating files on British personnel that would be passed on to enemy agents.

Everyone knew about the Japanese craze for photography. It was useful cover for spying, especially when many of the British forces were interested in this newish 'art' and pastime. Young Australian private George Aspinall was one of several enthusiasts in the 30th Battalion. Several studios sprang up at the base at Batu Pahat to meet their demand. He recalled that one of the better studios was run by a man calling himself Mah Lee, a Japanese posing as a Chinese. Troops would have shots taken there. Mah Lee visited the battalion camp to take company and platoon photos.

Aspinall recalled him taking one of his transport platoon in front of their vehicles. He bought a copy and sent it home to his mother. On one occasion, Aspinall was over-charged for some prints. They had 'a few cross words'.

'Mah Lee was always finding ways to get into the camp to take pictures,' Aspinall noted, 'either with his big half-plate camera, or his shoulder 35 mm camera. I'd say he knew more about our camp at Batu Pahat than we did.'

Later, when the British were in this camp, it was bombed heavily.

Aspinall kept a photo taken by Mah Lee after a dinner at the Batu Pahat Chinese Chamber of Commerce. It included officers and NCOs of the 30th Battalion and the Chinese businessmen who entertained them. (Most of the Chinese in the photo were later executed by the Japanese.)[3]

In addition to intelligence, there was the much underestimated Japanese military precision. Bennett noted in his diary the number of times that the enemy pinpointed British or Indian troops. Japanese reconnaissance planes accounted for some of this laser-like identification.

12 December 1941 was a typical Bennett diary entry:

'The [krocol] front [in Malaya's north] experienced a black dawn. As day broken extremely heavy bombardment was concentrated on the positions held by the Indians.'

Reconnaissance planes had located their positions. Then the Japanese began a much repeated manoeuvre. They attacked, gaining a foothold on a hill. Then, using artillery and machine-guns, they bombarded the Indians' flank facing a river, and their right rear. This was followed by the Japanese moving round the weakened flank and 'threatening to cut off this battalion'.[4]

The other flank was hit in the same fashion. Then enemy reserves were brought in to cut off the Indians' retreat.

This basic military tactic was the method of Lieutenant-General Yamashita, a big, heavy officer, with plenty of command experiences but none until now on the battlefield. He had led military missions to Italy and Germany between the wars, but Malaya was his big test. Yamashita was determined to make it work. He was ambitious and aggressive. His sheer size—a bit more beef and he could have been a sumo wrestler—commanded fear and respect. He also was a bit of a risk-taker, a gambler. This came out in the campaign. He had been allocated fewer than 35,000 men, which meant he was on paper outnumbered nearly four to one. A worry that he later admitted kept him on edge, was that the more he stretched his supply lines and the longer he fought, the less likely he was to pull off a victory. He had to win as quickly as possible.

But Yamashita had a deeper secret concern that gave sleepless nights. If they were drawn into street fights, real hand-to-hand stuff that meant dragged-out encounters right into Singapore, his force was sure to lose. Yamashita learnt from his German mission that close fighting was just what some of the British troops, particularly the Scots and Australians, revelled in. It had to be avoided at all costs. Intelligent strategy, smart tactics and courage were required.

Through the early weeks of the campaign he wondered if he was on a suicide mission.

Wanted: One Digger Division

Yamashita's tactics on the battlefield, Japanese air superiority and coerced (and in some cases, willing) spies, made all British defending activity hazardous. Not the least problematic was shipping at Singapore's Keppel Harbour bringing essential food and equipment for the troops. It was continually hit. Vehicle transport was strafed. All the trucks in Chitty's convoy had bullet holes from low-flying enemy planes. There was little protection on the roads carved into the thick jungle. Drivers became familiar with the roar of the planes as they dived, the whistle of the falling bombs and the flash of the explosion on impact. Trucks would often be driven off the road into rubber plantations if they were fortunate enough to be passing them.

On 16 December 1941, the Japanese hit Burma from southern Thailand, aiming at capturing the British airfields at Victoria Point and Mergui. The plan was to cross the mountains on the Thai–Burma border at Three Pagodas Pass and at Mae Sot, with the aim of pushing the limited British force west towards Rangoon.

*

There was still a long pause before direct Australian contact with the enemy on the ground as the Japanese infantry moved relentlessly south over the next five weeks. They fought, defeated and pushed back the British and Indian forces with a little too much ease for the Australians' liking.

Trucks full of wounded and dying being transported to dressing stations and hospitals south of the action were an indicator of the course of the war. Australian Field Ambulance and truck convoys, including Chitty's, were kept busy in this period ferrying people south. The medical facilities were also being herded towards Singapore.

'When the bombing finished we filled the ambulance and off we went to the hospital,' Lemke recalled. The drivers were often asked to go straight back. 'One of the worst experiences of the war was driving in a blackout. You couldn't even smoke. The trip seemed to take hours.'[1]

Major-General Bennett, with more urgency than ever, was pleading for an extra division to be sent from the Middle East. On 17 December 1941, he wrote to Australian Army HQ in Melbourne:

'The situation in the north [of Malaya] is very grave indeed . . . I have seen a total absence of the offensive spirit [by the British and Indians], which after all, is the only great remedy for the methods adopted by the Japanese. Counterattacks would put a stop to this penetration . . . I am convinced that an advance of more Australian troops to Malaya . . . is a matter of paramount importance.'[2]

In the week since Pearl Harbor, the Japanese had made their intentions clear in the region by invading the Philippines and seizing Guam in the Pacific on 10 December. A day later, they hit Burma running. On 16 December, they were into British Borneo. They planned to take Hong Kong on 18 December.

There was time, just, for the Australian Government to ship 20,000 soldiers to Singapore to bolster the defence. But Bennett was not receiving support from his British commander in Malaya, the unassuming Lieutenant-General A. E. Percival, for whom Bennett was experiencing a dwindling respect. There was no doubting the Englishman's strength as a staff officer. He was not so impressive in the field. One problem was that Bennett had been under Monash in World War I, and Percival fell short on every comparison. His appearance didn't help. Tall but thin and poor in physique, he had a little moustache and protruding, rabbit-like teeth that earned him the nickname 'Bunny'.

The *London Times* war correspondent Ian Morrison believed Percival did not know how to deal with men. He saw 'the difficulties to any scheme before he saw the possibilities.'

'He was a negative person, with no vigour, no colour and no conviction,' the journalist further observed, 'As a leader he did not appeal to either the troops or the general public.'[3]

Bennett described Percival as 'weak'. One reason for this was his lack of support for that needed extra Australian division. But Percival was not alone. There was no support from Churchill. Australian Army HQ in Melbourne was equally cool to the request, which was not surprising given Blamey's self-serving ambitions in the Middle East. The last thing he wanted was a precious division, that might otherwise be under his command, being sent to Singapore.

That island, which Churchill had claimed was impregnable, would have to live up to this claim—with the 130,000 British troops that were already in defence of it. He was looking at the soldier numbers on paper without proper analysis and consideration for their fighting capacity and the experience and skill of their commanders. Churchill's belief that Singapore could not be taken was based on the big artillery guns. But the flaws in that argument had already been exposed. The fixed guns pointed out to sea and could not be turned around. The Japanese had already come a long way on land. Any possible enemy naval attack and engagement was irrelevant.

Matters looked grim for the defenders on 16 December 1941, when the island of Penang fell on Malaya's north-west coast. The Malayans were wondering which side would win. Now there was further uncertainty. The invaders were making headway.

The Japanese turned their focus to the Slim River another 200 kilometres further south. It was held by British and Indian troops. The roads were clogged with refugees fleeing south, military personnel moving in the opposite direction to all points of the compass and the various fronts the Japanese were creating. There was a sense of panic from the locals, and concern from the defenders.

Chitty and his compatriots in the ambulance convoys were moving the trucks and ambulances among the throng, transporting and helping out their Indian and British counterparts, who were struggling to keep up with the building numbers of casualties. The Australian 2/10th hospital at Malacca was in potential danger. Decisions had to be made to move it further south. At least 800 tonnes of equipment had to be shifted. That would need all the trucks available in one long convoy.

More important were the patients, who would have to be transported to the (13th Australian General) hospital at Tampoi in the south of Johor near the causeway.

The Red Cross marking on the trucks and ambulances was no guarantee that the Japanese planes would not aim their bombs and machine-guns at them. It depended on the mood of the pilots. If they had had a few hits that day, they might line up and scare the truck and ambulance drivers without firing or letting go a bomb. Ammunition was yet to be rationed by the Japanese. Each one knew that it was more 'productive' to strafe a marching battalion or British HQ than perhaps 'score' one truck in a convoy. On the other hand, the enemy pilot might not have been lucky with strikes on a given day. Any British force ambulance truck, Red Cross markings or otherwise, might well be a target. Major (Dr) Alan Hobbs from the 2/4th Casualty Clearing Station was concerned early in the new year that the Japanese airmen were becoming ever more dangerous.

Yet a diary entry in the first week of 1942 indicated there was some hope:

'Raid on aerodrome, 10 bombers at 7 a.m. Lasted on and off about 45 minutes. Many guns and much AA [anti-aircraft] fire. Only one military casualty, abrasions and cut scalp. From slit trench could see 10 planes, 3 fighters & AA fire and hear whistle of AA shells. Reports of 2 [British]—bombers not reaching base—crashing on way home . . . To Swiss Road Rifle Club. Solitary Jap plane flew low over us, commenced a machine-gun burst but apparently stopped on seeing the red cross.'[4]

This was in contrast to the convoy drivers.

'You never knew whether they would fly over us or have a

go,' Frank 'Titch' Lemin said, 'but we kept going. Peter Chitty was our [convoy] leader. He would go anywhere. Peter was a real man of iron. But he would not ask us to do anything he would not do himself. He was tough, fair and a good mate. Peter gave us courage to carry on our missions regardless of the enemy overhead.'[5]

All the drivers at this time experienced attacks from Japanese ignoring their Red Cross status. More and more they were sent slewing off the road from a strafing machine-gun swooping over them. They saw many ambulances from their British and Indian counterpart units that had been bombed or hit. On top of that, word came back that many of the vehicles were being captured by the enemy.

Suddenly in early January the non-combatant drivers were just as vulnerable to a non-discriminating enemy as the fighting men.

12

Ambush at Gemas

Gordon Bennett's warnings about the Japanese advance and how to tackle it were not heeded. Now, in charge of defending the southern state of Johor, he was left with the main responsibility of stopping the invaders as they fought their way down the west coast of the Malayan peninsula. They had not had it all their own way in certain battles. Their commander General Yamashita would have had nail-biting moments as here and there the British forces put up stiff opposition and delayed his determined force. But one by one the key places fell to the Japanese in December 1941 and the first half of January 1942: Battle of Jitra, December 11th–12th; 13th Balor Star; 14th Gurun; 16th Sungei Patani, Penang; 23rd Taiping, Port Weld; 24th Kuala Kagsar; 26th Ipoh; 30th Kampar; 31st Kuantan; 2 January Telok Anson; Slim River; 3rd Kuala Selongor; 10th Port Swettenham and January 11th, Kuala Lumpur.

Outside Malaya, the British had given the Japanese a Christmas present of Hong Kong on 25 December. Early in the New Year, the enemy had taken Manila and the US Naval Base at Cavite, and had attacked Bataan in the Philippines. On 11 January, the same day that Kuala Lumpur had fallen, they invaded the Dutch East Indies and Dutch Borneo. That week they planned an advance on Burma. Japanese diplomats were on their way to Berlin to sign a military agreement with the other fascist powers, German and Italy. The intensity, ferocity and spread of their invasions, attacks and advances were frightening for an unprepared Allied world.

So far, the Japanese had not received the sort of setback in Malaya that could turn a battle. Yamashita's high-risk strategy was working.

Bennett wanted to appear upbeat facing the coming challenge. He told war correspondents that his men were 'as happy as sand boys at the thought of being able to get at our new enemy, "the yellow Huns of the East".' This caused some of his staff to recoil. Bennett had taken the private 'speak' at the bar at Raffles into the world public arena. Then he added a comment that had them cringing: 'One Australian is worth ten Japanese.'[1] In the rarefied atmosphere, this was reported and given prominence without much reaction. It was propaganda, the sort of absurd comparison meant to inspire that was uttered by battle commanders, or football coaches every other Saturday afternoon when talking about the opposition. Given Bennett's front-line efforts in the last war, the words would be taken well by most of the men he would be sending into action. The rest would be blasé about any propaganda. But his enemies and those on his staff who disliked him would store away the remark for future reference if battles did not go Australia's way. Later, out of context, it could be made to look like bragging, racism and plain stupidity.

Bennett was left to tackle the flow of enemy troops. Yamashita's specialty of coming around behind their opponents through the cover of jungle was working well. Bennett would attempt to counter it two ways: first by attacking rather than waiting to be caught in the Japanese web; second by spreading his defensive flanks to make it tougher for the enemy to creep by.

After the fall of Kuala Lumpur, he chose Gemencheh Creek, about 11 kilometres west of Gemas village in Johor's north, 55 kilometres north-east of Malacca (on the west coast) as the place not just to make a stand, but to counterattack.

Bennett was aware that this battle would be crucial. It and those sure to follow close on its heels would incur extra casualties. He called for more medicos and ambulances. Chitty was quick to put his hand up to switch temporarily on loan to the 3rd Motor Ambulance Convoy for this special mission.

Bennett had looked at suitable sites from Gallipoli to Flanders and northern France in battle. He considered the wooden bridge across the Gemencheh Creek as just about right. The road on which the Japanese were expected to come twisted through dense jungle for about half a kilometre. Once the force crossed the bridge, it had to travel another 250 metres in the open with no cover either side of the road before reaching more jungle. Bennett considered it perfect for an ambush. He put Lieutenant-Colonel Frederick 'Black Jack' Galleghan, the commander of the 2/30th Battalion, in charge. His nickname came from a part West Indian background and misleadingly indicated a cavalier approach and aggression in his make-up. Galleghan was a careful planner and a good leader. His initial reaction was that the bridge area was too small for a battalion (about 1,000 men). He opted for a company (of 250). All company commanders wanted the mission. The only fair way to make a choice was to put names in a hat. D Company, led by Des Duffy, won the draw.

Galleghan put the rest of the battalion across the road a further 5 kilometres back. They were geared up for the inevitable flanking stealth and surprise by the Japanese. Indian troops were kept at the ready.

It was raining on the night of 13 January 1942. The soldiers crept up to their positions. Sappers moved to the bridge and set it up with explosives. The entire battalion waited all night and until 4 p.m. on 14 January. Then the Japanese appeared. There were about 1,000 soldiers on bikes, riding eight abreast. They began to cross the bridge, smiling and chatting. They were relaxed and enjoying themselves. They had good reason to be pleased. Their invading army was winning.

Duffy and his men were hidden close to the winding road. They let 300 of the happy throng pass by and over the bridge, leaving 700 in the vulnerable zone. Duffy signalled. His engineers blew the bridge. Wood, men and bikes were hurled in the air. Duffy's men tossed grenades and opened up with machine-guns. The Japanese had nowhere to run. They were cut down, the dead and the dying littering 300 metres of road among the debris.

The initial action took 19 minutes.

Duffy's men made it back to the battalion position 5 kilometres away west of the bridge. Only one Australian was killed, making it in every respect one of the most successful ambushes in the entire war to that point.[2]

The Japanese recovered. Percival and the other British commanders no sooner received the news about the unique success than 15 January dawned and it was the war as it had been. Other parts of Yamashita's force kept coming. They reached the Muar River about 65 kilometres south of Gemas. It was 500 metres wide and was the last hurdle in the thrust to the causeway at Johor. The Japanese gathered north of it. They engaged two Indian companies that were overrun. At night, the Australians attacked with heavy artillery fire. But it could not stop the enemy who used boats they had brought with them. By the end of the day they had crushed the terrified Indian opposition on the south bank of the river.

The Japanese also made it across the river 50 kilometres further south of Batu Pahat. Bennett's sensitivity at being one division short was at its height. He would somehow have to stiffen his defences at Johor.

He committed the 2/19th and 2/29th Battalions to battle.[3]

The enemy set patrols forward, looking for the Australian positions. When located on 17 January, they hit them with accurate mortar fire, which the diggers were forced to endure through the night. It did some damage to the guns of the 2/4th Australian Anti-Tank Regiment, which indicated that Japanese intelligence was as pinpoint as ever.

At first light on 18 January, they sent tanks down the Muar Road heading for the digger battalions. The Australian gunners fired armour-piercing shells, which did their job, technically speaking. They ripped right through the lightly built tanks, going in one side and out the other. The astonished gunners reloaded and fired. Three tanks kept sliding forward. They passed the frustrated gunners, who were looking down the road for the next group of tanks. But the 2/4th commander, Lance Sergeant C. W. Thornton, ordered his men to keep firing at the three tanks, this time using high-explosive rounds. The tanks became trapped in a cutting. They tried to manoeuvre out. The anti-tank shells roared at them. One struck home and exploded inside one tank, then another. They blew up like a thunderous firework displays, ammunition and metal flying off like sparks from a Catherine-wheel.

The third tank endured the same fate. Another seven faced similar destruction in the next few hours.

Ten tanks in all were obliterated. The Japanese infantry, shocked and demoralised for the first time, were beaten off.

They brought in fresh troops, unscarred in battle, to assist. Many assaults were attempted but repulsed. Yet the Japanese were relentless and their expertise at jungle flanking moves by stealth was successful, especially with the inexperienced and frightened Indians not up to facing them.

The Japanese built a roadblock between the positions of the 2/29th and the 2/19th Battalion at the rear. A valiant attempt by commander Lieutenant-Colonel J. C. Robertson to link up the battalions failed. He was cut down by Bren-gun fire from the roadblock and died an hour later. This stunned the battalions. At first, the soldiers were demoralised by their leader's demise. But they regrouped and held off assaults from the south and west. The Japanese continued to mass around them like angry hornets.

The diggers, without support on the flanks, were left vulnerable.

If the enemy needed any inspiration to carry through to victory in Malaya, it was provided by their brothers-in-arms in North Borneo when they took that country on 19 January 1942.

13

The Hunter and the Hunted

Robertson's place was taken by the no less distin-guished commander of the 2/19th, the bespectacled Lieutenant-Colonel Charles Anderson, 44. He served in the King's African Rifles in World War I and won a Military

Cross fighting pro-German Askari tribesmen in the jungles of East Africa. That experience prepared him better than most for war in Malaya. He also shot big game in Kenya for pleasure. Now instead of being the hunter he was the hunted. Anderson was given the tough task of leading a fighting night withdrawal 8 kilometres to the bridge at Parit Sulong. On 20 January, the battalions had to retreat through swamps and go wide of roads where the Japanese had set up road-blocks and prepared ambushes. Anderson's aim was to clear each roadblock so that his force's vehicles—ambulances and trucks—could move forward.

It was slow going. The fatigued men dragged themselves through the mud. They had gone 2 kilometres when they met Japanese troops dug in on a marshy knoll 50 metres off the road. They would have to be removed so that the trailing vehicles could move through. An estimated 100 Japanese manned the knoll.

Anderson swung his forward company into action in an attempt to remove the enemy. A battle ensued. The Australians could not make headway. Anderson ordered another company to assist in the conflict.

A digger began singing 'Waltzing Matilda'. A huge chorus of voices lifted above the mangroves as the two companies attacked. The inspired force of the assault dislodged the Japanese, who were soon surrounded and forced to retreat into the jungle. The vehicles carrying the growing number of wounded troops rolled forward.

Anderson and his men waded on. They were soon faced with another block by Japanese on a hill. Armed with a pistol and several grenades, he led seven hand-picked men around the south side of the enemy while others created a diversion in the north. Anderson's group crept up close behind the Japanese, then tossed grenades at their position. He led the charge at this block, firing his pistol. The action cleared the way again.

There were other blocks on the road that had to be cleared. The diggers were struggling. Casualties were mounting and filling the convoy of trucks and ambulances under the command of Major Dick. Chitty and others volunteered to join and help the stretcher-bearers. They braved the machine-gun and rifle fire to retrieve fallen diggers and Indians from the battle zone.

The two medical officers in charge of the estimated 400 already wounded—Captains (Richard) Cahill and Brand—were becoming more concerned with every passing hour. Some of the injured were in need of urgent medical treatment or they would not survive.

Anderson had ordered his medical officers not to leave any wounded in the 'hot' battle areas. The Japanese were known to show little mercy to prisoners, especially the wounded who were regarded as liabilities and executed.

Ammunition was low. To preserve it, Anderson had to order his force, comprising the 2/19th and 2/29th Battalions, and the Indian 45th Brigade, into fixed bayonet charges.

After 18 hours on the run with stop–start 'marches' and battles, he and his depleted force reached the outskirts of Parit Sulong about 130 kilometres from Johor Bharu and the causeway. The Japanese now controlled most of Malaya's west and spine. They had leapt ahead of the Australians. They were digging in at Parit Sulong, waiting for these desperate diggers.

*

The aim of Anderson's column was to smash through the last block at a bridge in the village on the road that would take them north to Brigade HQ at Yong Peng, 60 kilometres away on the coast. The men were rested through the night. Anderson planned an assault on the town set for 11 a.m. on 21 January. In those 14 hours, the Japanese dug themselves well in, and waited. Anderson's force attacked for two hours but could make no headway. He got news to a British contingent moving close by. It made a move from the west, but it failed to distract the Japanese enough.

Anderson pulled back his men. They were outnumbered and running out of supplies. He sent an urgent message to Bennett to rush him ammunition.

A message came back: 'Look up at sparrowfart.'

It would have had the enemy interceptors scratching their heads, but the Australians understood. Supplies would be dropped into the region at first light. At dawn on 22 January, five old planes—two Albacores and three RAAF Buffaloes living up to their name—lumbered into the sky and followed the road to Parit Sulong. They dropped cases of tinned food, morphine and other medical supplies by parachute, then doubled back to drop bombs on the Japanese manning the main bridge. But they had forgotten something even more important at that moment than food and medicine: the ammunition, the reason they had received the urgent message in the first place.

Anderson had an agonising decision. The alternative to the road was through the jungle. None of the wounded, except those who could walk, would have a chance of making it back to base. If he could not fight his way through, he would have to leave the wounded.

Anderson attempted to liaise with the Japanese in the hope that they would let the truck and ambulance convoy pass through the block and over the bridge to Yong Peng. The enemy refused.

The second approach was more daring, and dangerous. A truck carrying 13 of the worst wounded diggers and Indians, with a conspicuous Red Cross flag flying, would be directed onto the bridge. There were no guarantees that the truck would not be fired on. The Japanese so far had demonstrated a cavalier attitude to neutral flags, the Red Cross workers and their vehicles. Some respected them. Others did not.

The wounded, nine lying flat and four sitting, were loaded on board. The driver eased the vehicle the 70 metres to the beginning of the bridge. He edged up to the top of the bridge's rise, stopping short of the hump in the middle. He was aware that at any moment a burst of machine-gun fire could rip through the vehicle. The driver applied the brake and stopped the engine. Seconds later, a Japanese sentry approached. The driver was then escorted to the village to front a Japanese officer.[1]

The driver informed the Japanese, who understood a little English, that he was transporting only the most seriously wounded. The officer responded in cold, direct terms that the entire Anderson force had to surrender. Then, and only then, would the wounded be allowed to pass.

The driver walked back over the bridge to convey the message to Anderson, who was put in an invidious position. He had very little fire power. He could not fight to take the town. He told the driver to tell the Japanese officer that there would be no surrender. The driver made the delicate march through no-man's-land once more. The officer was furious.

He informed the driver that he could not drive the truck forward or back. It had to be left where it was. The driver was stunned. He asked for confirmation that the truck and the wounded had to stay in the middle of the bridge.

The Japanese officer nodded curtly. He added that the driver was not allowed to return to the truck. The bemused driver was dismissed. He walked to the truck, and explained the position to the wounded. Turning his back to the roadblock, he tossed the keys onto the floor under the driver's seat. Two sentries ran from their block waving rifles at him. He walked, unhurried, over the bridge to the Australian camp.

The truck remained where it was through the long, hot afternoon and into the cooler night.

Meanwhile, fighting resumed.

The wounded inside the truck were in despair as night fell. With the machine-gun fire going on around them, Lieutenant Austin, the senior officer among the wounded, struggled into the driver's seat. He released the brake, letting the truck reverse back over the bridge. Once it had rolled thirty-five metres, he picked up the keys, slipped them into the ignition, started the engine and reversed the truck to the Australian/Indian camp.[2]

Anderson had time to consider his dwindling options again. His men would have to leave the road route and all the vehicles and heavy equipment in order to make a detour north to base. This would be through jungle all the way, which meant he would have to leave the most incapacitated soldiers. Only those who could walk would be taken, if a mate would assist. Chitty and 50 other of the very fittest men volunteered to lend a shoulder. After medics had comforted the 110 diggers and

35 Indians that could not be moved, they were left with food for a week and plenty of morphine. In an act braver than any of the fighting, 10 of the slightly wounded volunteered to stay with their mates and act as medical orderlies, knowing that they would soon be taken prisoner and be at the mercy and whim of the Japanese.

In the most painful decision of his career, Anderson ordered his men to slip away from Parit Sulong and into the swampy, malaria-infested jungle.

A Japanese contingent crept over the bridge the next day and surrounded the vehicles cautiously, unsure if they had been set a trap, such as a booby-trapped truck. Realising that the lorries were full of wounded men, they approached with fixed bayonets. They ordered everybody out of the vehicles. Those who were too sick to move were dragged out and pushed to the ground. They were left for several hours before orders were barked. The captured men were to be placed in a small building, the remnants of a farmhouse nearby where they were left for another night.

The rough treatment and the delays indicated that the Japanese were not sure what should be done next. The more than 150 captured men were a big haul of prisoners.

The morning's activities indicated a renewed urgency. Soldiers bustled about. A guard formed outside the building. Half an hour later a car pulled up. The bulky General Yamashita stepped out. He was escorted around the building. The general peered in through windows at the wounded men. There was urgency in his step and manner. He grunted a few observations, then returned to his car and conferred with senior officers. Yamashita conveyed that there should be no delay or impediments to the push to the causeway and the attack on Singapore.

All the POWs should be disposed of.

Yamashita was then driven away. The POWs were clumped together in groups of five, tied with wire and dragged, pushed or carried outside to a clearing. They were then machine-gunned and bayoneted until there was no movement among them. Similar acts were repeated in the clearing by the end of the morning. When the carnage was over and all seemed dead, petrol was poured over the bodies. They were set alight. Some had faked their deaths, but there was no faking the screams that followed as the diggers and Indians were incinerated.

Lieutenant Ben Hackney of the 2/29th Battalion had been wounded in the fighting at the bridge, just before Anderson's decision to pull out. When the prisoners were being forced from the building, he had collapsed on the ground short of the killing space, his wrists bound. He was unconscious then. When the Japanese guards returned to him after murdering some other prisoners, he had awoken but pretended to be dead. He endured a couple of kicks to the ribs. Then his boots were pulled off him. Perhaps the guards were happy with the footwear acquisition or too lazy to set him on fire. Whatever the reason for their neglect, he was left lying where he was for another 10 hours. When it was dark, Hackney crawled into the jungle and staggered on until he felt he was safe. Then he stopped and worked free his bound wrists.

Two days later travelling north, he met three other digger escapees from his battalion, who had made the same lucky escape. One was Private Reg Wharton. He had been shot and bayoneted, and looked lifeless to the captors. Another was Sergeant Ron Croft. He had a slight bullet wound from when he was lined up for the machine-gunning. Perhaps his mates had taken the brunt of the fire, or maybe the machine-gunner was inaccurate. Again, he was beyond caring, especially when he escaped death a second time. He still smelt of the petrol that had been thrown over him. For some reason, he and a seriously wounded mate had not been caught by the flames. Croft had dragged his friend clear of the funeral fire and into the jungle. But minutes later the mate died.

Croft made his escape but did not return to Yong Peng. He joined Chinese communist guerrillas making their own stand against the Japanese in Malaya.[3] Hackney and Wharton were less fortunate. They were recaptured by the Japanese, but not the same unit that had carried out Yamashita's orders. The two said nothing about the massacre from which they had escaped, fearing they would be executed for witnessing such an atrocity and surviving it.

They were sent to a prison camp. Their lives were spared.

Anderson and the 'fit' remnants of the battalions pushed their way through swamps and staggered over open ground here and there. The Japanese noted their movements. Unaware that the diggers were out of ammunition, the enemy, going on the diggers' aggressive acts in the past two days, thought this was another manoeuvre to attack. The Japanese withdrew.

This left a small window of opportunity for the Australians of just 400 metres, which they had to negotiate. They slipped through and on to the Brigade HQ at Yong Peng, just before the base had to be vacated. The Japanese were closing in fast. From there, transport trucks drove them east and then south down to a 'safe' Australian brigade position.

Despite, or perhaps because of the tough decision not to capitulate, Percival later said Anderson's effort was 'one of the epics of the Malayan campaign'. It would earn him a Victoria Cross to accompany his MC. But it was the last gasp for that campaign.

Percival had no option but to withdraw the remaining forces south across the causeway.

14

Singapore Siege

On 27 January 1942, General Wavell was given permission by Churchill for the entire British force in Malaya to withdraw to Singapore Island. It was a humiliation for everyone from Churchill down to the lowliest private, and a massive psychological boost for the Japanese. The impatient, bull-necked Yamashita was thrilled. He felt his promise to the emperor to deliver Singapore to him now had a strong chance of fulfilment. Yet still his concern was time. As ever, his nightmare was the thought of his so far triumphant force being caught in the street-by-street brawling that would delay and stretch supply lines for everything from fuel and ammunition to food and arms.

That nagging fear caused him to be even more aggressive. The Japanese Air Force would bomb everything on the island without discrimination. Hospitals would be targeted rather than spared. The civilian population would be attacked as much as British military bases. Prisoners would continue to be savaged. Machine-gunning, beheading and torturing would be increased. The aim was to force the British command to capitulate. The propaganda appeal, or emotional blackmail, from the cunning, ever-gambling Yamashita would be aimed at the British commanders' humanity to spare civilians, the wounded and the fatigued soldiers. If surrender was not accepted, the Japanese promised to annihilate both civilians and soldiers alike. No-one would be spared. And going on the history of the war so far, no-one believed this to be an idle threat. British commanders, especially a vacillator such as Percival, would be forced to consider his place in history. If there were a massacre, it was put to him that he would be held responsible for it.

There was a rush to cross the kilometre-long causeway, which was 20 metres wide at the waterline and wider at the base, and enter Churchill's 'fortress' island. It was flat apart from three hills. The main one, Bukit Timah, rose 176 metres just north of the village of that name, which was nearly in the centre of the island. Another hill lay north of that. A long ridge about 30 metres high ran along the south coast towards Singapore town. The rest of the island was low-lying. Outside the built-up areas it was covered with jungle, rubber and other plantations. Small villages were scattered every few hundred metres.

Singapore town on the southern shore merged inland into areas of well-manicured parkland, interspersed with homes of the rich. Bukit Timah, the main road, ran from Singapore north across the island to the causeway and beyond into Malaya.

Chitty found himself caught up in the mayhem as the wounded and the sick in the last Johor outposts had to be hurried onto the island. This was as much a challenge to his fitness as anything he encountered in the jungle. There was no stopping sometimes for 36 hours at a time. Driver fatigue was not even considered as he and scores of other ambulance and truck drivers transported casualties to the newly created hospital sites at various locations, including the local golf courses and clubhouses.

The air raids continued as dressing stations and makeshift hospitals sprang up in the north-west sector in support of the Australian battalions, which were placed there to defend the coast.

Often they were in a mix of jungle, forest and cultivated land. The 2/9th Field Ambulance began setting up a dressing station at Hill 80 in this sector, not far from a pig wallow. The Japanese bombed in a heavy raid. Private Jack Sammons stopped putting up a tent and ran for the nearest cover, which was the bank of the wallow. It was too slippery. Sammons slid down the bank and into the mud. After the raid, he was ordered by a sergeant to be hosed off before he could continue his duties.

The causeway seemed to shrink to a narrow-way as dispatch riders, troops, ambulances, trucks and cars flowed chaotically around and through the vast throng of refugees. Would this bridge linking the two countries become a road to salvation or an artery to nowhere?

Random Japanese air attacks caused panic. The ambulance drivers only stopped to grab fuel for their vehicles as medical posts were set up along all Malayan routes to the causeway. They were created to assist the casualties straggling in. Some needed immediate operations.

Major Hobbs, a doctor, captured the intensity of the withdrawal:

'Tues 27 [January]—Operated all night—6 cases. Most needed transfusion some with serum and some with blood in addition. Amputated arm, two fractured humerus. Fractured humerus and abdominal wound from entry wound over pelvis—died. Could not close abdomen. Facial wound. Compound fracture R. femur [leg], tibia and fibula.'[1]

Many died before Chitty and Co. could reach them. Others could not take the ride to safety. They died en route. Instead of being driven to overworked doctors they were taken to morgues that became just another destination point. Other casualties were taken to the dispersed hospitals.

*

There were terrors for medical staff and ambulance drivers that would leave mental scars, perhaps for life. Orderly Bob Owen, 20, experienced his first Australian casualty. Machine-gun bullets were right across the young soldier's back.

'How bad is it?' the young soldier asked, barely conscious.

'Don't you worry,' Owen told him. 'The main thing is for you to rest. We'll patch you and have you up and about.'

The soldier died moments later. Owen pushed a trolley down a pathway through trees to the makeshift morgue in a tent. He was there alone. He kept talking to the body as he rolled it onto a slab and straightened it up.

'You'll be comfortable here,' Owen said, 'everything will be all right.'

Owen ran out of the tent and kept running along the path. The experience had been confronting.

'I was working in intensive care,' he said. 'It stuck with me. I had been talking to him the whole time.'

There would be many more situations similar to that.[2]

Sounds too, would haunt drivers and medical staff until long after the war. Even more indelible than the gasps and cries of the badly wounded were the screams of the shell-shocked. Soldiers would demand their rifles, still believing they were out on the battlefield. The drivers and medical orderlies learned how to cope and did their best for the ailing diggers.

The last military contingent to cross the causeway on the night of 30 January 1942 was the Argyll and Sutherland High-landers. These Scots, as ever, had fought as hard as anyone on either side. Their commander, Colonel Duncan Stewart, brought up the rear. The moment they stepped onto the causeway, their pipe band began playing 'Highland Laddie'. Contingents ahead of them were alarmed. They had been told to be as quiet as possible, just in case enemy artillery, which was being brought to the invaders for the first time, was set up. Then came the stirring tune, beautiful to some, just shrill noise to others. It split the night air as only bagpipes can do.

But the Japanese were not quite aware, or didn't care. They were coming after the British one way or another.

The worst sound of all came at 8 a.m. on Saturday 31 January when the already tense island residents were unnerved by a massive explosion in the north. It rattled windows and caused chairs to jump. The city had been hammered for two months. But this detonation was as loud as it was symbolic. It came from the charges set in the causeway linking the island to Malaya. It signalled the British concession that it had no hope of defeating the Japanese in Malaya. Singapore was to be the last stand. Water rushing through the gap would stop the Japanese bicycle assault. They had used this transport method right down the peninsula, with their supporters and fifth columnists collecting bikes for them everywhere. But it was hardly the last means of invading the island. The first way, regardless of their bicycles, was to catch boats and barges across the Johor Strait. The Japanese had to come. They were not going to leave the British troops there without surrender. They wanted the excellent harbour in the south; the naval facility in the north-east.

The British command, in permanent disbelief and even shock that Malaya had slipped from the Empire so quickly, was not planning to give away Singapore quite so readily. It carried prestige as the British Empire's Asian Gibraltar. The lives of one million people on this small sea-bound outpost, just 40 kilometres long and 23 kilometres wide, were at stake.

Bennett's Australians would be part of the defence. His troops included the two AIF brigades and a recently landed Indian brigade, the 44th. They had made a final withdrawal from Malaya the night before the blast and there was disgruntlement about it. The Australians felt a real stand should be made from their bridgehead in the southern tip of Johor state. They believed their defensive positions were well sited for a real shoot-out, despite the disadvantages from lack of air cover and support.

That was not going to be possible on the island.

Bennett was stunned too but in a different way to the British generals. It hurt his military pride, especially after his World War I experience. He had been part of the evacuation from Gallipoli, where 30,000 diggers lived to fight another day without disgrace. And he had been in the victories of 1918. Yet this was a new experience.

His diary for 31 January 1942 reflected his incredulity:

'Thus ended the retreat to the island. The whole operation seems incredible: 550 miles [885 kilometres] in 55 days, forced back by a small Japanese Army of two divisions, riding stolen bicycles and without artillery support.'[3]

He expressed his disappointment at not being allowed to hold Johor, blaming the British and Indian troops for the demise. He and his men, and some of the British troops, were keen to defy the invaders and to take them on. Bennett was certain the war would have gone a different way had the Australians been allowed to fight the Japanese from the start. The enemy had lost just 2,000 men with another 3,000 wounded.

They had annihilated three of the seven Indian brigades, with their combined Indian and British battalion make-up.

15

Softening Up

By 3 February 1942 there seemed nowhere to hide from Japanese air assaults and artillery as the softening-up process intensified prior to the enemy infantry attacks. The medicos were working round-the-clock coping with the casualties among the military and civilians during this lull before the expected big battle. Hobbs' work as a surgeon hardly gave him time to scribble in his diary. The entries had to be brief.

'Tues: 3 [February]—Air raid on oil tanks 8/10 miles north of us at 0530. Bombs sounded very close and shook the building knocking cups off the table but not windows broken. Machine-gun fire from planes. One [oil] tank set on fire making a landmark for a raid of 20 [Japanese] planes.'[1]

Medical teams worked under horrific conditions. One make-shift hospital was in an old Chinese school. Its courtyard was roofed with canvas creating a big surgical ward. One part of the school housed 'medical' casualties with malaria, dysentery (which struck the intestines and caused diarrhoea, the passing of bloody, watery stools, fever, nausea and severe abdominal cramps) and other cases of disease. There was a ward for 'psychological' casualties, those with 'shell shock' who needed quiet conditions for rehabilitation. But there were sirens blaring, bombs falling close by and a battery of Indian artillery firing from the school's garden. Such a frightening cacophony meant that the right treatment was impossible.

Doctors could do little except prescribe tranquillisers. It was up to the nursing staff to calm these patients as best they could. A doctor was operating one day when a shell shrieked overhead. A patient remarked how close it was. A nursing sister agreed.

'I was holding an aspirin in my fingers leaning out the window,' she said. 'The shell carried it clean away.'

Her comment caused everyone to laugh. The tension, for a moment, was eased. But not for long. The scream of shells and whine of planes diving created a perpetual tension.

A wounded young man from the Western Australian 4th Machine Gun Squadron was waiting for surgery to remove several bullets. He asked a nurse for a cigarette. She lit it for him, puffed it herself and placed it gently between the man's lips.

'Thanks darlin',' the digger mumbled in gratitude. He coughed then inhaled. As he exhaled, three streams of smoke emitted from his riddled chest. The nurse smiled as if it were normal. The soldier smoked for a minute, then collapsed.

He did not make it to the operating table.[2]

The skies belonged to the enemy more than ever before in the last two months. Most of the island's planes had been withdrawn to the Dutch East Indies (Indonesia). Two of the three airfields were within Japanese artillery range, which made taking off or coming in hazardous. Air support for the defence of Singapore had to be forgotten.

Apart from ruling the skies, the Japanese had an observation balloon tethered near the Sultan of Johor's palace on the mainland. This afforded a fine view of Singapore and indicated where to shell and bomb the British forces, sever communications and interrupt defence preparation. Percival directed that the palace, now occupied by Yamashita and his Command, was not to be fired on, mainly because he wished to preserve ammunition for a three-month siege.

The Japanese commander, worried about supply lines, had the opposite approach. He was gathering all his ammunition and artillery for one all-out assault. Three months would be perhaps two months too long for him. Yamashita, the risk-taker, was putting all his chips on a quick and decisive strike. He reckoned he had no choice. He was stretched to the limit down the Malayan peninsula as it was. A prolonged battle would end in defeat for him and a major psychological set-back for the entire Imperial Japanese Army.

Each of his 168 guns had up to 1,000 rounds to fire.

Percival had 85,000 troops left and fit (about half were experienced combatants) for the defence, and two choices: he could fight them on the beaches or allow them to come ashore and then counterattack with a strong and mobile reserve force. The British commander-in-chief opted to meet them on the beaches. His reasoning was simple. There was no room to position a reserve force. Percival was not confident about the British forces fighting in the jungle, which covered most of the island's centre. The record so far had been nearly all the enemy's way in Malaya's mangroves and undergrowth, where stealth and encirclement had ensnared the defenders.

Repelling a mass Japanese attack on the beaches had its own problems. The force would have to disperse too thinly unless intelligence could be sure where the assault would come from. The experienced Wavell, who had flown in for just a day to assess the situation, calculated it would come from the north-west where the Australians were stationed and covering almost half of the western sector. Percival thought it would be too tough for the Japanese to invade there. He was convinced it would be from the north-east, where he had placed the bulk of his artillery.

Wavell and Percival dropped into Bennett's HQ in the western sector. In the middle of the meeting, Japanese planes dive-bombed the building. The three generals ducked for cover.

'The unedifying spectacle was seen of three generals going to ground under tables or any other cover that was available,' Wavell noted. 'There was a good deal of debris and some casualties outside, but the party of VIPs escaped untouched, though I lost my car and my field glasses.'[3]

The accuracy of the attack was no fluke. Once more the Japanese fifth column had been working overtime to locate the generals' meeting place.

Wavell would have been in no doubt about the seriousness of the situation. He would have been more than pleased to be out of the war zone that evening.

Bennett's command area would make communications tough. It was part jungle and dissected by rivers, and he had half the number of men that had been allotted to the north-east sector. He placed the 27th Brigade in the causeway sector, with the 30th and 26th battalions forward and the 29th Battalion at the rear. The 22nd Brigade was west of the 27th Brigade; the Indians were further west still.

The positions brought a quiet despair for all officers and men. Most faced areas thick with mangroves with streams converging on the coast's foreshore. Unless the diggers stood at the water's edge, there was no field of vision to see an enemy coming, and no natural fortifications or defences. There were just a few foot tracks on which to move. They wound through the wilderness, and provided no direction or protection.

The terrain was unsuitable in every way for defence. Because of the huge region to patrol, battalion posts were several hundred metres apart. There was thick jungle in between. Each post was isolated and vulnerable. On the other hand, the vegetation afforded the Japanese the perfect cover for their method of fighting by stealth.

Despite Yamashita's haste, his officers were doing everything right to prepare for the invasion of Singapore. Gun emplacements were being dug 50 metres well back from the Johor Strait and in rubber plantations on the Malayan coastline. Big kitchens were being trucked in to feed the troops before their assault.

Intelligence on these developments was passed to Bennett, who agreed with Wavell, that his sector would be the target. He informed Percival, who responded that the same build-up was going on opposite the north-east sector.

The Japanese began their barrage on 8 February 1942. The invasion of Singapore had begun.

16

Falling Fortress

The Japanese hit the Australian sector in the west with the greatest intensity. The artillery fire was accurate all through the first day. Soldiers who had experienced German heavy shelling in World War I said that the Japanese attack was worse.

Veteran Lieutenant-Colonel A. L. Varley had been on several Great War fronts in four years. He was now commanding the 18th Battalion and had never seen a heavier pounding over such a period. He wrote in his diary:

> '80 shells were counted falling in D Coy area in one minute. One platoon area had 67 shells in 10 minutes and this was typical of the whole area. Battalion HQ had 45 shells in seven minutes; half an hour's spell then another similar dose and so on throughout the whole area all day.'

Despite the ferocity of the attack, Percival, when informed, refused a counter-battery from the heavier British guns. The position was so critical that the artillery liaison officer with the 20th Battalion said simply: 'Bring down fire everywhere.'[1]

Percival and his jittery Command, going on hunches and guesses, thought that the shelling would continue for several days and shift to the causeway in the middle, and then to the north-east.

Japanese accuracy had come from aerial reconnaissance, but also from infiltration onto the island. They had sneaked in. Some had been 'sleepers' waiting for the instruction to attack; others had come across by boat at night. They were in their element in the thick jungle on the coast, spreading out to avoid detection by defending patrols. The secret invaders in the first week of February had been hard at work mapping the Australians' positions and passing them back to Japanese artillery commanders on the mainland. The defenders' slit trenches and the soft soil saved many lives, but there was chaos when communications were cut by the shelling.

On the night of 8 February, the Japanese invaded in big numbers, crossing the Johor Strait in barges, armoured boats and rafts, landing in the western sector as Bennett and Wavell had predicted. The fierce day of relentless shelling had been the key indicator. The 20th Battalion was the first defending force to encounter them. Gunners of the 4th Machine Gun Battalion were parked right on the shore-line, and barely in the jungle. Burning oil tankers in the strait afforded just enough light to see the silhouettes of the Japanese invasion vessels. The gunners' commander waited until the enemy was just 30 metres away from the shore. Then he ordered:

'Fire! Fire!'

The Vickers machine-guns opened up, shredding the barges' flimsy sides. But they had less impact on a second wave of armoured landing craft, which the Japanese had plenty of. After the first Australian pulverising, the enemy soldiers scrambled away and headed further west. Their invasion vessels kept coming across the strait from every angle and spread right across the north-west coast.

The Australians kept their weapons spitting into the dark at the unwelcome shapes through the night. Yamashita's two best divisions—the 5th and the 18th—poured out 13,000 men at night and another 10,000 at dawn. This huge invasion was being held up by about 1,000 Australians, who inflicted heavy casualties on the Japanese.

The sudden, horrific losses on both sides brought out the differences in the mentality of the fighting men as opposed to the Field Ambulance people, from the drivers such as Chitty to the doctors working overtime from that early morning.

One soldier, separated from his unit during the fighting, wandered into a hastily prepared hut dressing station. He seemed quiet at first when speaking to the medicos. Then he became animated as he told David Boardman of the 9th Field Ambulance that he had killed seven Japanese. It had been exhilarating for the young soldier, who looked about 19. He said it was the most important moment in his life. Boardman was stunned and wondered if this was the normal reaction to killing in war. He had not thought about it before the mayhem of 8 February. Boardman questioned his own response to this excitement. He asked himself if he was abnormal for not sharing the enthusiasm for the slaughter of the enemy. It made him realise that he was unsuited for battle.

'Men such as Boardman and Chitty were courageous,' Frank Lemin said, 'They proved it as much as any soldier in countless actions and activities through their years of service. But taking human life was not their—our—thing . . . But someone had to do the fighting, just as someone had to the healing, like the doctors. We all served in our own way.'[2]

In these critical moments, the Field Ambulance personnel understood fully why they had not become combatants. One mentality was to kill, and keep killing. Some did it as if on a kangaroo hunt. Others had to be stimulated, encouraged and pushed. Still others would be dogged for life by their actions. In the end, they were to take lives. By contrast, the medical staff and ambulance workers were there to save lives, even those of the enemy, if the situation arose.

There was a cost for the Australians' fierce defence: 334 killed and 214 wounded. The forward battalions, who took the enemy head on, fared worst. One company of 145 diggers right at the front lost 57 killed, 22 wounded and 66 taken prisoner.

22nd Brigade's forward posts were similarly overrun. Its survivors were forced back behind Tengah airfield, 6.5 kilometres from the coast. It had been shelled relentlessly from Johor across the strait through the night.

Its brigadier (Taylor) formed a defensive position.

Repairs to Australian communication lines ran through the night and into 9 February. Ambulances were in greater demand than ever in the Malayan conflict. At first light, the 9th Ambulance's medico Captain Donald Shale and a crew of three—Privates Wilfred McCulloch, Arnold Gardner and Roy Sparks—set out in a marked Red Cross lorry to find wounded diggers. They found themselves on a jungle track heading for the Lim Chu Kang road. Their base with the 19th Battalion was already inside enemy lines as the Japanese swept inland. Shale and his crew were trying to leave the area, while still looking out for injured infantrymen. They had gone five minutes when they were hit by fire from three machine-guns from both sides of the track, and heavy artillery shelling. All on board were killed, and several of the men were burnt beyond recognition.

One feature on the lorry was recognisable: a shredded Red Cross flag. It had been flying from the front of the vehicle.

At 5 a.m. on 9 February, Captain John Park of 9th Field Ambulance gathered many of the drivers about 500 metres from the action. He told them they were going to withdraw to the main dressing station deeper into the island at Hill 80.

While waiting to make the move inland, Chitty's ambulance received a call. He responded. Moments later another call came in from the opposite direction. It was from the ambulance of medical officer, Captain John Catchlove. He had been attending the wounded of the 20th Battalion, which had been in the thick of the fighting in the night. Catchlove himself had received a serious hip wound. Instead of asking Chitty to switch missions, Park himself decided to go forward to find his mate 'Catchy'. He took with him drivers Harold Ball and William Lewis, and ambulance orderly Alf Woodman. This unit had been active through the previous day evacuating the wounded.

Catchlove appeared to be near the Tengah airfield, which had been shelled heavily and which the Japanese infantry were in the process of securing. The ambulance, with large Red Cross markings clear, was driven by Ball. The intrepid four were all wearing Red Cross armbands. They reached the outskirts of the bomb-ripped and cratered aerodrome, over which a black pall of smoke hung.

Then they ran into a Japanese patrol.

The four Australian non-combatants were taken prisoner. They had their hands tied with wire behind their backs. Perhaps they put up some resistance; maybe they refused to answer questions. It was almost certain that Park in particular would have pointed out their neutrality as medicos and ambulance men, which was self-evident by their vehicle and armbands. But for some reason, or perhaps none at all, the four were tortured. Then they were taken to a remote part of the aerodrome close to the jungle. The Australians were pushed to a long mound of yellow mud. They were made to kneel in line with each other. If they were offered blindfolds, they refused them. One of the Japanese drew his samurai sword.

One by one, he beheaded them.

The fates of these two ambulance crews on the same morning delivered two clear messages to the 8th Division: First, the Red Cross flag was being ignored by the enemy. Second, medicos and ambulance staff members were in just as much danger as infantrymen now that the lines between the defenders and the invaders were blurred in the rush of battle.

The remains of the captain's lorry, crew and wounded were discovered in the 19th Battalion's rush to pull back inland. But the whereabouts of Captain Park and his crew was unknown. When they did not return to base, Chitty had his first bout of survivor's guilt, which was often experienced by those who had narrow escapes in war, when others did not. In the close-knit ambulance group, everyone feared the worst in Park's case, especially with the knowledge of other atrocities and the mixed attitude of the enemy to Red Cross workers.

All four were popular, particularly Ball and Park on sports arenas. Park's skills as a doctor and leader were soon to be missed. A sombre, demoralising mood enveloped the Field Ambulance group. It was not improved by a peculiar and unpopular directive soon afterwards from British HQ.

The 9th's dressing station had just pulled back to Hill 80 by the end of that day when Chitty and other ambulance staff learned they had to hand in all firearms and weaponry. None knew the fate of Park, Ball, Lewis and Woodman, but there were suspicions. Field ambulance people were non-combatants, but drivers like Chitty, who were crack shots, may well have been able to avoid capture by enemy patrols. Without the weapons they were defenceless.

HQ argued that the Japanese were respecting the Red Cross, and the weapons were needed for combatants. But no-one agreed with the judgement. Apart from the two lost crews on 9 February, ambulances on Singapore in the previous week had been strafed and bombed by planes in daylight when their markings were clear to pilots.

The confiscated arms included machine-guns, rifles, grenades and revolvers. Knives could be kept. In the confusion of war now close upon all defending units, no-one seemed to know what to do with the haul of weaponry. Then they were directed to surviving sailors from the sunk *Prince of Wales* and *Repulse,* who were being seconded to fight as the numbers of the wounded and dead began to mount.

At least a couple of the drivers kept revolvers, which were hidden in their trucks. They would be of little use against an armed enemy patrol. But it gave the owners a thin veneer of security as they went about their work of gathering the wounded from dangerous spots and battlegrounds.

There was a store of a hundred 44 gallon drums near the Bukit Panjang railway stop 20 kilometres west of Singapore town. Chitty was driving with Lemke on another mission to pick up casualties in the thick of the fighting. They had to drive into the battlefield fast, load up with the sixteen soldiers and leave.

'We had the back [of the ambulance] full of stretcher cases,' Lemke said, 'and some [of the walking wounded] hanging on to the bonnet or wherever they could. The Chevie was pulling in pit [bottom] gear. The roads were choked with people. We couldn't go any faster.'

They seemed to take an interminable time to crawl past the petrol dump. The fear was that the Japanese, in close pursuit, would hit the dump with artillery fire.

'It was so hot I thought we would burn or explode,' Lemke said, 'and when petrol drums explode it's quite something.'

The wounded were yelling, 'Hurry up or we'll burn!'

There was a sudden lull in the truck as it struggled on. Then Chitty piped up: 'Wouldn't it be a bastard if we got a puncture!'[3]

Every Field Ambulance person was having his narrow escape. Ken Topliss was driving medico (psychiatrist) Major John

Cade to a battalion HQ where there were wounded who needed attention. They were travelling along a road in the western sector when they came across a long column of marching soldiers. It was dark as their vehicle, lights out, rumbled up next to the soldiers. Both men had their heads out the window to make sure they kept on the road.

'Topliss, I think we are going in the wrong direction,' Cade said quietly. 'Next chance you get to turn around, turn around. Nice and slowly, no hurry.'

'Righto, sir,' Topliss said.

'We won't worry about finding Battalion HQ tonight.'

They turned around and drove back to their camp.

'That was a close shave, wasn't it?' Cade remarked.

'What?'

'They were Japanese!'

'God! Why didn't you tell me?

'You would have ditched both of us!'[4]

Cade believed that they were saved by the Red Cross flag, but for the wrong reasons. In the dark, the Japanese may well have mistaken the insignia for that of the Japanese national flag, with its red bull's eye.

On returning to camp, Topliss was physically sick at the thought of what might have happened.

Chitty had a close call when travelling in an ambulance convoy close to the front. The four trucks came under intense shell fire and all passengers and drivers were forced to dive for cover under their vehicle. Shrapnel rained down, hitting Chitty in the knee and killing a fellow driver.

Chitty was this time himself ferried to a dressing station

for medical attention. Within a day he was back in action, walking, and soon jogging, with a pronounced limp.[5]

17

End-Battles

More than 120 nursing sisters at the Australian hospitals rose to the moment as the pressure mounted from enemy attacks and the increasing number of wounded needing urgent attention. Their steadying influence and calm in the crisis was evident to all. But on 10 February, fears were held for their safety as the Japanese pressed closer. The Field Ambulance command decided that six of the sisters should be evacuated from Singapore to Sumatra on the Chinese ship *Wah Sui*. They would be leaving with a select group of Anglo personnel and would look after the wounded on board.

The sisters were disappointed. They did not want to leave their fellow nurses at the two main Australian hospitals, pointing out that they had faced the dangers just like the men. Most wished to stay and help the wounded and suffering. The women had been efficient at running the hospitals, and compassionate with the injured, especially those with mental anguish and shell shock. By their grit and endeavour, the sisters had bolstered morale among the doctors and patients.

Their tearful departure was one stark reminder for those remaining that this war was coming to an end, one way or the other. Another was the formation of X Battalion, speedily put together from among the rear echelon and support troops such as 4th Reserve Motor Transport Regiment. Within hours of formation, members were being killed on the ever-fluid and inward-pushing front-line.

Half of them (about 400) were casualties within a day.

By 11 February 1942, the defenders were pressed back into a shrinking perimeter around Singapore town in the south. The high point at Bukit Timah hill and the town, with its considerable oil and food supplies, were in Japanese hands. Wavell, away from the battle zone after another fleeting visit the day before, sent a plaintive 'Order of the Day' via a dispatch rider to all troops on Singapore Island:

> 'In some units the troops have not shown the fighting spirit which is to be expected of men of the British Empire—the spirit of aggression and determination to stick it out must be inculcated in all ranks. There must be no more withdrawal without orders.'

These late platitudes from an absent commander did nothing to boost morale. They demonstrated either a lack of comprehension of events or an attempt to circumvent criticism of him and his command, should the Japanese succeed in taking Singapore. The implication was that the Australians had 'run' from the battle. Waiting for 'orders to withdraw' would have ensured that every one of the soldiers and non-combatants of the 22nd and 27th Brigades would have been slaughtered.

Wavell's hollow cry was thrown in the bin.

Half the remaining nurses were next ordered to leave. Matrons at the two hospitals chose about 30 from each. Chitty and Len Lemke (who was now teamed with him after the death of his former driving partner) were assigned to ferry them to the *Empire Star*, which was a much bigger boat than the *Wah Sui*.

'One nurse, Thelma Bell, was someone I'd known well in Albury,' Lemke recalled. He had dated a friend of hers and they used to go to dances and the cinema together.

'It was a sad goodbye. I helped her onto the boat, amidst the tears. She said: "When I get back to Australia, first chance I get, I'll visit your mother and father." ' (Thelma fulfilled her promise.)[1]

On board were about 2,000 evacuees, including another group of military personnel and more wounded. Even as they gathered at the docks, the ship was rocking from bombs hitting close by. After waiting all night and unable to sleep because of the flash and crash of artillery, the women were put in the ship's hold. They were all appreciative of the hooks for their bags (the boat had once shipped frozen meat).

Their last view of Singapore on 12 February was black smoke blocking the sky and a yellow oil slick covering the emerald sea. Enemy aircraft whirred overhead. One forlorn, broken British plane could be seen on the beach. Acrid smells stayed with the ship as it ploughed away from the stricken city. Fire in the town was so fierce it seemed as if it would engulf the entire island.

It was rough sailing. A wave of Japanese planes spotted the vessel and did their best to destroy the *Empire Star*, bombing and strafing the decks with machine-gun fire. They made three direct hits, killing 17 men on the deck and injuring 32, among them the ship's second officer. His arm had to be amputated.

The battling marine crew tackled the fires and helped keep it afloat. The ship's captain steered a zig-zag course, making it harder for the attacking planes. Modest anti-aircraft guns directed by the injured second officer brought down two planes. The beleaguered passengers applauded.

During the raids a group of nurses were in a cabin with some wounded men. The fumes and smoke began to asphyxiate the casualties. The nurses waited until they believed the attacks had stopped. Then they stretchered the men onto the deck. To their horror the planes returned, machine-gunning the ship. Nurse Anderson refused to leave the helpless men. She attempted to shelter them. As one plane roared in, guns spitting, she placed her body over one wounded soldier, protecting him. After further attempted slaughter, the plane flew off.

The nurses were as busy as they had been on land, tending the many more wounded from the air attacks.

From the air, the ship would have looked ready to sink. It was ablaze at several points. Smoke billowing from it would have added to the impression. After four hours, the Japanese dive-bombing ceased.

The boat limped on towards Batavia on Java.

Just as the *Empire Star* appeared to be out of danger on the afternoon of 12 February, the 65 remaining nurses on

Singapore were rounded up and taken by tug to the more mod-
estly sized *Vyner Brooke*, owned by the Rajah of Sarawak, Sir
Charles Pembroke. There were 200 on board, which was well
beyond its capacity.

The boat was held up in Keppel Harbour. A departure was
planned for the next day.

Also on 12 February 1942, Percival noted it was:

> 'a day of heavy fighting on the whole front. The enemy, which had
> now been reinforced, launched strong attacks at several different
> points . . . Japanese aircraft and artillery were both active. The town
> area came in for much attention and there was a large number of cas-
> ualties . . . Throughout the day the 22nd Australian Brigade group
> (much below strength) continued to hold its advanced position in
> the Pandan area in spite of all attempts by the enemy to dislodge it.'

There was a lot of fighting at close quarters, just what the
Australians wanted and the Japanese did not. But the weight
of numbers tackling the 22nd Brigade told by the evening.
The invaders seeped around to the south and isolated the brigade. It had to be withdrawn after dark.

The Australians, Percival noted, fought 'a gallant action for
48 hours and had done much to hold up the enemy's advance'.[2]

A conference of Percival's generals including Bennett was
held at Fort Canning in south-east Singapore on the morning of 13 February. It was agreed that further resistance was
hopeless. Morale, especially among the Indians, was lowering
as fast as the ammunition.

The command generals were sure the Japanese would take

the fight right into Singapore town, which meant the civilian population would be wiped out. They could not escape the Japanese cordon. The heavy bombing and artillery fire had already created severe dislocation among the people, killing and wounding thousands.

The generals decided to send a message to Wavell, asking permission to capitulate.

Gordon Bennett and the others planned to escape among the AIF allotment of just 100 personnel of all ranks. His world at that moment had come crashing down. Instead of being involved in the first defeat for the enemy marauders of the Asian–Pacific region, he was a key part of a humiliating loss. The Japanese, so long degraded in the propaganda as 'little yellow men', were having a golden moment. They had proved superior in planning, strategy, tactics and fighting techniques for the terrain. Bennett's boast about every Australian being worth 10 of them would haunt him. He had experienced the highs of the 1st AIF's triumph under Monash in 1918 when the diggers took on 39 German divisions (equivalent to eight armies) and beat every one of them, including the crack Prussian Guard. Bennett knew the lows too in the frustration of Gallipoli in 1915, and never wanted to visit that sense again. But Singapore was far worse.

After the demoralising meeting, Bennett walked back to his HQ through the deserted streets of Singapore that had once teemed with commerce. He could see the devastation and smell the blast of aerial bombs.

'There were holes in the road,' he wrote in his diary,

'churned up rubble lying in great clods . . . tangled masses of telephone, telegraph and electric cables strewn across the street . . . smashed cars, trucks, electric trams and buses . . . the shops were shuttered and deserted . . . Hundreds of Chinese civilians refused to leave their homes . . . bombs were falling in a nearby street . . . the side of a building had fallen on an air-raid shelter, the bomb penetrating deep into the ground, the explosion forcing in the sides of the shelter.'

Chinese, Malays, Europeans and Australian soldiers were shovelling and dragging the debris away. A boy emerged, bleeding and lacerated.

He cried, 'My sister is down there! My sister is down there!'

The rescuers dug frantically in the fallen masonry. The top of the shelter was uncovered. When pulled aside it exposed 'a crushed mass of men, women . . . and young children, some still living . . .'

One desperate Chinese man worked harder than anyone. His entire family was in there. His wife and three of his children did not survive. One 10-year-old daughter did.

'This was going on hour after hour, day after day,' Bennett recorded, 'the same stolidity and steadfastness among the civilians was evident in every quarter of the city.'[3]

As Bennett surveyed the ruins of a once proud town before making his own escape, the *Vyner Brooke* made its bid for freedom and Batavia. The captain's aim was to cling to the coastline south of Singapore and attempt to hide in the waters of the many islands studding the area.

At one point, he planned to make a dash for the Straits of Malacca, the open sea between Singapore and Sumatra.

General Yamashita was on Singapore on 13 February, having left his safe haven at the sultan's palace. His troops had captured much of Singapore town's water supply. Bennett, even before Percival, had known the end, one way or the other was nigh. His troops and the rest of the British force were now squeezed into a tighter and tighter semicircle. They were running out of ammunition, weapons, food and water. All the British planes had flown away. There were very few means of escape from the island and certainly not for more than 70,000 troops.

There could be no face-saving mass evacuation; no Gallipoli.

One of the two main Australian hospitals had to be withdrawn from the town's outskirts at Oldham Hall, a boarding school, when artillery defences were set up. The Field Ambulance doctors could not afford to let their workplaces become main targets, endangering them, the nursing staff and the patients. The Cathay Theatre in the heart of Singapore town was chosen as a new site. Once a sweet haven to watch a movie, its lower floors were converted into a theatre of a different kind. Other parts of the Cathay complex were transformed into a convalescence depot for 500 patients, which would grow soon to three times that number. But the same problem arose. The Indian III Corps had shifted its HQ there. This meant the Red Cross flag could not be flown from the building.

The new hospital site would be in danger of artillery and air attacks.

18

Capitulation

Just after lunch on Saturday 14 February 1942, Japanese soldiers burst into the grounds of the British Alexandra Hospital in Singapore. They headed first for the sisters' quarters. A British lieutenant in the reception area was warned of their approach. He assembled a white flag and waved it as soon as the first three soldiers charged in. Ignoring the surrender, they bayoneted the lieutenant to death and rampaged around the hospital. Staff waved Red Cross signs at them and cried: 'Hospital!' 'Hospital!' but it had no impact. There was no stopping the invaders who seemed intent on barbarity as they fired their rifles or swung their bayonets. Medical staff threw their hands up. Ten of them were herded down a corridor and then, seemingly on a whim, they were butchered. The mayhem continued on several floors where more than 200 were murdered.

Nothing in the underworld of Chicago in the 1930s could match the horrors of this St Valentine's Day massacre.

The severity of this indiscriminate killing of non-combatants and wounded soldiers drove home the danger to all as the Japanese seeped into the town. It put enormous pressure on the British Command to capitulate. In the meantime, life and death went on. While the feverish acts were being perpetrated against British medical staff, across town St Andrew's Cathedral was being converted into a hospital by the Australian Field Ambulance for civilians as well as troops. Pews were removed. Apartments were transformed into surgical operating theatres, first aid wards and recovery units. The Adelphi Hotel across the road was seconded. A special section for traumatised patients was created in that building's basement in the hope of lessening the nerve-shattering noise of bombs and artillery.

The Japanese were swarming closer. Snipers had infiltrated the town. They were lodging on building window sills, firing at every presented target. No civilian, not even a child, was safe to wander the streets. Japanese artillery and mortar fire was more penetrating with every hour.

'The noise was terrific,' Len Lemke said, 'with everything concentrated in such a small area. You would stand close to a person and speak up real loud. When the artillery guns went off your shirt would flap against your body [with the vibration].'

The shells rained in on the St James Cathedral grounds.

'Everything was happening so fast,' Lemke recalled. 'Even the tiles were slipping off the roof of the cathedral with the vibration of the shelling.'

He and Chitty were sitting in Lemke's Chevrolet truck eating bully beef and biscuits. 'One of the nose caps of a shell came screaming down and went through the bonnet of the Chevie. It took half the engine out. As the head piece [of the shell] got closer and closer, we scrambled out of the truck.'[1]

It was demolished. The two men dashed to Chitty's truck, their meal rudely interrupted. They were lucky. The shelling killed drivers, nurses, orderlies, patients and soldiers. Chitty, Len Lemke and other drivers rushed into the cathedral with casualties. The attack had ripped off the cathedral's heavy rear door at the rear. A huge fig tree in the garden had been split clean in two as if a giant had taken an axe to it.

Chitty kept running, with all the dedication of the teenage kid he once was setting rabbit traps at Cudgewa. His face and clothes were black. He had taken one 'wash', a swim in the pool of the deserted Swiss Club, the day before it was taken by the invaders. Minutes were running into hours and days. The noise made it impossible to think beyond the endless duty of ferrying patients to the ever-changing hospital sites.

He and Lemke attempted to drop six wounded soldiers off at the Cathay and were told there was no way they could be treated. He manoeuvred his vehicle through the streets of rubble to the cathedral. Chitty left the vehicle, trotted into the grounds past the stricken fig tree again and through the doorless back entrance, only to be given the same sorry tale of rejection. The beds were all full; no doctor was available. Chitty returned to the truck, telling Lemke to start bringing the wounded in. They stretchered the patients into the anteroom to the cathedral's vestry, where operations were going on. The doctors and their staff would have to walk through the anteroom to leave the church. The patients would then be their problem. Chitty and Lemke had many more calls to make.[2]

On the next round two hours later, they went straight to the cathedral just as another mortar attack looked likely to destroy it. People in the grounds were hit again. The building was spared. Chitty and Lemke rushed from the truck and carried two injured civilians into the vestry's anteroom. It was empty. The other six wounded had been catered for. Perhaps some were being operated on by a team of doctors led by the indefatigable Frank Cahill at that moment in the vestry. Cahill had been a leading surgeon at Melbourne's St Vincent's Hospital. But he had never encountered anything like the pressure in this makeshift theatre. There was no time to think; no time to worry; just do.

The drivers were doing enormous physical work. It took its toll. Dave Klein, who had been running as hard as anyone, staggered up to Lemke in the cathedral grounds.

'Lemke, I'm buggered,' he gasped, 'I can't go on. Can you give me a drink of water?'

Lemke obliged. Klein stumbled to the cathedral wall, lay down and slept despite the noise and chaos.

'Snipers were very active,' Lemke said. 'They were in the buildings and you could not see them.'

They had not gone very far on their umpteenth rescue mission when a sniper struck. A bullet ripped into the vehicle's rear. Chitty tried to veer down a side street and realised he had a flat. He steered the limping vehicle into the side street out of the sniper's sights. They jumped out and examined a front tyre. It too had been struck. Two hits at either end of the truck meant two snipers. They changed the tyre and drove on. Calls were not coming in so much now, but it didn't matter. The walking wounded were making their own way into town. Chitty, Lemke and the other ambulance drivers knew where the action was, and where the stricken soldiers would be. If the phones were down, they didn't have to travel far. Casualties among the soldiers and civilians were everywhere.[3]

Chitty, after eight hours straight driving, running, carrying and lifting, slumped in the front passenger seat and tried to doze off while Lemke drove. It was impossible to rest. He could drift a little but not really sleep. The intermittent whistling of shells overhead kept him alert. If a shell stopped whistling and emitted a noise like someone being throttled, then it was falling. That was the moment to look up. Not that it would help. It didn't when he and Lemke were caught in the Chevrolet in the cathedral grounds. But gazing skyward was what everyone did. The truck would keep going. If they had been on foot and they heard the dreaded gurgle, they would dash for cover.

Late on 14 February, they needed rest. A little 'haven' was discovered when they delivered a shell-shocked soldier, who had been wandering the back streets, to the Adelphi Hotel's basement. The two men found an empty store room and lay on the stone floor. There were the muffled sounds of the mortar. The building shook a couple of times. Traumatised patients cried out now and then. One kept yelling for his rifle.

Chitty and Lemke rested for an hour, then it was into the truck for another mission.

It was becoming dark. The choking smell of cordite was everywhere along with the dust. Chitty dozed off while his mate drove. He heard machine-gun fire, lifted his helmet and gazed into the road they were travelling. Chitty asked Lemke to pull up and turn around. They were beyond their own perimeter and in the ever-expanding Japanese zone.

The truck was driven back the way it had come as fast as it would go. They reached the town centre, perhaps away from any immediate danger. In the semi-darkness, the truck hit a fallen stone wall. Lemke fought the wheel and crashed the truck, buckling the right fender. It was jammed against the wheel. Chitty took a hammer from a toolbox and did some panelbeating. The mangled fender was difficult to budge. They had no wish to stay with the vehicle in the dark, especially with the Japanese advance and their unpredictability. Chitty and Lemke removed the truck's rotors, disabling it, but leaving the key under a foot-mat, just in case they could return and fix it.

They then moved at the trot through the streets towards the town's centre. They had noted abandoned vehicles from the Australian convoys. Finding one that seemed in reasonable repair, they affixed the rotors, found the key and moved off, relieved at the protection of their 'new' truck and that they were still able to work.[4]

Fighting continued during the night. Chitty and Lemke were called to the coast south of Kallang Airfield. Reports of a shipwreck and injured passengers were coming in. They found no-one.

Chitty drove slowly on the road overlooking the sea near Keppel Harbour. He would not try to leave while the fighting was on. But he didn't fancy staying if the Japanese were going to win. He did not like the idea of being a prisoner of war like Phil and Ron. Stories that Phil had been 'treated well enough' in Stalag XVIIIA, Austria may or may not have been true. It was most likely German propaganda. There were rumours about flouting of the Geneva Convention in the handling of POWs. But unless you were in a camp in Europe, you could not be sure.

Chitty and all the servicemen could only go on what they knew of the Japanese and how they treated prisoners during the conflict. There had innumerable stories of atrocities. How would they treat the vanquished, especially when it was believed that in their culture 'surrender' was frowned upon? It was claimed that the Japanese would rather commit *hari kari* than be taken alive themselves.

The burnt but still standing post office was behind them as Chitty and Lemke lingered a few minutes. Light from it and other burning buildings allowed them to see many vessels, all of them on fire. Nobody could be seen in the water. The beach seemed deserted. Most of those locals and British force personnel deserting or running had already made their moves. Or they had drowned in the attempt.

Chitty was thinking of escape. He was confident that he could live rough and survive anywhere. He thought he would have to do it by sea for the initial break from Singapore.

But on the night of the eventful 14 February, all the avenues appeared blocked off.

*

On the same day, the *Empire Star* staggered into Batavia (Jakarta) on Java, south of Sumatra. The nurses bought limited supplies with their few Malayan dollars. After repairs were made to the ship, it set sail for Fremantle.

Meanwhile, their fellow sisters were still on the struggling, top heavy *Vyner Brooke* when its captain made his bid to slip away from the small islands, giving it flimsy protection, and into a more vulnerable stretch of the Straits of Malacca.

The ever-present fifth column, or the Japanese Army, spotted the vessel. A squadron of six single-engine fighters dashed to sink it.

They made contact at 2 p.m. The Japanese pilots dipped and then veered towards the vessel and made their runs at it. The ship's captain, showing nerve and verve, manoeuvred the smaller craft, avoiding more than 70 bombs, which fell either side of the ship and only served to lurch it left and right. Frustrated by this skilful avoidance, one pilot flew very low. Skimming over the boat, it strafed its hull and deck. 'Kills' were easy on the overcrowded ship. The captain was hurled around the bridge just as another plane buzzed low and dropped a well-aimed bomb amidships right down a funnel. This blew up the engine room. Glass and timber flew everywhere. The ship came to shuddering halt.

The stricken *Vyner Brooke* was in chaos. The nurses, on autopilot, hurried on deck to attend the many men, women and children injured all over the ship. They carried morphine, bandages and other medical essentials. Not quite sated with their kill, the Japanese pilots returned for another run over the crippled vessel, this time machine-gunning the deck and lifeboats, which clattered down the ship's port side and into the sea. Most sank. The wounded and elderly passengers joined nurses with the medical equipment in two boats that were not damaged. Blankets and army coats went with them.

The *Vyner Brooke* began to list. All on board were ordered to abandon ship. The nurses again slipped into 'work' mode, making sure wounded men were taken from below deck and lowered into the water. They took control, showing others how to inflate their lifejackets and helping them to timber from the ship with which to keep afloat.

Nurses, some wearing tin hats, were last to leave. They removed footwear and climbed onto the railing of the listing ship, which was about to keel over and sink. Moments after everyone had swum away, the ship's stern pitched up, throwing out a big wave. Then it disappeared with hardly a whimper.

Japanese planes swooped back, diving low at the small congregations of survivors on the lifeboats and those clinging onto makeshift rafts. They strafed the water, killing and injuring some. Their headgear offered a little protection and strong swimmers dived down as far as they dared, surfacing when the planes climbed away.

Through the mayhem came the sound of voices. One group sang 'Waltzing Matilda'. Fifty metres away a nurse began singing a rendition of the theme song from *The Wizard of Oz*. Those with less heart were lifted by such humour and cheer as they struggled to survive.

Everyone in the sea needed inspiration. Once it seemed the enemy pilots were over their lust for easy strikes, spirits were high. Perhaps it was the adrenaline rush of survival, or maybe it was just the thrill of being alive with hope, or a combination of both. But within minutes, the rafts and lifeboats were pushing together. Survivors began lifting each other's hopes once more. Matron Olive Paschke, still the leader in the crisis,

Peter Chitty, 2/2nd Motor Ambulance Convoy, in 1941.
(*AWM P04441.001*)

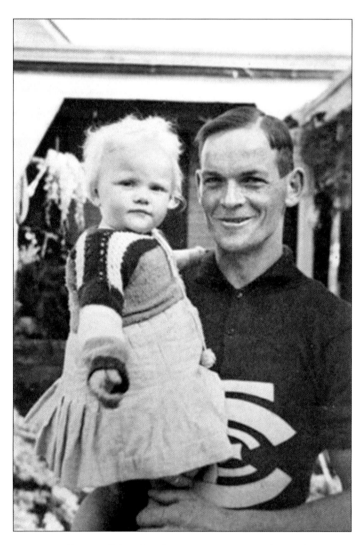

Peter Chitty with his daughter Norma, wearing the Cudgewa
(his local club) football jumper. (*Chitty family*)

The Changi Brownlow Medal – Peter Chitty's
most treasured possession. (*AWM REL32808*)

'Chicken' Smallhorn with Harold Ball, before a football match in Malaya,
June 1941. They were captaining service teams. (*Carl Johnson*)

'Chicken' Smallhorn, a former Fitzroy wingman, in action.
(*Chitty family*)

Peter Chitty, in later life, with the Changi Brownlow.
(*Chitty family*)

Left to right: Peter Chitty, Reg Lemke, Nelson Potter and Des Glover, just before the fall of Singapore. (*Chitty family*)

The proud ambulance driver: Peter Chitty, Singapore. (*Chitty family*)

Harold Ball (*front row, third from left*) captained this Ambulance Unit team in Malaya, 1941. (*Carl Johnson*)

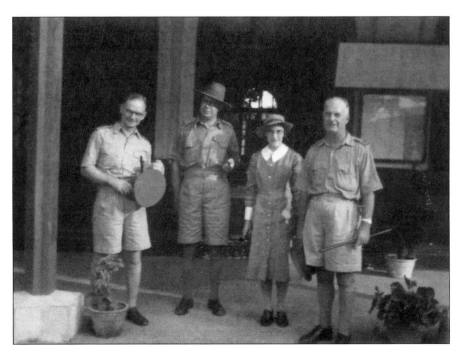

Colin Hamilton (with some doctors and a nurse), in Singapore before the Japanese attacked. (*Carl Johnson*)

Harold Ball, killed in action, Singapore, February 1942.
He played in the Melbourne Football Club premiership
teams in 1939 and 1940. (*Carl Johnson*)

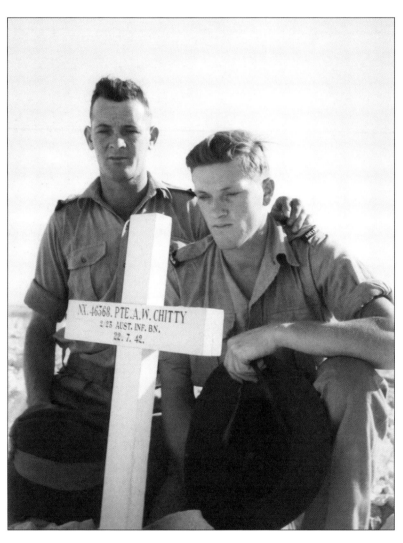

El Alamein, Egypt. 11 November 1943: Phil (*left*) and Ron Chitty pay their respects to their brother Arthur ('Toxa'), who was killed in action on 22 July 1942. (*Chitty family*)

gave up her position on a raft to a nurse in difficulty. No great swimmer herself, Paschke moved from group to group, hurling words of encouragement. She had been awarded the Royal Red Cross for her initiative as Singapore fell and was carrying on as if she was in a casualty ward.

Plans of action were yelled. Someone called how lovely it was to have a cool wash. It drew laughs, but many agreed. There had been no time for such niceties. In the last days, the water supply had been cut off in Singapore town.

The impromptu gathering realised they had to make for land. The nearest island, Bangka, looked as if it were the best prospect. Some estimated it was only a short distance off.

It was 16 kilometres away. They were all in for a long swim.[5]

19

Day of Infamy: 15 February 1942

Singapore was at cracking point on 15 February. Heavy shelling and bombing began at daylight aimed at the defended parts of the town. The British artillery batteries and anti-aircraft gunners were active, bringing down three Japanese planes. But it did not deter the attackers. The planes kept dropping their bombs. The enemy artillery inched closer and fired more than ever.

The hospitals at St Andrew's Cathedral, Cathay and Tanglin Road were hammered, almost as if the Japanese were demonstrating to Percival that non-combatants were being targeted. They sent planes to bomb a battery located 300 metres from the cathedral. Two bombs landed in the cathedral grounds.

One killed ambulance driver Roy Keily. It caused Chitty to reflect on his luck, and how it might run out sooner or later with incessant attacks and the infantry closing in. All of them had been moving through those grounds at some time during any day. But reflection did not last long as the fury continued. He and the other drivers were living with death every minute. (Only later would he and the others who survived have moments of anguish over the death of mates. Once more a sense of survivor's guilt would leave an impression. Much later in their lives the cumulative impact would leave scars.)

It was Sunday. There was a church service mid-morning for anyone who wished to pray for salvation. After it, Field Ambulance staff went back to their duties. Just after some arrived at the Cathay building, artillery shells pierced the theatre's roof and dropped among the medical staff and patients. Plaster and wooden beams crashed down. Those left standing went into action tearing away the rubble in a frantic effort to help their fellow workers. Sixteen were killed. Thirty-five were injured, including many who were in the theatre for treatment for other wounds.

Frank Regan of the Field Ambulance was there:

'Cleaning up was a job,' he recalled. 'Pieces of flesh, gore and blood had to be collected and buried; then a coating of lime placed over the whole area. It was the first time I had seen pieces of human beings swept up with a broom, and I hope it is the last.'[1]

All seemed lost. Some of the Australian non-combatants in the 9th Field Ambulance began to curse the British Command for carrying on.

Early afternoon, perhaps because of the devastation at the Cathay building, Percival was aware his fight was over on Singapore. A deputation of military and civilian leaders approached the Japanese front-line along the Bukit Timah road. Yamashita, revelling in his moment of glory for the emperor, sent a message back that Percival himself would have to make the surrender. This was most important for the Japanese general's own image in front of the ubiquitous Imperial Army camera crews and journalists. No second-rate major bending the knee to the general, and therefore the emperor, would do. Forcing the top British commander into the picture, literally, also ensured maximum humiliation for the vanquished and a lowering of the Allies' morale. Such subjugation had been rare in Britain's 400 years as the most powerful nation in the world. It was certainly unusual on such a scale where 70,000 British Empire prisoners would be taken.

Yamashita, with his keen sense of history and his place in it, viewed this moment as the transfer from one imperial power to another.

By mid-afternoon, fighting began to stop. A strange silence descended on Singapore town. The only army in operation now was the corps of doctors, nurses, orderlies and ambulance drivers. Their war—against death—had to go on. Any cessation of hostilities meant to them only that they could go on with their 'fight' without the annoying interference of bombs, artillery, snipers and crazed enemy soldiers.

The 13th Australian General Hospital at St Andrew's was busier than ever as the patients built to more than 1,200. Wards were full of soldiers and civilians in critical condition. Doctors stood in several centimetres of blood as they operated; a Chinese civilian here with his shoulder shot away; a digger there with a chunk of his upper leg missing. Volunteer stretcher bearers waited to carry patients to a ward, or the mortuary, which with the moveable front-line was now found at nearby Martia Road.

Yamashita's request for Percival to turn up with the British flag and another of surrender caused a delay. But in effect Japan on the afternoon of 15 February 1942 had taken control of Singapore. It had added to its euphoric and frenetic run of territorial acquisitions in the last 10 weeks: Hong Kong, the Australian Territory of New Britain (Rabaul) and Malaya. The Japanese occupied Manchuria, about 30 per cent of China (in the east), Korea, French Indochina (Vietnam) and Thailand. This year they planned to control Burma, the Dutch East Indies (Indonesia), the Philippines and New Guinea. Australia was on its hit list too. The abundance of resources to feed Japan's war machine and industry was an attraction it could not ignore. First glance at a map would make any military observer think stretching that far south would present supply-line problems. But with Asian, South-East Asian and Pacific countries falling like dominoes to the ambitious imperialists, the Japanese command was super-confident. There was no reason for it to believe Australia would not submit too. First, however, it had to destroy much of Australia's and the Allied forces' air and sea defences. This would secure resource-rich countries in South-East Asia and allow the Japanese to build strong defences against expected counterattacks from the US in particular, and Australia.

Darwin, the biggest town in the country's north, was a key defensive position. The Australian Government had developed its military ports and airfields. Coastal artillery batteries and anti-aircraft guns had been put in place. Darwin's garrison of troops had been enlarged. This city was seen as a key port for Allied ships, planes and forces defending the Dutch East Indies (Indonesia).

With their spies working overtime in Darwin, the Japanese were aware of the build-up of the military there and the decrease in the civilian population. From 16 December 1941 about 2,000 women and children were moved away by sea. Others departed by plane, road and train.

On Sunday 15 February, the last hot and overcrowded ship, *Koolama*, carrying female and child evacuees, left Darwin with everyone on the lookout for enemy mines.

Just as those on board the ship observed a blackout to avoid Japanese air detection, the British officially surrendered Singapore. It was 8.30 p.m. The capitulation stunned most of the defending troops.

'It was unreal, just like a dream,' George Aspinall of the 30th Battalion said. He had just taken six wounded soldiers from the town's Tanglin area to St Andrew's when he heard the news. 'It was so bewildering that we just carried on normally. It wasn't as though we stood out on the road and put our hands in the air . . . We just stayed at our different posts.'[2]

Chitty, Lemke, Frank Lemin and their fellow drivers were exhausted, not having had real sleep for eight days. They were out of petrol, food and hope. They heard shouting and singing from enemy lines.

'We knew it was over then,' Lemin said. 'I looked over at Peter Chitty, who just shook his head in disgust. I don't think anyone said a word.'[3]

Silence in the Australian camp spoke volumes. The 8th Division had 1,919 men lost or unaccounted for since the Malayan conflict began on 8 December. Another 6,000 cases of wounded or ill personnel from the force had been reported.

It was a heavy price to pay for what the world would view as an abject failure.

The diggers hated their captors. But the next morning, Monday, they had to admit a grudging respect for the way the Japanese soldiers marched into the town. The main description was 'orderly'.

Chitty, Lemke, Lemin and some of the other drivers wandered into the main street and stood on the footpaths as the Japanese paraded by in their battle dress. Lemke lit a cigarette and observed them.

'They were cheering and happy, very orderly even though they were front line troops. The tanks came rolling along. The men were standing up in them, cheering. After all, they had taken the great fort of Singapore. After this we went back to the cathedral and had our bully beef and tea and a smoke . . . we wondered "what now?" '4

There had been fears after all the authentic stories about behaviour in Malaya and Singapore, not to mention the barbarous acts in Nanking, Hong Kong and many other countries. Would they continue to murder, rape, loot and pillage? Probably not in front of the huge media throng and countless witnesses. The Japanese acts of inhumanity would be confined to war or remote regions where there would be no observers. Yamashita had made it clear to his troops that anyone caught committing crimes, such as abuse of the female population or looting, would face the death penalty, which applied to the local Chinese as well. This was to make sure the Imperial Army was seen by the world as 'benevolent'.

It was the image the face-saving conquerors craved, even if it did not fit with the integrity of events.

During the day, Chitty slipped away from his mates and found the broken-down ambulance truck that had been donated by the people of Corryong. He unscrewed the plaque inside and placed it in his pack, telling fellow POW Charles Edwards: 'That stays with me until we're out of this mess.'5

Plight of the Sisters

Seven of the 65 nurses drowned within a day of the *Vyner Brooke* going down. Among the lost was Matron Paschke. This brave, selfless woman, typical of the sisters, had put everyone else before herself. But when she needed help, no-one was there for her.

The darkness and the rips in the Straits carried the little knots of survivors away from each other and in different directions. The closer they came to Bangka Island, the more treacherous were the currents. After much struggle, some were swept in. Others were washed further down the small island's coast.

In the end, the survivors of the 18-hour ordeal in the Straits made it to shore in two groups. After lighting fires and attending to the wounded, the 22 nurses of one group on Radji Beach, led by straight-backed, no-nonsense Matron Irene Drummond and the *Vyner Brooke*'s captain, made decisions on their next move. After a night huddled together, they thought it best to make contact with the island's rulers. This way, help could be brought to the wounded. A delegation went in search of a village. The nurses were shocked to learn that Singapore had fallen to the Japanese in the two days since they left it.

The delegation made contact with the new conquerors, who had just taken control of Bangka Island. The Australian nurses led their 'captors'—a young, tight-lipped Japanese officer, a second officer and six armed soldiers—back to the beach. The officer's coldness and officious manner soon brought uneasiness to the survivors.

After a brief, silent survey of the beach, he snapped orders at his men. Perhaps it was the isolation on the beach where there were no local witnesses; maybe he was a psychopath. But his demeanour was menacing in its dart-eyed deliberation.

The prisoners were segregated by sex. Each one was searched for documents. Matron Drummond, banking on her authority and appealing to the enemy's sense of fair play, demanded that the wounded be taken to a hospital. The young officer did not react. Pointing to her armband, she then indignantly reminded him that they (the nurses) were Red Cross personnel and therefore protected under the Geneva War Convention. He may have understood, but it didn't matter. The apparent worthlessness of the prisoners to the Imperial Japanese Army led him to a quick decision. He ordered all the able men to stand. Drummond repeated her pleas but she was brushed aside. The 25 male prisoners, three on stretchers, were taken along the beach to the other side of a rocky outcrop and away from the women's view. The men were told to stand in one line. Those on stretchers were left on the ground. The Japanese soldiers were ordered in a semicircle around the prisoners.

The order to fire was given.

The soldiers let go with rapid-fire rifles and sub-machineguns. The men crumpled from the onslaught. The soldiers then fixed bayonets. Without any directive, they hurried forward screaming. They ran through any of the men who may have given some twitch of life. Each victim, who may already have been dead, was skewered at least once. This organised way of brutality began in earnest against the Chinese in Nanking in 1937. It had become common practice for some officers, and ill-disciplined, callous soldiers, especially if they believed there were no witnesses to report such atrocities. The isolated beach and the 'thrill' of their first 'British' captives would have conspired to allow such a depraved act.

The execution job done, the officer led his soldiers back to the women.

The nurses were in shock. They had heard the screams and gunfire. They saw the Japanese soldiers coming towards them, some smiling and laughing as they wiped their bayonets clean.

The officer barked an order at the women. They were told to turn around and walk to the water. The terrified nurses had no choice but to obey. The ever-courageous Drummond talked to the girls either side of her, trying to keep them calm.

With hand signals, the officer ordered his six men to line up and take aim. He then dropped his hand. The soldiers fired. The sub-machine-guns spat at the nurses. All collapsed. Soon a red pool filtered around the bodies as they bobbed in the water.

One nurse, Vivian Bullwinkel, feigned death, lying on her side. She had been hit in the hip, and was bleeding. In shock, she could hear the soldiers splashing around her, thrusting bayonets into anyone that may not have been killed by the intense fire.

Minutes later, she heard the men leaving the water. Orders were yelled again, and the little Japanese contingent departed the beach, content that there were no witnesses to their mass murder.

Certain that the Japanese had left, Bullwinkel waded among the sisters, herself now searching for any sign of life, hoping and praying that one of them, like her, had been spared.

But all her friends including Matron Drummond, with whom she had been through so much, were dead. Stunned, isolated and alone, Bullwinkel hid in bushes near the beach and dressed her wound.

A few hours later, she made her way to the bodies of the slaughtered males on the beach and came across a survivor from the massacre of the men, a British soldier, Private Kingsbury. He was one of the stretcher cases, with three bayonet wounds and much of his left upper arm shot away.

Bullwinkel could not leave the man. She decided that the only course of action was for them to give themselves up when Kingsbury was well enough to move. They planned to avoid the village where they had first found the young Japanese officer and his execution squad. Bullwinkel and Kingsbury would surrender to the enemy at another place.

By not admitting to being witnesses to the atrocities, they might be allowed to live. Bullwinkel could not have known of the fates of diggers Hackney, Wharton and Croft at Parit Sulong Bridge in Malaya, when they too cheated death by pretending to be dead. Wharton and Croft had been recaptured but not by the same enemy unit. They did not mention the executions they had witnessed.

Similarly, the gutsy Bullwinkel was savvy enough to gamble that not all the Japanese would be as inhumane as the grim young officer she had just encountered.[1]

Changi

C hitty and the other ambulance drivers were idly having kick-to-kick outside the burnt-out St Andrew's Cathedral early in the morning of 19 February. A dozen armed Japanese soldiers were on the opposite side of the road. They gesticulated and grunted *'Kurrah'* (Come here), indicating that a contingent of Australian soldiers should form up near them, pick up their haversacks and start moving. Their destination would be the former British barracks at Selarang 19 kilometres away at Changi in north-east Singapore. It was an arduous command given the distance and condition of the 8th Division force. Chitty would have made the trek without complaint, but was content with the need to drive a truck-load of wounded men and supplies.

He drove forward and back past the long snake of POWs. There were about 15,000 diggers marching to their prison quarters. More than 70,000 British, Australian and Indian prisoners shuffled along on foot towards their designated Changi destinations. Chitty became familiar with the landmarks along the east coast road. He jolted along with his loads of sick and supplies through low hills rolling down to the sea fringed with bamboo fish traps. Small green islands studded the horizon. Attap-thatched huts and small roadside markets were folded into gaps in rubber and coconut plantations.

Many of the marching Australians were still in shock. As they straggled along, some wondered what had happened.

'When you came up a long hill you'd just see this line of humanity behind you,' Don Moore, marching on his 22nd birthday observed. 'It made us puzzled, why couldn't we have done something? Look at us!'[1]

It was a hot muggy day, which accentuated the stench of rotting bodies. At one point, a few kilometres out of Singapore town there was a line of bamboo poles. On them were the decapitated heads of alleged Chinese 'communists'—the arch enemy of the Japanese imperial fascists. Yet it was Chinese locals who offered food and water to the Australians when the Japanese captors were not looking. Even children caught doing this were beaten by the guards, but there were so few Japanese on the trek that only a few sympathetic onlookers were harmed. They received a smash from a rifle butt for their trouble.

Bananas, coconuts, duck eggs, buns and pieces of bread were handed to the straggling diggers. The Chinese had no love for the invaders. Plenty of the locals had experienced their cruelty. All of them knew of the atrocities in Singapore, Nanking and other places. There was something audacious and defiant about the Chinese actions as they rushed forward to press their offerings into the Australians' hands.

The Japanese planted flags in many houses along the route for the benefit of the film crews and photographers in abundance to document this most amazing of Imperial Army conquests. The shots of so many British prisoners shuffling their way to oblivion would be wonderful propaganda for the victors.[2]

A Scottish piper was near the front of the line. Whenever a

village was reached, he would start up again, drawing people to the road. As night fell, the villages became more and more spread. But still the lone piper blew, lifting the flagging spirits of the men. Once at their destination, the weary soldiers drank chlorinated water and threw their groundsheets on the shell-marked concrete of their allotted barracks among the green vegetation. They took in their new 'home'—three-storey barracks with tiled roofs and broad balconies—and slept where they were.

More than 12,000 wounded would have to be transported from Singapore town to the Changi area over the first week of captivity. The chief Japanese medical officer, Colonel Sekiguchi, refused to allow the Australians to take any medical equipment. The inhumanity of this decision shocked the Australian medical staff, but seemed on reflection to be consistent with the military madness witnessed, especially at Alexandra Hospital.

The callous Sekiguchi seemed only to be in Singapore town a day before he was off with General Yamashita, who was away on another mission after his moment of triumph. He would begin planning his next invasion. It had taken him just 70 days to conquer the British in Malaya and Singapore. The general wanted to invade Australia but he had been overruled by the Japanese High Command. India was a better bet as his next conquest, he was told. It would not require the long lines of sea communication or present the supply problems in tackling Australia. Yamashita would have to wait for his crack at the biggest island in the Pacific.[3]

Sekiguchi's replacement was Lieutenant Nakamira, an

infantry officer. Similar to all the Japanese command, he had little idea of how such a huge number of prisoners should be managed. There was no manual for it and little precedent.

Sensing this, the wily and bold chief medical officer in the 8th Division, Lieutenant-Colonel J. Glyn White tried bluff when Nakamira asked him what his orders from Sekiguchi had been. White replied that he had a week *each* to shift the Australian, British and Indian wounded, meaning three weeks in all. Nakamira accepted this. White had bought time to circumvent Sekiguchi's cruel, even sadistic decision not to allow medical supplies at the prison hospital.

White then gave secret instructions for Chitty and all the ambulance and truck drivers to move as much equipment as possible. They had 76 vehicles and worked two runs a day. They visited all the hospitals in Singapore town and scavenged 4,500 beds, 7,000 mattresses and a hidden hoard of medical supplies and equipment. Reading material of all kinds was also purloined, as were two pianos, wirelesses, bags of sugar and chocolates. Vegemite was part of the haul. Chitty's vehicle was checked on one run. The Japanese guard made a cursory inspection of the items in the back of the ambulance. His eyes settled on Vegemite jars.

'What this?' he demanded.

'Boot polish, mate,' Chitty said, sitting in the driver's seat. Lemke was in front with him. The guard motioned for Chitty to open it. The guard starred at the black substance.

'Boot polish!' Chitty repeated. He put his finger in the vegemite, smeared it on his right boot and made a polishing motion with his hand as the Japanese peered in the driver's window.

'Arrh so!' the guard said and waved him on.[4]

*

White was in awe of the ingenuity, energy and dedication of Chitty and his 75 fellow drivers. None of the 12,000 wounded and sick was forced to make the march to Changi.

It was a prodigious and inventive beginning to a period of unpredictability.

The Australians moved into Selarang, which was between Changi jail and the township near the north-eastern tip of the island. The British, Indians and Dutch had their own barracks. The main hospital was at Lord Roberts' barracks. It became 'home' for the 9th Field Ambulance. Selarang had been occupied by 900 Gordon Highland Regiment soldiers and their families before the war. It had six three-storey reinforced concrete blocks. One building served as a kitchen.

A small building at the other end of the square housed a clock-tower. It had already been put on Tokyo time, as had all other timepieces in Singapore, and the island had a new name: Syonan-to or 'Light of the South'.

The vast number of POWs had their first glimpse of their new 'holiday camp' the next morning. At first glance, it was palatable. Many had been impressed when they first saw the Changi area on arrival from the sea nearly a year earlier. It featured green rolling hills. The vegetation was lush. Two months of pounding from bombs and artillery had destroyed the atmosphere. Buildings were flattened; farmhouses were charred; fields were crater-marked.

*

On the first day, prisoners mingled in the square, looking for mates. The Japanese were still undecided on a plan for what to do with POWs, and they were left to their own devices and organisation. Barbed wire to keep them in had yet to be rolled out. Their captors knew that there was nowhere to run or hide if they did try to leave.

The penalty of death by firing squad or beheading for attempted escape was a deterrent for most inmates.

Chitty retrieved a football from his ambulance. The ball's leather surface was almost peeled off. But it was inflated. The sight of it flying in the air on a field, and the familiar 'thump' of a punt or 'ku-dung' of a drop kick had scores of heads turning. Four drivers—Chitty, Lemke and two others—turned into ten then 20 who were soon playing 'kick-to-kick'. The flashier ones were flying for spectacular high 'marks'—the outstanding feature of Australian Rules. Chitty was happy to leave his transport chore for 20 minutes. For a few moments, he and the beleaguered POWs were boys without a care.

The growing group of men decided they had a quorum. Tomorrow two groups of 20 would play a game with four upright bamboo poles as goals and 'behind' posts at each end of the field. A field umpire was appointed. He would be sole judge and jury on any indiscretion in the field. There was also a selection panel, which tried to make the height, skill and speed of the two teams as equal as possible.

Chitty was disappointed not to be able to play. He had the wounded to transport for days yet. On the second night, when arriving back at the barracks, he learned that the 13th Battery had won 13 goals 9 behinds to the Hospitals 10 goals 8 behinds.

Competitive sport gave the diggers a spark after less than

48 hours in Changi. Within a few days, football fever ignited other sporting enthusiasts. Most of the men loved the races, and a bet. There were no horses, so the diggers settled for the next best thing: frogs. Not to be outdone by the admirable football organisation, which avoided brawls and kept a fine crowd of about 500 interested, the well-known racing identities among the POWs formed the CFRC—Changi Frog Racing Club. Everyone from committeemen to stewards and bookies were appointed. This had been inspired by the use of scorpions in the Middle East in World War I. Frogs were more fun and less dangerous. They would be dressed in quaint, colourful bands and placed in an upturned bucket in the middle of a circle. Bets were called for. The starting steward would then lift the bucket. With plenty of encouragement from the betting yard, the frogs would head for the circle.

On the first 'meet', a steward picked up the winning frog, which seemed much friskier than his competitors. Examining the buttons that kept a red band in place, the steward received a sting in the finger. He discovered a drawing pin aligned with the buttons. The frog had received a nasty prick, which enhanced his leap and took him to the line first.

The CFRC committee sat. It imposed a life sentence on the winning frog's owner. He could only view the next meeting as a spectator.[5]

One morning the Japanese arrived at Selarang in trucks carrying concertina wire in 50 metre pieces, iron posts and hammers.

'We were about the only POWs in history to fence ourselves in,' Lemke observed dryly. 'They told us where to lay the fence, but we didn't care.' When they came to a ditch or a cutting they just set the fence over them, making it easy to escape under the wire, if any were brave or foolhardy enough to attempt it.

'It was our first time with the Japanese watching,' he added. 'Rings were taken off in case they wanted them. We took our time with the fencing. When the Japanese were having their dinner, we would ask: "Tomorrow you bring more rice? Can't fence on little bit of rice." '

Their pleas were ignored.[6]

Buoyed by the success of their blitzes and invasions through Asia, South-East Asia and the Pacific, the Imperial Japanese Army turned its attention further south to Australia. Just as the POWs were settling into a strange new life, on 19 February 1942, 188 Japanese planes were launched from four aircraft carriers in the Timor Sea. Darwin's military build-up made it the prime target in Australia's remote north. The planes were accompanied by 54 land-based bombers. Darwin's harbour was full of Allied ships. There were two attacks, both planned by Admiral Yamamoto, who was behind the attack on Pearl Harbor 10 weeks earlier.

In the first run, which began at 10 a.m. on a Thursday, the harbour and town were pattern-bombed. Dive bombers escorted by Zero fighters then attacked shipping, military and civil aerodromes and the hospital at Berrimah. The blitz was over in 40 minutes.

The second attack began an hour later. There was high-altitude bombing of the Royal Australian Air Force base at Parap, which lasted 23 minutes. The official death toll figure put out by the Australian Government was 243. Locals put it at around 1,000. Twenty military aircraft were destroyed.

Eight ships at anchor in the harbour were sunk. Only four enemy aircraft were brought down.

Most civil and military facilities in Darwin were obliterated. It was the first ever attack on Australia. It was also mission accomplished for the Japanese. For the time being, Darwin would not provide a threat from the Americans and its allies to the consolidation of Japanese imperial conquests in South-East Asia.

22

There Goes Bullamakanka

The Japanese prison guards made little contact with the Changi POWs in the early days of captivity, but they were quick to let the inmates know of their attack missions on Australia and Allied countries, some mythical, others exaggerated.

'Darwin, boom, boom, boom! Finish,' one guard informed Chitty, other Ambulance Corps personnel and some of George Aspinall's 30th Battalion.

'What about Brisbane?' one digger asked.

'Brisbane, boom, boom! Finish.'

'What about Woop Woop and Bullamakanka?' Chitty asked.

'All finish! Boom, boom, boom!'

'Not Woop Woop too?' Chitty said.

The guard nodded emphatically.

'All finish!'[1]

This verbal propaganda was meant to undermine POW morale. But no-one believed they were being told the whole truth. The Japanese began their own English-speaking newspaper, *Syonan Times*, shutting down all the other presses in Malaya and Singapore. This was propaganda with exaggerations, some of them such stretches that they amused the diggers. A classic was the story of a Japanese pilot who ran out of ammunition. He dived on the British forces, pulled out his samurai sword and swung it at the troops, killing plenty. Other pilot 'sons of Nippon', when badly wounded, were saved miraculously by planes that would take them home and land them safely, *automatically*. Japanese technology and efficiency had surprised the British troops, but this futuristic development amazed them.

Reading the *Syonan Times* became like solving a jigsaw puzzle. The Australians, with a well-honed sense of cynicism, learnt to read between the lines, and perhaps believe the reverse of what was written. If a huge number of Allied ships were said to have sunk in a Pacific battle, then it was guessed that the British had held their own. If the Germans were said to be winning the battle in the skies over England, then it was assumed that they were losing.

The specifics were too specific; the facts were too dry; the numbers and lines thrown out about Allied losses became clichés.

*

Not long after gloating about the attacks on Darwin, the *Syonan Times* and the guards were telling the POWs that Japan had 'taken' the Dutch East Indies (Indonesia). The Australians in Changi knew the enemy had landed troops on Dutch Borneo and in the Celebes in early January. They met little resistance. One by one Ambon, Sumatra and Bali fell to the Japanese. Timor, including the Portuguese sector of the island, was a more difficult proposition as a combined Australian/ Dutch force fought a guerrilla-style campaign in the island's rugged interior.

Inside Changi, a smuggled radio, kept in the brush end of a broom, let the inmates know that by the end of February the Japanese had isolated Java, where the Dutch Government and most Europeans were based. It was defended by about 30,000 Allied soldiers—Dutch, indigenous Indonesians, Australians, Americans and British. But this loose alliance was poorly trained and equipped. It was no match for the over-exercised, well-oiled Japanese machine, which had been boosted by its successful rampage through South-East Asia.

The Japanese invaded on 1 March 1942 with 50,000 infantrymen. A week later Java surrendered. The enemy took another huge batch of POWs.

The news was a blow to the Changi inmates, who only had scratchy reports over the radio, which were disseminated through the camp. The Dutch East Indies was uncomfortably close to Australia, and the Japanese occupation of all its islands cut off an important avenue of escape home.

*

Frustration built over not knowing what was really happening in the war. The Australians began early in their enforced stay to think about how they might acquire more radios, even though anyone caught with them would receive severe punishment. But some things, such as obtaining the news, pushed the prisoners to take high risks. Another was food.

The meals were dominated by rice in small rations. The men and the medical staff were aware that this had to be supplemented with vegetables, but they were not easy to acquire. Attempts were made to cultivate gardens with valiant efforts to grow tropical vegetables such as sweet potatoes. The leaves of tapioca and sweet potato plants were boiled in the hope of extracting vitamin B. Troops were not allowed to pick coconuts from the palm trees, yet there was no rule about taking those that had fallen. The milk and fibre were needed for the sick soldiers, which led some of the Queenslanders to help along the harvesting. They shinnied up the trees and hooked the coconuts with a device attached to their feet.

The Australians gave their tins of bully beef to the cooks, who made a rice and meat hash. Soon it was down to just the rice, which was unappetising to almost all the POWs. The rice had been mixed with lime to avoid weevils. It was gritty and was at first presented in a sticky type of soup, which developed an early disgruntlement among the men. Its exterior was soft but the interior was rock-like. Diggers with poor teeth found it hard going.

One of them said he could not stand the sight of the gelatinous mush. Many complained graphically that it reminded them of a 'wet dream'.[2]

Only a few hardly souls such as Chitty would devour everything they could, without complaint or trouble to their systems.

'He'd eat a blow fly if necessary,' Lindsay Chitty commented. 'His adaptability to any food was part of his survival kit while a POW.'[3]

Not all the inmates had such versatile stomachs or inclinations. The doctors were concerned. The nutritional value was low. Constipation was an early problem. They sent men out to collect lalang grass, a more reliable source of vitamin B, which was put in 44 gallon drums and boiled over a fire for three hours. Then devices similar to a coffee grinder were used to mince it up into 'grass soup'. The POWs were supposed to drink it with the rice. They found it revolting, but it eased their bowel problems.

There was also a salt deficiency. Working parties were organised to fetch beach water, which would be boiled with the rice. This went a little way to improving the quality and taste of the staple diet. Some of the men took advantage of the beach run and had a swim. This way there was no shortage of volunteers for the water assignment. Along the way too, they did some dealing with the locals, especially the Chinese, whom they trusted. Cigarettes were exchanged for just about anything. Food was the key acquisition.

Pressure from the inmates forced the cooks to fast-track their ingenuity in preparing rice. The soldiers helped by spearing fish, buying prawns from the locals, gathering snails and catching big frogs (scratchings and even winners from the Melbourne Cup) and sizeable lizards. They were all grilled and mixed with the rice.

More mastication was needed than normal, but the POWs pretended it was chicken.

*

By 26 February, Vivian Bullwinkel had tended Private Kingsbury for 10 days on Bangka Island. She had fed him with the rations of their dead companions and by 'borrowing' vegetables from local village gardens at night. There was enough morphine for them both to stave off the pain from their wounds.

When Kingsbury was able to be helped along, they struggled through the scrub to the village of Muntok, a few kilometres from the place where they had first encountered their new conquerors. They asked locals where they could find the Japanese and were directed to a guard post. They surrendered and were taken to a naval officer. From the initial conversation, it was clear he had no idea of the massacre carried out on Radji Beach by the depraved young army officer and his men. The naval man accepted that their severe wounds had come from the attacks by Japanese planes and the sinking of the *Vyner Brooke*.

Kingsbury was sent to a prison. To her joy, Bullwinkel was placed with the other 31 shipwrecked nurses who had been washed up some distance from Radji Beach.

The contingent of survivors was later transported from Bangka Island to Palembang in southern Sumatra. After refusing to 'entertain' (sexually) Japanese officers at a newly formed club on the island, they were housed in flimsy, crowded huts and fed on meagre rations.

They were to be held in these primitive conditions indefinitely.[4]

After all the POWs and wounded had been transported from Singapore to Changi, the Japanese ordered that all of the 76 trucks and ambulances had to be stripped down to their chassis to avoid any mass attempt to break out with the vehicles.

Chitty and his fellow drivers were saddened about this destruction of their ambulances, which had done so much good for the force before, during and after the fighting. It seemed to them an unnecessary waste, especially since the Japanese always appeared short of functional transport beyond the ubiquitous bicycle.

Only the chassis and steering mechanism were left on each vehicle. They had to be pulled over sand and rough terrain to the beach to collect salt water for the food or firewood for the kitchen, and stores such as rice which came in heavy bags.

The chassis were hauled by 20 men with ropes.

The Japanese organised more barbed wire to be laid around the barracks, marking the perimeters and enhancing the sense of a prison. Many Sikhs among the Indians troops hated it more than the others; enough to change sides when offered the choice of becoming guards rather than prisoners. The (Nepalese) Gurkhas, when offered the same option, to a man remained with the POWs. They formed a loyal, proud regiment with a fierce reputation for fighting.

The Sikhs who opted for disloyalty were called 'gutless' and 'turncoats' by the POWs, which did not make them any more lenient when dealing with their captives. Some even became as officious and vicious as the worst of the Japanese and Koreans. They were just as free with their rifle butts in delivering the odd bashing to the inmates.

'Aussie humour was alive and well in those early weeks,' Joe Jameson said, recalling the day when a gold-braided Japanese officer ordered most of 8th Division out on parade. The men had to bring with them their drinking mugs. Standing on a raised platform, he fingered the sword by his side and told the POWs that it was the emperor's birthday. It should be celebrated. Guards carrying flagons of sake wandered down the lines dishing out a splash of this favourite Japanese drink. That task completed, the officer ordered the diggers to drink to the emperor.

'He took a swig out of a glass,' Jameson said, 'but no Australian mug was raised. It was a really tense moment. The officer called for his glass to be topped up. Then he bellowed at us to "drink to the Emperor!" He took another swig. Just as he finished, a big Tassie bloke [Vern Rae, an intelligence officer] from the Australian 15th battery stepped forward. He yelled:

'"Boys, we drink to the Emperor—faaaarrrk the Emperor!"

'It brought a tremendous, spontaneous roar from the lads as if it had been rehearsed:

'"Faaaaarrrk the Emperor!!" they cried, almost in chorus. They downed their sake. Then the officer, pleased with this response, and showing his deep knowledge of the Australian/English language, drained his glass and bellowed: "Ahso! Faark the Emperor!"

'This brought another roar from the assembled diggers, having toasted the most important man from the conquering force, in their own delightful and inimitable way.'[5]

Food was sustenance to the body as humour was to the diggers' souls. Without either, they would be finished.

23

Mind Games

The bored inmates were looking for mind nourishment too. They created Changi University. Brigadier H. B. Taylor was appointed Chancellor. Sir Adrian Curlewis was made Dean of Law. Every conceivable study course sprang up. Some aired their knowledge of history from World War I to ancient Egypt. Others lectured on mathematics and engineering. Languages were popular; business principles and accounting were taken up by the practically minded with an eye for careers post-war. Talks on sport were well attended. Tactful, charming Ben Barnett, who was a wicketkeeper for Victoria from 1929 to 1940, and for Australia in the 1938 Ashes, told of his first-class playing days and what it was like to play under Don Bradman. He organised a small panel of footballers, including Chitty, Chicken Smallhorn and Lou Daley, to talk about their experiences in the top leagues and in the bush.[1]

Colonel E. R. White of the 10th Australian General Hospital organised a postgraduate medicine course. The 9th Field Ambulance offered complete medical and dental examinations for the inmates, which was a big enterprise and took much time and organisation. The dental check-up was less appealing. Many POWs had teeth problems and had to be cajoled into being looked at. The examiners had one old-fashioned foot-drill, which made a fearful sound. Fillings were painful operations, but those who braved them were appreciative of the results.

Russell Braddon thought the most bizarre self-improvement course was delivered by Alec Downer. Alec was the son of Sir John Downer, an architect of the Australian Federal Constitution (and father of Liberal government minister Alexander). He put his Oxford University 'toffy' accent to use by giving elocution lessons to 'volatile' Australian privates, who murdered their vowels at every opportunity.

'How now brown cow!' Braddon recalled instructing the lads with rounded vowels. 'It was magnificent!'

Most surprising was the fact that neither party ridiculed the other.[2]

Clubs sprang up. A scout group was formed, then some philatelists got together. A few of them even had their most prized stamp collections in tins and books with them. They were soon discussing the merits of 'Penny Blacks' and how to spot the most valuable ones. Not to be outdone, motorbike enthusiasts grouped and discussed their passion, without the objects of their desire being there. They were able to compare, however, the Japanese sidecars and bikes they had glimpses of on trips to Singapore. Men of the cloth became active, holding sermons under palm trees. The Catholics were the most dedicated of the religious groups. The garrison church at Changi had been belted by the Japanese air force, but a new chapel was created. The stained glass windows from the destroyed church were salvaged and used in the new building. The Catholic POWs gathered to recite the rosary every night. Religious instruction was twice weekly. Benediction was given on Wednesday and Sunday nights. Mass was celebrated with some altar wine received from home just before Singapore's collapse. A high mass was held once a month. Discussion groups gave these men a strong focus and a vague sense of normality.

Freemasons also congregated, and a secret lodge was formed. A story circulated that may or may not have been apocryphal. They were holding a clandestine meeting in a hut. The door burst open in the middle of their rituals and a Japanese officer marched in. After taking a few seconds to assess what was going on, he stepped up to the grand master. Shaking hands in the Freemason manner, he bowed and said:

'Grand Master, I see nothing!'

He then wheeled around and walked out.

Whether or not this tale was true, it served to depict some of the Japanese in a more charitable light.[3]

The beliefs of all religious groups were reinforced. Many claimed this strengthened their resolve and helped their attitude to their captors, at least in the early period. Services dominated Selarang on Sundays, which was a traditional time for most religious groups in Australian communities.

The Australians in Selarang had a library of more than 20,000 books. Men who had never been inclined to read, now did. There was time in the early weeks in Changi and for many the desire stayed with them. Books on travel, sports and technical subjects were plentiful. The classics were devoured.

Romance, perhaps because there was very little to be had in the barracks, was popular.

Some men were found to be illiterate. A class was begun. In an odd way, their incarceration was a salvation. About 450 men learnt the basics or reading and writing. Worlds were opened up. Many of them were never without a book after the experience.

Concerts were well attended. Crowds of more than 10,000 men would sit on the grass outside their huts and listen to gramophone records of music that wafted through the warm, balmy nights. Even the Japanese would stop and listen. In a rare generous concession, they agreed to obtain more records and books, and were true, in this instance, to their word. Professional singer George McNeilly was the music man. A wooden studio was built to shelve the records and store the precious gramophone. He made sure than Bach, Beethoven, Mozart and Chopin were listened to. Operas were played often. McNeilly lectured on them and their composers. This increased the appreciation, despite a majority wanting to hear 'swing' music. Many tough men, who previously would have branded anyone showing an inclination to like classical music as 'effeminate' at best, had their minds broadened and souls deepened.

Interests in jazz developed. A true theatre sprang up. Technicians converted a garage into a crude version of something like Sydney and Melbourne's glitzier auditoriums. Innovation was the key. Seats were made from planks laid across coconut tree stumps. Different colours of clay taken from boreholes for the latrines were used to paint bright backdrops. English and Dutch POWs were allowed quotas. Japanese guards insisted on having front-row seats and were seen to laugh at the more slapstick drama. They were there partly for the entertainment and party for censorship reasons. Any insults to the emperor, the troops were told, would lead to instant beheading.

The organisers wanted a better piano than those smuggled into Changi earlier. Some of the English POWs knew of one at a brothel in Singapore, which they had frequented before Singapore fell, and now was a favourite haunt of a Japanese officer. The POWs knew about his 'habit'. One of the Englishmen made a request for the piano. The Japanese officer would not let the POWs have it. The Englishman fronted the officer and told him that his 'habit' might be mentioned to the most senior British officer in the camp. This was a brave, risky confrontation. Apparently the Japanese officer thought more of his reputation than his ruling on the piano. He relented. It took 12 strong men more than a day to get the piano into Selarang.[4]

A few professional actors, some amateurs and still more who had never dared perform before, gave their all to appreciative audiences. The problem of a total lack of female actors was solved by some men doing female impersonations, complete with wigs and dresses. This never failed to stir laughter in the onlookers. But as the actors began to apply make-up and play up to their parts, the POWs stopped laughing. The men playing women really looked like the opposite sex. So much so that Hedley Hatch observed radio personality John Wood when he 'dressed' up and commented:

'He is the goods, and sure gives the boys ideas . . .'[5]

Black Jack Galleghan had become the senior officer of the division after those senior to him were taken elsewhere. He seemed loved and loathed in equal measure. He thought he knew how to keep up the morale of the troops by insisting on soldierly disciplines even when the men were fast losing a sense of military ways and bearing. They were inmates in a remote, strangely lax yet sometimes brutal prison rather than men of battle. And as they were all volunteers, there seemed no need to carry on like soldiers in this camp.

Black Jack directed that a concert be put on right in the middle of Selarang Square. A stage was set up. The orchestra included violins, clarinets, saxophones, French horns, guitars, drums, harmonicas and that hard-earned piano. The size and concept of the proposed show concerned the Japanese. Two hundred guards rimmed the square to deter an attempt at a mass break-out. The audience built steadily. When it passed about 5,000, the Japanese installed mortars facing into the spectators. At 10,000, the guards brought out machine-guns, and with good reason. They were outnumbered in a way that would have put on edge even the bravest of them. The crowd grew to more than 15,000 onlookers. There was a typical concert atmosphere with music and performing artists. At the end of the show, Black Jack strode to the stage and ordered the manager to play 'God Save the King'. Every soldier stood and sang with gusto. If the senior Japanese officer in attendance wished to prevent this forceful rendition of homage to another emperor, it was too late. The guards looked bewildered and more nervous than ever. Would these POWs now attempt anything? The Japanese stood by their mortars and gripped their weapons knowing full well that they would be overwhelmed in any stampede.

Black Jack knew what he was doing. It was the most

unifying and stirring moment in Changi to that point for most of the men. They had mixed hopes and feelings about their plight, but they still had powerful emotions. Sensing the mood, accomplished lyricists, including composer and tenor, Slim De Grey went to work and came up with appropriate verse and music. They touched romantic and nostalgic nerves. An instance was his 'Waiting for Something to Happen':

> I'm waiting and praying for you
> I still hear you saying, 'I love you.'
> Knowing I will be coming back to you soon.[6]

'Soon' was the operative word. Almost all the POWs believed that they would be liberated before long. Rumours abounded about rescue missions by fellow divisions hitting Singapore. Another to have initial credibility was that a government-to-government deal was being done to exchange sheep for men. It seemed somehow plausible given Japan's purchase and need for Australian wool. But the rescuing army did not materialise in the first few weeks. Nor did the sheep.

Black Jack had heard all the rumours. But, no matter what the future held he kept up the division's physical training. He wanted his men fit just in case they would be forced to fight again, which might well be an option if there were an effort by the Allies to free the Changi POWs. There was logic in his dreams. The entire British force was equivalent to three divisions with about two-thirds of them well trained and battle hardened. Such a force would be vital as the war progressed.

But for the time being, the Japanese had use for them.

Early in March 1942, the 6th and 7th Divisions returned to Australia from North Africa and the Middle East. They were three months too late for Gordon Bennett's purposes. But these crack, experienced shock troops gave the nation some comfort, especially with Japan marauding around the region so far unchecked.

Each day there was news of another exploit. On 7 March 1942, the British abandoned Rangoon, Burma. The enemy took it two days later. They also invaded Salamaua and Lae in New Guinea.

Australia was fearful it would be the next sustained target.

24

The Force's Forced Labour

Peter Chitty and his fellow drivers had been left to their own devices ever since the destruction of the ambulances. In the first few weeks after the surrender, they had been kept busy transporting goods, the sick and the wounded. Then their right to 'work' was removed. They were left as idle as all the other POWs, which did not fit with Chitty's mentality. He thrived on physical labour.

When the Japanese announced they would create 'work parties', which were to be sent around Singapore to do different jobs, he was interested in the concept and comfortable with it. Like thousands of others, he was restless in Changi, despite all the activities being set up by the inmates themselves. These were leisure-time pursuits. Men like Chitty wanted more. There were attractions too in leaving the perimeters of the barbed wire prison.

Their captors began to oblige.

Hundreds were housed in Singapore town's entertainment centre, 'The Great World'. Gangs of 150 men were organised. On his thirtieth birthday on 12 March, Chitty found himself in a group at the docks, where Japanese guards taunted him and the other Australians, claiming the Dutch on Java had surrendered to Japan. The POWs were not sure, but learnt soon afterwards that a claim such as this, for once, was true.

The docks' massive storage sheds—'godowns'—were full of goods from Japan's initial systematic looting of Singapore and Malaya. There were crates of cars, trucks, aircraft, rubber and just about every other item imaginable, including kitchen sinks. Australian gangs had to move the crates to the dock to be hoisted by crane into ships' holds. This was heavy work, even for Chitty and former wharfies among the POWs. If they erred or slowed up, it invited a rebuke from a guard that would often lead to a punch in the face, or a rifle butt to the head. Some guards, both Korean and Japanese, were more sadistic than others. Many were 'verballed' or worse by Japanese officers for not enforcing rules on the docks. Among the guards was the odd decent man, who showed it by an act of some kindness when an officer was not in sight.

Once two of Chitty's 9th Field Ambulance workmates dropped a crate down a flight of stairs. A guard approached with a thick stick. He belted them both across the back and forced them to struggle with it up the stairs to a landing. After they had completed their task, the guard confronted them once more, this time with soft drinks. He lingered almost apologetically.

This kind of act confused all the Australians, who assumed the less vicious guards wanted to show they were 'nice guys' under strict orders.

The jobs at the Nestlé products factory were cushier in every way. The men stole and devoured as much chocolate and condensed milk as possible short of making themselves sick. They made the most of it, but not for long.

A big project was organised at the golf course, where the Japanese wanted to build a road and shrine to their war dead. The POWs were housed in a Singapore suburb, Adam Park, which provided better conditions and opportunities than at the isolated Changi. They had bungalows to live in. There was no barbed wire. The more enterprising men would take advantage of the easier contact with the Chinese in a nearby village. They still had to deceive the guards, but as food, apart from rice, became scarce, ways were found. Some would slip away at night. Those that had Red Cross armbands would put them on and pretend to be assisting a sick or injured worker. When the guards were out of sight they would take off for the village to trade anything they had, including precious tobacco rations.

An abandoned trench system, which had been in the thick of battle in the last days before Singapore's fall, was searched with the intensity of beggars at a waste dump. Some gems, such as watches, wallets and discarded clothes were discovered and traded. There was also some looting to be done in numerous empty houses that had been left in a hurry. The men would slip away in the early hours, break in and 'borrow' whatever they could, then sell it to Chinese traders. The brave thieves and local 'businessmen' developed a nocturnal bond based on survival and a mutual desire to, if not beat, then cheat the new conquerors.

The POWs took other risks. One visited the Japanese store and asked for a gallon of petrol every morning to start a steamroller. It was wood-fired and did not need any petrol. The fuel was traded.

Four members of a gang, two British and two Australians (Corporal Rod Breavington and Private Victor Gale), took the ultimate risk in the middle of the night early in April 1942. They made a dash to leave Singapore, using a raft over the Johor Strait to evade Japanese guards. The men stole bicycles and rode up the west coast of Malaya. Breavington and Gale split from their English escapee mates and hid in a village. Chinese Malayans helped them obtain a canoe. They stacked it with tinned food and then attempted to reach Ceylon (Sri Lanka) over the Indian Ocean. After six weeks at sea they were about 65 kilometres from their target, Colombo, when they spotted a naval vessel. They paddled towards it, waving their arms. The warship came alongside them.

It was Japanese.

They were taken on board and later deposited back at a Changi hospital where they encountered the two British escapees who had also been rounded up.

The men were informed that they would be executed, but were not told the date. They were left in Changi wondering when and how they would be killed.

Also in April some of photographer Aspinall's unit in 30th Battalion were working on the shrine the Japanese were building on top of Bukit Timah Hill, Singapore. During a break for a smoke, fellow POW Kevin Ward told Aspinall:

'You'll never guess who the interpreter is on the job . . . it's Mal Lee! [the photo studio owner].'

He was a captain, and wore a big sword. He didn't like the Australians and gave them the 'dirtiest' jobs, claiming some of them had not paid for work he had done for them.

Remembering their heated exchange when Mal Lee tried to cheat him over the cost of prints, Aspinall kept well away from the spy.[1]

By mid-April 1942, the Japanese captured Burma's Lashio and the railhead there, which cut the supply of Allied aid to China. The invaders gave themselves a month to drive the British forces across the Burmese border into India. Nothing seemed likely to stop them.

*

Early in May 1942, the Japanese decreed that the Changi prisoners had to be as self-sufficient in food as possible. This could be taken several ways. The POWs were doing it their way, purloining and trading where they could. They also started more vegetable patches, the produce of which was to supplement their worrying rice-dominated diet. But when they succeeded, the Japanese demanded a hefty quota of all produce for themselves.

They wanted, it seemed, a massive slice of everything. They were preparing a sea invasion for Port Moresby, New Guinea. A support force included an aircraft carrier, *Shoho*, and several cruisers. The Japanese planned also to extend their control of the Pacific by setting up a base at Tulagi in the Solomon Islands for long-range amphibious aircraft. Taking the port and airfield at Port Moresby would mean that islands under their control would be safe from land-based air attacks. In turn, the Japanese Air Force would be free to attack Australia's northeast. No northern airports or ports would be free from attack. Sea links between Australia and the US would be cut. There would be no movement of Allied troops and supplies.

Japan could rule the Pacific unchallenged.

After securing these objectives, the Japanese planned to destroy the main American fleet at Midway—between Pearl Harbor and Japan. This would put the US out of the war in the Pacific.

The enemy's confidence was at a peak as they swept towards New Guinea after making further strides in April to conquer the entire region. On 9 April, after a six-day battle, they forced the Americans into unconditional surrender on the Bataan Peninsula in the Philippines. This led to the Bataan Death March, during which 76,000 Allied POWs, including 12,000 Americans, were forced to walk 96 kilometres to a POW camp under a blazing sun and without food or water. More than 25,000 died, including 5,000 Americans.

On 29 April, thousands of kilometres away, the Imperial Army had taken central Burma, almost on cue. When, if ever, many in Australia wondered, would this frenzied, merciless enemy force be checked?

Most Australian observers, from Prime Minister John Curtain down, saw this coming ocean struggle off the nation's north-east corner as a key battle for survival. The Americans regarded it as a big test too. For the first time in the Pacific war they were well prepared. They had intelligence after intercepting and decoding enemy secret signals. And they had radar, a recent development (by Australian scientist Mark Oliphant in England) that could identify incoming aircraft in time to scramble their own planes into the air to tackle them.

On 4 May 1942, the Japanese were confronted by the 'Allied Task Force 44' off Australia's north-east coast. It consisted of Allied (American and Australian) vessels, including HMAS *Australia*, a heavy cruiser, and HMAS *Hobart*, a light cruiser. It was commanded by Australian Rear Admiral Crace.

The fight, the Battle of the Coral Sea, was between opposing aircraft that were trying to destroy each other and opposing carriers. It was the first aircraft carrier battle ever fought. It was also the initial naval battle in which the enemy forces of surface ships never sighted or fired at each other. The planes (from the carriers, with some land-based) did all the attacking.

The battle went on for five days until 8 May. There were huge losses on both sides: the Allies had one carrier destroyed, one almost crippled, one oiler and one destroyer sunk, 66 aircraft lost and 543 men killed or wounded. The Japanese lost one carrier and had one crippled. One destroyer and three small naval ships were sunk. Seventy-seven of its aircraft never came back and 1,074 men were killed or wounded.

The Allies won on points. But more importantly they delivered the Japanese their first major defeat of the war. They had prevented them from achieving their objective in New Guinea and the Solomon Islands, for the time being. Japan, with its incredible, sustained, efficient and brutal onslaught in the Pacific, South-East Asian region had received a shock setback.

Just when Allied morale was at a very low ebb in the region, the imperial warrior army had been shown to be less than invincible.

Undaunted elsewhere, however, the Japanese machine pushed on relentlessly. By the end of May 1942, it had driven the British back into India and taken Burma. They planned to challenge for India. This would also further isolate Australia, and increase a siege mentality.

The Japanese needed a secure supply line to Burma. The sea routes were too dangerous. The Allies had one powerful asset in the region: submarines. They were doing damage and would be disastrous for enemy shipping. The only way to open up supply lines of men, weaponry and essentials for a fighting army in Burma was by rail. It had to be built. The Japanese saw the chance to put to use most of Changi's POWs in constructing the line. It would run from Burma, down through Thailand's west and across its south to Bangkok.

In the late 1930s, the British had surveyed a route for a railway from Bangkok to Thanbyuzayat in Burma. Japanese intelligence had long since garnered this survey. Now they would implement it. The proposed Japanese-built railway would follow the eastern bank of the River Maeklaung from Bampong west through the towns of Kanchanaburi and Tha Makham, where two bridges would be constructed. Once across the River Maeklaung the railway would turn to the south-west to meet a smaller river, the River Kwai, at Chung-kai. The railway would then follow the eastern bank of the Kwai towards the Burmese border.

Without specifying the mission, the Japanese called for 3,000 AIF volunteers for a party, which became known as 'A Force'. The information supplied was that this party would be taken 'up-country'. Better food and conditions were promised. Rumours abounded once more and created excitement among the POWs. It was claimed that the 3,000 men would be swapped for Japanese POWs. Bets in the Australian camp were on this outcome, although canny punters took the longer odds that there would no repatriation.

The prospect of going home encouraged many to volunteer. Chitty was among the many sceptics. He reckoned that if an exchange of POWs were to be made it would not be so secret. Discreet yes, but not clandestine. He thought that if a swap were in the offing, then Australian officers would be quietly informed so that the 3,000 most worthy—meaning primarily those wounded and ill—would be chosen. Calling for volunteers did not sit with the logic of a well-thought-out repatriation. They were more likely to be used for a project. A railway had long been rumoured.

Chitty and many others in the Singapore working parties had not found their early work assignments too arduous. They were driven by their captors but it was bearable. He and others found the work a less difficult proposition than being shut in Changi. But a trip back to Malaya or Thailand or Burma was less predictable.

Another factor tempted him. Ever since the night before the fall of Singapore town he had thought about escaping. In Selarang, he had listened to all the options from other prisoners. Many had theories about the best route to take and how it should be done. Chitty was attracted by a possible escape to India. It seemed the best of several poor options. The Japanese were crawling all over the region and the seas between Singapore and Australia. Better, it was believed, to make for India and sit out the war there.

Could a trip to another country provide the chance to make a run for it?

On 9 May 1942, an Australian working party made the grisly discovery at Tengah Aerodrome of the bodies of John Park, Harold Ball, Alf Woodman and William Lewis. Their remains had not been buried.

Private Don Moore, one of the prisoner working party, noted that the four men had been tortured and executed.

They had figure-eight wire around their wrists. The party's sergeant in charge from the 2/20th Battalion wanted to give them respectful graves. The Japanese at first refused and wished to force them to another work area. But the sergeant persisted. The Japanese relented and a burial was arranged.

'The sergeant took the identity discs,' Moore recalled, 'and handed them back to the POW camp commander, Major Schneider.'[2]

Park was recommended for a posthumous Victoria Cross for the selfless, courageous act in going forward to find and assist his mate Captain Catchlove. (But such a prestigious decoration was never going to be allowed by General Blamey, who wished to give as little recognition to any 8th Division achievements as possible.) Despite this attempted gesture, nothing could salve the feelings of the 9th Field Ambulance and the many mates of these four.

Brigadier Kent Hughes was grief-stricken with news of the find. He penned a eulogistic poem to close friend and protégé, Park:

To John

The Tengah field, bomb-torn, smoke pallid and black,
Resounding with barbarian Banzais
Undaunted, undismayed by hostile cries
He turned to help his team-mates down the track.

A long, low mound of sun-baked yellow mud,
Marks where he broke the tape in his last race
And finishing fell forward on his face
To write his record in his own warm blood.

No laurel wreath he won—Olympia's crown
To hang within the nation's hall of fame—
But on the honour roll another name
Will be inscribed in letters of renown.

The record which he set at Singapore
Will stand throughout the ages evermore![3]

The Japanese had to take the land route to supply their size-able army now in occupation of Burma because of concerns over their vulnerability if Pacific sea battles did not go favour-ably. Much preliminary activity of constructing a railway to run 415 kilometres from Kanchanaburi in Thailand to a base camp at Thanbyuzayat Burma had already been done by Major-General Hattori Shimpei, commanding officer of the Japanese Southern Region Army's Railway Control. His way had been paved by the Japanese and Thai governments sign-ing a cooperation agreement in February 1942. Within weeks Hattori had overseen calculations and assessments over ter-rain, climate and health conditions, and logistics. Heavy construction machinery had been ruled out.

This meant a workforce of more than 260,000 men would be needed over five years to dig the cuttings and remove 3 million cubic feet of rock, erect 14 kilometres of bridges, raise four million cubic metres of embankments, lay hundreds of thousands of sleepers and rails, and drive home countless spikes.

In addition to the Changi POW manpower, captured Dutch and Americans would be made to join the gangs along with another 200,000 mainly conscripted men and families from Burma, Malaya and the Dutch East Indies. Thais too would be included despite the 'agreements' with the Japanese Government.

The first Japanese construction engineers arrived in Bangkok on 13 May 1942. Aerial photographs and other data were waiting for them. Three days later, they began a detailed survey.

After weeks of rumours, potential members of A Force were told that they would be taken 'overseas' to a place where conditions would be much better in terms of food and living conditions. That ended the dreamy visions of repatriation. Bets were settled. The unmentioned location was made to sound like Paradise, which was what caused Chitty and others to opt out. Reading the *Syonan Times* and the general commentary from the Japanese helped conclude the opposite from what they were told. There was no trust. He decided not to go.

But 3,000 other men, some of them already 'stir crazy' at Changi, thought they needed a change, any change.

A medical unit was assigned to A Force. Concern built when the Japanese would not allow tools, equipment or medical supplies to be taken on the trip. Medicos were assured that everything would be waiting for them at their destination. Scepticism was justified the moment the volunteers spotted the rusty old merchant ship *Celebes Maru*.

A Fremantle wharfie was shocked when he recognised what he called 'old blue-bottle'. He exclaimed that they would be herded into sheep pens. He had helped load thousands of sheep into it.

'The poor old sheep had barely enough room to stand!' he said with anguish, 'Boy! Why did I break my resolve never to volunteer for anything in the army?'[4]

One man had fallen and broken his leg on board ship. He was returned to Changi to tell the tale of what it was like: the men were crammed into the vessel's lower deck, 'more like sardines than sheep'. The journey would be 480 kilometre test. They would only be allowed to emerge for a 20 minute 'smoko' or a meal of rice. The man with the broken limb reckoned it was the luckiest break of this life. He reported the strongest rumour back to Changi camp: the destination would be Burma. If so, it was more bad news for the POWs. Burma was in Japanese hands and this would cut off any chance of the Allies being aware of A Force's plight.

25

Subs in the Harbour and Headway at Midway

In the middle of the night, a small 'float-plane' emerged from the built-in hangar of a Japanese submarine 13 kilometres from Sydney Harbour. The date was 30 May 1942. The plane then took off from the sub for a reconnaissance mission. In an exciting moment for the air crew, they spotted the American heavy cruiser USS *Chicago* in the harbour. The intelligence was radioed back to the sub, one of a fleet of five clustered off the New South Wales coast. The float-plane also noticed three other largish vessels. It was enough for the Japanese admiral to make a decision: three midget submarines would be launched the next night, 31 May, from three of the 'mother' subs. Each carried two torpedoes and was manned by two submariners.

The three midgets made it through Sydney Heads. One was picked up by electronic detectors that evening but was thought to be either a ferry or just another surface vessel passing by. At about 9 p.m., a Maritime Services Board watchman spotted an object caught in an anti-submarine net. No-one was disturbed, or even suspicious. A full-size submarine would have caused panic, but this strange object created more curiosity than worry. It was bigger than a shark and more like a whale, although whales rarely entered the harbour.

After investigation found it was a foreign midget sub, the general alarm was raised just before 10.30 p.m.

A few minutes later the midget's crew blew it up, killing themselves. At 11.45 p.m., sailors on board the USS *Chicago* spotted a second midget. They turned a spotlight on it and opened fire, but it escaped. Later, gunners on the corvette HMS *Geelong* shot at what they believed was another midget.

Naval search parties were hampered by limited vision at night. Normal shipping, including ferries continued to operate in a bizarre period just after midnight.

The Japanese submariners on one of the two remaining midgets lined up to torpedo the USS *Chicago*. They fired, missed their target but scored a direct hit on a naval depot ship, HMAS *Kuttabul,* a converted ferry. Nineteen Australian and two British sailors died. Survivors were hauled from the sinking vessel.

The submariners let go their second torpedo, but were off target again. This time the wayward weapon ran aground on the rocks on the eastern side of Garden Island. It did not explode but was found intact later.

The submariners took off for their mother-ship submarine, which was waiting for them. Perhaps they too caused their vessel to self-destruct. Or maybe they ran out of fuel. But the midget, which had done collateral damage rather than making a substantial hit on the USS *Chicago* never reached its destination.[1]

The third midget failed to make it far into the harbour. It was spotted in Taylor's Bay and attacked with depth charges by Naval Harbour Patrols. The two submariners on board shot themselves.

The bodies of four of the Japanese submariners were recovered. They were cremated in a ceremony with full naval honours at the direction of Rear Admiral Muirhead-Gould, in charge of Sydney Harbour defences. The ashes were sent back to Japan. His decision brought criticism in the press, which was unaware of the conditions at Changi. He hoped that by showing respect to the submariners it might improve conditions for the POWs under Japanese control in various parts of Asia and the Pacific.

A month after the Battle of the Coral Sea, the Americans and Japanese engaged in another titanic Pacific struggle, the Battle of Midway. Midway was a small, insignificant atoll. Admiral Yamamoto aimed to draw out and destroy the US

Pacific fleet's aircraft carrier forces. The Japanese had been stunned and embarrassed by the outcome of the Coral Sea battle. They wanted to crush the US fleet before it could challenge them in the Pacific. First they planned to break down Midway's defences, invade the atoll's two small islands and set up an air base there.

But once more the US's superior communications intelligence operations delivered it an advantage. Aware the Japanese were cruising their way, American Admiral Chester W. Nimitz developed an ambush plan.

The trap was sprung on 4 June 1942. The Japanese fleet, led by the carrier *Soryu*, attacked the atoll. The Americans stationed there fought back, launching five torpedo and bombing attacks on the enemy. This was followed by three torpedoes from American carriers. The eight assaults inflicted minimal damage on the big Japanese carrier force, but they threw the enemy off balance. Dive bombers from the USS *Enterprise* and USS *Yorktown* took advantage of this and inflicted fatal damage on the *Soryu*.

The Japanese retaliated on the afternoon of 4 June and sank the *Yorktown*.

After a three-day arm-wrestle, the enemy was beaten off. It had lost four irreplaceable fleet carriers to just one by the US. The base at Midway was damaged by Japanese air attacks, but it remained operational.

This was another rebuff and prevented any possible immediate attempts to invade Hawaii and Australia.

Hidden radios in Changi were tuned in to the BBC Delhi news each night from 10.00 to 10.45 p.m. The listeners, tucked away in secret cupboards, beneath floorboards and disused water tanks, scribbled down the highlights, memorised them and destroyed the paper. Then they passed on the news verbally. The camp learned by mid-June 1942 that the Japanese had experienced setbacks in two big Pacific battles. It was not seen as a turning point in the war.

But after six months of depressing news about enemy successes, it lifted the spirits of the POWs. The outcome of the battles also meant that there could be no more Japanese carrier-based forays into the Indian Ocean to prevent Allied naval forces operating there. The long sea voyage around the Malay Peninsula to Rangoon had become an even more dangerous trip for enemy merchant transports.

By early June 1942, the emphasis on developing the Thai–Burma railway became urgent. More than 12,000 Japanese soldiers in two regiments were sent to both ends of the proposed line.

The ambitious plan began badly when the commander of the 9th Railway Regiment, Lieutenant-General Shimado Nobuo, and 11 other senior engineers and officers were killed in a plane crash on the mountainous Thai–Burma border at Three Pagoda Pass. Their up-to-date survey maps were destroyed with them. The project would be left to inexperienced army officers using a 19th century map. There would now be educated guesswork on where the rail line should be constructed either side of the border, which did not augur well for the POWs. Any amateurish engineering mistakes in surveys and construction would be disastrous for the labourers, especially as work would begin simultaneously from opposite ends of the proposed line.

*

Rear Admiral Muirhead-Gould's humanitarian act concerning the Japanese submariners in Sydney Harbour appeared to have no impact. It did not help the men crammed into the *Celebes Maru*, who were taken to the Burma end of the proposed railway. At Changi, food rations continued to be alarmingly small. They were still limited to rice with a few variations of poor quality meat and vegetables here and there. After nearly half a year of incarceration, the poor nutrition, uncertainty and fear about the future in the camp, were beginning to lower the mental and physical fitness of the POW collective. Morale had reached a very low point.

26

Good Sports in Changi

Concessions unrelated to Admiral Muirhead-Gould's largesse were granted for the development of sport in Changi by mid-year. These were mainly given by the Australian and British officers, who ran the camp under guidelines from their captors. Japanese commanders would let these circumstances run on until they needed more labour forces, similar to A Force now in Burma.

By mid-June 1942, most POWs had become sports obsessed. Competitions began. Cricket was the first. Ben Barnett started an 'Ashes' competition between Australia and England. The standard was high with several accomplished cricketers from both countries taking part. Equipment was obtained from the only club in Singapore; the rules were modified. Emphasis was on aggression with bat and ball in 30-over competitions, which were completed in an afternoon. This truncated version attracted crowds of several hundred. Soccer started up in England's barracks and several 'clubs' were soon formed to meet demand. As in the cricket 'Test' matches, these were 'friendlies'. There was no malice or fierce rivalry. The British POWs didn't see much point of making war on the pitch inside a prison camp.

Cricket and soccer games inspired rugby, basketball, volleyball and golf. Sydney's Lieutenant Fred Harvey taught some in 2/2nd Motor Ambulance Convoy to play baseball.

'He was a beaut to us,' Lemke recalled. 'We formed teams. Harvey taped tennis balls together to make them heavier so they would pitch better.'[1]

'Over at Selarang they play baseball and basketball,' Hedley Hatch of the Hospital staff noted in his diary, 'but over here we play volley ball, a very enjoyable and not too strenuous a game. We have two courts, one belonging to the officers, who entered two of the 20 teams in the competition. There are six in each side . . .'

The names of the teams reflected humour, feeling, frustration, aspiration and over-ambition: the Whitebait Wanderers, Red Sox, Vitamin Bs, Spine Bashers, Dragon Slayers, Babblers & Starvers, Corinthians, and the Harlequins (the officers' team).[2]

Plenty of prisoners were talking about playing Australian Rules. Even during Australia's involvement in the Boer War in South Africa (1899–1901) a competition was created.

Veterans of World War I spoke of successful games played during that conflict.

One in particular was an inspiration. The match took place at the Queen's Club, London on 28 October 1916 between the Australian 3rd Division and the Combined Training Units serving in England. The 3rd Division had been built by its commander, Monash, into an entity ready to go into battle on the perilous Western Front. The game featured some top league players, including the Swans' Bruce Sloss, Fitzroy's Percy Trotter and Geelong's Hughie James and Bill Orchard. Monash instigated the game to help build the Division's *esprit de corps*. The diggers needed plenty of it before being flung into battle at a critical juncture in the war.

Around 3,000 watched the contest, won by the 3rd Division by 16 points. All proceeds went to the Red Cross.

There were differences from the considerations at Changi 26 years on. The London match had been played in friendly surroundings well away from the battlefront. In 1942, any proposed games would be in a tough prison atmosphere in an air of hostility.

The other sporting codes already underway in the prison were more or less recreational affairs. But the Australian Rules aficionados in 8th Division did not think they could afford any slapdash events; not with 36, if not angry, then disgruntled young men tramping on a field while incarcerated.

Four of those with top sporting experience—Chicken Smallhorn, Ben Barnett, Les Green and Roy Fox—got together. Chitty was called in as a consultant. Barnett spoke of the 'Ashes' cricket at Changi. They were playful, half-serious matches. He believed a Rules competition would need something stronger, more rigid. Otherwise, he thought matches could become farce

at best and at worst, all-in brawls. 'Rules' was a fierce contact sport, somewhere between non-contact soccer and rugby
(league). But the rules as constituted allowed different types
of violence not even seen in rugby or gridiron (American football). The shirt-front was an instance. The legitimate crashing
of an opponent five yards (4.5 metres) off the ball was another.
Thuggery too was just as prevalent in Rules as the other codes.
The Victorians often played in winter mud. This led to close-
in, harder and slower action than in Western Australia, where
games were played with more speed and grace on harder sur-
faces. Western Australians such as (future) world champion
yachtsman Rolly Tasker, on pilot training in Victoria in the
war years, were amazed at the style of the VFL game.

'They don't play football at all,' he observed in a letter to
his parents in Perth after watching a VFL match. 'They just
chop one another around with rabbit-killers, punches and
trips. They get around in bunches battering the other side.
[Jack] Dyer, the captain of Richmond is one of the dirtiest
players I have seen . . .'[3]

These discrepancies in style across Australia had to be
catered for, Barnett warned, otherwise the (Australian) officers would shut them down fast. The organisers settled on the
concept of a serious competition that limited foul play.

A committee was formed. It created the framework for a
'tribunal'—a three-man panel that would stand in judgement
on any player reported for misdemeanours on the field. If a
player transgressed by, for example, punching an opponent
behind play, he would receive a severe penalty. A 'king-hit'—
the bashing of a player from behind without warning—would
see the perpetrator fined and banned from the competition
altogether.

The penalties would be tougher than any code in Australia. The committee knew that there was ill-feeling between some units. Because of the general misery at Changi, some men were 'down' or 'depressed'. Any flare-up in a tough contact sport could lead to an onfield catastrophe. No-one wanted to see an all-in brawl, which would need intervention from the more trigger-happy Japanese and Korean guards. The more sadistic among them would take advantage of any excuse to machine-gun a melee before it got out of hand. With this in mind, an 'order-off' rule was considered. But it had never been used in Australian Rules. The committee decided against it.

Smallhorn was so concerned about violence that he volunteered to be the Changi competition's number-one umpire, despite being stricken with severe dysentery in recent weeks. He was a fair, pleasant, strong-minded individual, who had everyone's respect. He was also a 'legend' in the camp as the only Brownlow Medallist there. Roy Fox then decided he would be another umpire. One only was needed for field work. Single-minded, strong characters would be called on to be boundary and goal umpires.

Smallhorn suggested that they should strike a medallion to emphasise the importance of 'fairness' in the competition (and therefore shame for playing it too hard or outside the rules). It was to be called the Changi Brownlow. It would follow all the system, etiquette, rules and glory of the Brownlow Medal itself. It would be given to the best and fairest player over the entire competition, which was planned to run for eight months from August 1942 to March 1943. The umpires voted for three players a match, 3, 2 and 1 over a proposed 18-match 'season', which again replicated a VFL season.

Smallhorn conducted a search. He found a soccer medal

from British stores and had it modified. The end product was a silver medallion with a decorative scroll attached to the top. Its front had a hammered finish with a gold shield in the centre. A scroll was engraved with 'GEELONG FC'—in honour of Charles Brownlow's club. The medal's reverse was hallmarked with the maker's details and engraved:

'1943 [the year it was planned for presentation to the winner] Changi POW Brownlow Medal Won by . . .'

That name, it was planned, would be engraved before a proposed grand final of the competition in March 1943. It would be presented to the winner in a small ceremony before the big game.

There was much forethought in this planning and not all because of the need for a superbly run competition to distract young men and channel their feverish energy. The committee and all concerned with setting up this elaborate prison enterprise wished it to be a show of strength, even defiance to their captors.

It would demonstrate an unbreakable spirit to carry on a culture and institution in the face of deprivation and adversity.

The teams were the next consideration. There were about 15,000 Australians in the camp. When applications were called for, more than 600 men expressed interest in turning out. Six clubs—copies of Victorian Football League clubs—were constituted. Melbourne and Richmond were to come from the hospitals. Collingwood, Geelong, Essendon and Carlton were to come from Selarang. Each team would have a list of 30 men, making 180 players with another 20 in reserve: 200 registered players in all. Each team would field 18. There would be one reserve, the 19th man, who could only play if one of their team was injured, which followed the VFL tradition. Transfers (for payment) between clubs would have to be approved by the ruling body, the Changi Australian Football Association—CAFA. Transfer fees would be standard—three bowls of rice, including a 'regular' (which meant very small) amount of the scarce vegetable commodities. This fee was solemnly debated early in July 1942. Many payment options were thought of, including cigarettes, money, clothing and other food from outside Changi. But only one 'commodity' was vital and worth really negotiating for: the staple, unreliable and monotonous rice.

Such a food fee would sustain a man for three days.

Every effort would be made to find suitable uniforms for the six clubs. The goalposts would be cut from the straightest, tallest bamboo. The boundary of the field would be marked by that useful coloured clay used for theatre performances. The ground itself was an initial hurdle. Soccer pitches covered a far smaller surface. Rules needed twice the area. The only suitable stretch of land was in 'no-man's-land': a paddock (padang) between Selarang and Roberts Barracks.

'It [the playing field] was in a big gully between Roberts Hospital East of Changi and Selarang,' Chitty recalled. 'It was flat. Rugby was played on it. It was also suitable for AFL.'[4]

Permission to move outside the barbed wire to watch and play it would have to be sought. The Australian officers were warned that games would attract big crowds once the competition was underway. The Japanese had to be told, as they were for the concert held in the barrack square.

A small railway ran from Selarang alongside the padang to the hospitals. Chitty suggested that permission be sought for loading it with the sick, wounded and amputees, who could be taken to the field to view the games.

There was also a minor initial drawback of the padang's condition. It was flat, but a few bumps, mounds and a few craters near the perimeter would have to be smoothed. That was rectified by 40 men with a few hours labour.

By late June 1942 everything was set for the start of the competition except for a few essential items: clothing, good quality footballs, and goalposts.

The quality of the balls became an issue. There were a few worn footballs in the camp. A full-blown competition with teams competing once each week (two games on a Wednesday and one on a Saturday and vice versa) would need at least one football a game. There were plenty of rugby balls in store. But they would not do. They were fine for the standard punt kick common to both codes. But they were not as conducive to the raking 50 metre drop kicks or 60 metre 'torps', where a ball kicked from the outside of the foot would spiral on its axis like a torpedo sometimes 15 metres further than any other type of kick. Nor were rugby balls best for the most spectacular feature of 'Rules'—the high mark. Bigger, heavier, slower rugby footballs did not provide the trajectory or 'hang time' for the leap onto an opponent's back or shoulders for a sensational 'grab' in mid-air.

'A lot of trading [for suitable balls] went on with the Chinese [outside the camp],' Les Green said, 'you could acquire anything in Singapore. What they didn't have they would make. We made others ourselves using old boot leather and [the skin of] wild pigs [boars].'⁵

The football's casing would be leather from pig or boar skin. The bladder would be made from rubber. The number of rubber plantations made the bladder acquisitions easy, although the organisers still had to make sure the specifications were adhered to when dealing with local merchants.⁶

Chitty volunteered to do work at one of the godowns and found a way to slip into Singapore town with Len Lemke to do business with the Chinese over the ball's pigskin outer casing. First the boars had to be found and shot, which was easier said than done. Chitty wondered when the boars could be found. He could not get a straight answer from the Chinese. The football competition could not go on without a store of quality balls. Chitty was adamant that the whole 'show' would be downgraded with second-rate balls.

'Not only would the [running and] bouncing be below par,' he said, 'the kicking, handpassing and marking would suffer.'

'We didn't want the umpires throwing the ball in the air to start a game or quarter or after a scrimmage,' Ben Barnett commented. 'On top of that, the whole look of the game would be better with brand new balls.'⁷ Chitty and Lemke took the initiative and organised a trip with Chinese meat traders into the jungle to find boars in Singapore's centre. They were taken to a small valley near a hill north of Bukit Timah. Chitty was offered a rifle but at first refused, knowing that if he were caught by the Japanese with a weapon it could land him into big trouble. But once in the jungle with Lemke and 10 local Chinese hunters, he accepted it. The Chinese led them to a stream in the jungle and told them to wait, hidden in the jungle, until near sundown.

At about 5 p.m., a herd of 120-kilogram boars came snorting and thrusting down to the stream for an early evening drink. The hunters opened fire and killed three. A fourth was wounded and turned his attention to the attackers. He pawed the ground and hustled towards them. The Chinese scattered, some shinnying up trees. Chitty stepped forward, aimed and fired. He hit the animal between the eyes, bringing him down at 20 metres.

When the rest of the boars made off, the Chinese butchered the dead animals, taking the meat for themselves, and later sale in their market stalls. They were careful to carve off the skin and take it to the craftsmen in Singapore town, who would create the leather.

Later, Chitty negotiated with the Chinese for more boar skin. Wild stories spread that some Chinese were killed attempting to catch boars in the jungle to provide this precious material for the footballs. Whether accurate or not, within weeks there was a store of 40 footballs with the chance to make more.[8]

Chitty, accompanied by Barnett and Smallhorn, went into Singapore's centre jungle region once more, but this time Chitty was armed with an axe. The mission was for the three of them to select a dozen sturdy, straight and tall bamboos, from which the best eight would be chosen for the games on the padang. Once chosen, Chitty turned woodsman. He felled the bamboo and stripped it down to just the trunks.

They now had nearly all the essentials for the competition. The final commissioning in Singapore town was for local seamstresses to produce 250 pairs of shorts, and tops in the six teams' colours.

By mid-July 1942 all was in readiness for the games.

27

End at El Alamein

Toxa's mother Hannah was distressed when she received a letter (as the designated 'next of kin' on his file) from the army informing her of his death. She and the family learned later of the circumstances of Toxa's demise.[1] It happened near El Alamein, a tiny Egyptian coastal railway stop on a ridge. His B Company was pinned down and being destroyed by an ambushing German contingent. Toxa dashed forward and made an attempt at a Bren-gun attack on the enemy, less than 30 metres away. He was shot and killed. At the same time, a few hundred metres away, his brother-in-law Corporal Horace 'Auber' Prowse (Lilian's brother), in C Company, was commended for gallantry for repeatedly rushing onto a battlefield under intense fire to bring in the wounded. Witnesses claimed he should have been given a Victoria Cross. On the same day and in nearby action, Private A. S. Gurney of 48th Battalion charged a German machine-gun nest and was killed. He received a posthumous VC.[2]

T. E. Lawrence ('Lawrence of Arabia') once observed that there was a thin line between courage and cowardice in war. If so, the line between death, and decoration and glory, was even more slender.

The fact that Toxa had fallen in battle for acting with the courage and determination he had always shown in anything he did was no consolation for his relatives. The most talented Chitty family member, and the one with the brightest future, was gone.

Hannah kept her grief about Toxa to herself, taking the lead from husband Allan, who locked in his emotions. They were stoic in the true tradition of country people and many Australians of their generation. Life was tough. You rolled with the punches if you were in a pioneering bush family, which had seen off the Great Depression of the late 1920s and 1930s. If you had 12 children and one died by any means—disease, accident or in war—you counted your lucky stars that you still had 11 who were healthy and had survived.

'Hannah would have really suffered when she heard,' Lilian said of her mother-in-law, 'but she wouldn't show it. Allan wouldn't either. They had suffered in the knowledge that sons Phil and Ron were in POW camps in Germany and Austria.'

There was the worry also for Hannah about Peter, whose whereabouts could only be surmised. Now came the news about Toxa, whose grand dreams had ended on a lonely ridge in Egypt.[3]

Lilian was anxious about Peter. There had been no word from Singapore. She believed he was in a POW camp. It was an intuitive feeling. She could not be certain.

Hannah dreaded that a fifth son, Dick, just 16 years old, was keen to follow the lead of his four brothers. He was not put off by Toxa's demise. Dick seemed spurred on by it. He could not wait until January 1944, when he turned 18 and was eligible to enlist. Hannah was relieved that daughter Nellie, the sergeant cook was not far away at an air base, and that Nancy was safe as a wireless operator at Lavington in Victoria. She was thankful too that her other five children, with the exception of Bob, were either female and not in combat, too young or not fit enough for service.

Bob would have felt Toxa's loss more keenly than most. He was well into another strong season for Carlton, in a VFL that was depleted by those who had enlisted. There was no stigma attached to those who chose not to volunteer to serve. For the million that enlisted, about the same number, who were eligible, did not.

Yet he would have dwelt on fate and critical decisions in life. Toxa lived in the country and felt the pressure from mates to join up. Bob lived in the city and experienced pressure from Carlton to stay and help it win premierships. In the end, Toxa sacrificed one, possibly two outstanding sporting careers, and his life for his country. Bob chose a career and life. He was no physical coward. His on-field grit, courage and leadership demonstrated this every Saturday afternoon in the winter. If there were any bad feelings directed towards him from those who enlisted, he would ignore them. White feathers (signifying cowardice) were already appearing in the post boxes of some young men who were eligible but who had not joined the armed services. If Bob received one, he would brand the person who sent it as gutless himself for not putting his name to the parcel, and forget it.

With possibly three brothers suffering in POW camps and one dead, he may well have felt justified in not enlisting. His family had suffered and done more than most for the war effort.

An Offer He Couldn't Refuse

Oblivious of Toxa's fate, Peter prepared himself for the 1942 Changi football season as if he were back in Melbourne playing for St Kilda. He ran around the camp for several kilometres a day regardless of any physical work he had been detailed to do. He made time too for exercises, particularly sit-ups and press-ups. He was a 'no pain, no gain' man, long before it became a cliché in the US. Peter's aim was simple. He wished to be the fittest of the 200 men who would pull on a football jumper in the Changi competition. His most outstanding asset was his stamina over four quarters—more than 100 minutes—of action in a game. He could go hard all day. Most observers believed he was best suited to be an 'on-baller'—someone in the play most of the time. He had played centre, half-forward and as a rover, someone to whom the ruckman tapped the ball. Yet he would begin the season at centre-half-forward, where thundering defenders would use your back as a target and crash knees, boots, fists, elbows and shoulders into it and every part of the body. If he was not in the play, he would have the option, as skipper, of switching positions to a more central role.

The padang was ready, with bumps and mounds honed off. It was baked hard like a centre cricket pitch and interspersed with patches of soft earth.

Chitty was preparing to play for the hospital teams Melbourne or Richmond when a delegation from the 'Geelong' club led by big Lou Daley from Selarang prison came looking for him. Daley had been a star for the real Geelong club before the war. The delegation found Chitty on his back under a Japanese truck doing repairs. They wanted to have a serious chat and suggested they meet at a room in the barracks. Chitty turned up, intrigued with what all the secrecy was about. He sat at a table opposite six POWs.

'We really want to win this competition,' Daley said. 'We want the best players we can get. We'd like to invite you to join the team.'

Chitty was surprised. He told them he was honoured by the offer. But he owed it to the hospital to play for one of its teams. Both Richmond and Melbourne wanted him. He was leaning towards Richmond. One of the players left the room and returned with a big bowl. He placed it on the table.

'That's yours,' Daley said, motioning to the bowl. 'Three portions of rice with vegetables if you join us. We can't give you more, because that is the agreed transfer fee.'

Chitty still declined the offer. One of the others asked if there was anything that they could give him that would change his mind. At first, Chitty demurred. The challenge to skipper a team was even more important than the food. He had been always a leader whether as an NCO, in the 1939 fires or in sport. Uppermost in his mind was his experience as captain and coach of Cudgewa, which gave him a taste of being an on-field skipper. He was to be the sole selector also. He threw in a third stipulation: Ben Barnett, a top-line amateur player for Old Scotch, and Heyne, a former team-mate at St Kilda, should also be enticed to join Geelong. When the others pushed him to respond he told them of the three conditions that would make him consider the move. Daley was unsettled. He wanted to lead. But the others said they would confer and get back to him.

The next day, Daley came to the hospital carrying a box. He placed it in Chitty's room. In it was the rice-dish transfer fee.

'You're captain,' Daley said shaking his hand, 'and sole selector at Geelong. Barnett and Heyne are going to join us too.'[1]

Chitty was in the modest crowd of around 3,000 for the first match of the 1942 season on Saturday 15 August between Essendon and Carlton. It was not a day too soon for all participants.

But just as the season began, a 'new' disease threatened to derail it. The last few weeks had seen a big increase in hospital admissions, mainly for skin diseases. Half a year of a terrible diet was taking its toll. Infections that would normally be cured were turning fatal. A POW had died from gangrene of the scrotal skin. The pathologist discovered the infection was diphtheria—caused by a bacterium that attacked throat membranes. It released a toxin that damaged the heart and the nervous system. The main symptoms were fever, weakness and severe inflammation of the affected parts.

In the past few months, the POW working parties around Singapore had experienced an epidemic of throat and nasal diphtheria. Scrotal dermatitis and ulcer cases were now getting this extra infection.

The men blamed it on the diet. They applied their 'gallows' humour to this dangerous 'new' disease in the camp and gave it a name: 'rice balls'.

This illness was one of a number afflicting the men in withering numbers. Others included the ever-present malaria and dysentery. Then there was pellagra (caused by a lack of niacin, a component of vitamin B complex) which was usually associated with a lack of protein, especially for those eating only rice or corn. It was characterised by skin changes, severe nerve dysfunction, mental symptoms and diarrhoea. Pellagra in the mouth manifested as split gums, which became raw and painful.

The accumulated impact of diseases threatened the general fitness of the entire camp and this most recent addition of rice balls seemed to be the last straw for officers and doctors. But delegations from several sports put their case. The cumulative impact should not have a big influence on sporting competition just yet. Officers and doctors conferred and agreed to let competitions, including the football, carry on.

But doctors warned that another year of the same nutrition would see a different situation. The Japanese were not helping by withholding vital medicine.

Still, the football was 'on', for the moment.

The weather for the football season opener was hot and sticky as usual. The Japanese guards increased in number to 'accommodate' the crowd. A machine-gun was more conspicuous than normal on one of the guards' raised platforms at one end of the padang.

'A few of the cripples [amputees] were placed in the trolleys and pushed towards the match,' Hedley Hatch recalled.[2] Bookies moved among the crowd, seeking out mug punters willing to bet on the match. There were plenty of takers.

The game, like war, was a great leveller.

'Padres, officers and men played,' Les Green noted, 'and I can remember a Red Cross chap too.'[3]

Chicken Smallhorn, who had been ill and was underweight, walked onto the field dressed all in white, flanked by two boundary and two goal umpires. He held the ball aloft; a cow bell rang. Cheers went up from the crowd. At 2.30 p.m., Smallhorn blew his whistle, the bell rang again and he bounced the ball on the rock-hard centre. The ruckmen leapt for it.

Changi-style Aussie Rules was under way.

Green was playing for Carlton. From that first game, he said, 'Believe me, they weren't picnic matches. It was very serious football. And the standard wasn't bad considering the difficult conditions we had to play under.'

A Carlton player was flattened by a shirt-front in the first minute. It was a show of strength by Essendon. The player did not move. He was concussed and had to be carried off the field. Opposing players began pushing and shoving. The crowd got involved. Smallhorn wagged his finger at a couple of players. They abused each other. He pulled out his report card. The players dispersed and went back to their positions. Diminutive Smallhorn had stamped his authority on this debut game, the competition and the season. There would be no melees or punch-ups if he had anything to do with it.

The Japanese guards watched on. At first they were curious, then amused.

'They laughed at us,' Green said. 'They thought we were silly bashing ourselves.'[4]

But they kept watching. Perhaps they had never seen anything so willing. There was a lot of crowd booing. Their 'involvement' concerned the guards. A second machine-gun appeared on the raised platform, just in case the spectators became too excited. The crowd settled to watch a hard-fought, close match, which Carlton won.

At the end of the game, bets were settled with the hundreds of punters who gambled on the outcome.

'The discipline the footy brought to Changi was very important,' Ben Barnett commented. 'It gave all the players a focus. It gave the spectators routines twice a week watching games and being such a part of the whole competition. It was played with ferocity at times and flair. Team-work was the key. It was instilled into teams by the champions such as Peter Chitty and Lou Daley. The lessons of combining well and selflessness were not lost on the spectators, who had to do this in day to day routines in the prison. The conditions were not perfect for matches, but the padang was hard enough for football skills to be on display. West Australian players, used to dryer summers, enjoyed the atmosphere.'[5]

Chitty saddled up for his first appearance for Geelong against Melbourne on Wednesday 19 August, the beginning of round two. The crowd was higher, perhaps 5,000, following the first three matches of round one in which it was clear that this competition was well-organised. Chitty's experiment at centre-half-forward did not work. With the opposition doing most of the attacking, he was left out in the cold. He switched himself to on-the-ball after half-time and helped swing the game Geelong's way. He stayed on the ball the next week (29 August) when Geelong beat Collingwood. Chitty played an outstanding game, collecting a raft of possessions. His game featured brilliant stab-passing (a sharp, low-skimming drop kick), and strong overhead marking, although his goal kicking could be inaccurate.

The feature that probably earned him three 'Brownlow' votes on the day was his capacity to run throughout the game without a break. Traditionally a rover 'rested' in a forward pocket after a spell on the ball. But not Chitty. He ran and ran and ran, similar to an early incarnation of Gary Ablett Jr.

Chitty was philosophical about his team's early efforts. Its members were made up of a 'foreign legion' of players from all states, with Victorians and Western Australians forming the bulk of the side. He was confident they would develop into a strong combination. More importantly, they had a focus that took their minds off the misery of prison life. The thousands of spectators too were transported 'home' in the football afternoon atmosphere with its betting and the occasional fight (in the crowd and on the field).

For the first time in months, Chitty and hundreds of others playing various sports were in reasonable spirits despite the poor nutrition, increased disease and growing feelings of helplessness about ever leaving Changi.

The hope that they might not be stuck in Singapore forever revived in August 1942 when the secret radio broadcasts from BBC New Delhi told of a further Pacific naval battle. The 1st US Marine Division had invaded Tulagi and Guadalcanal in the Solomon Islands on 7 August. The next day they took the airfield from the Japanese. Just when the marines were celebrating, the US received a setback out to sea off Savo Island, north of Guadalcanal. On 8 August, eight Japanese warships waged a night attack and sank three US heavy cruisers, an Australian cruiser and one US destroyer. Another US cruiser and two more destroyers were damaged. More than 1,500 Allied sailors were killed.

The devastation was made worse by its duration—about 55 minutes. But the American response was now multi-faceted. US marines started raiding Japanese-held islands. On 24 August, US and Japanese carriers clashed in the Battle of the Eastern Solomons, and the determined US Navy came out on top again.

By the end of the month, the Battle for the Pacific had reached a new level on sea and land as marines continued to invade islands held by the Japanese, who had dominated the region since 7 December 1941. Ten months on, their grip on the Pacific theatre had been loosened.

The Australians were just as interested in a battle going on in Papua. Radio reports mentioned the Japanese were attacking in New Guinea's Owen Stanley Range, the barrier separating the north from Port Moresby—Papua's administrative centre—on the south coast. The rugged series of mountains were crossed only by a few foot tracks. The most important was Kokoda. In July 1942, the Japanese landed troops at Buna and Gona on the Papuan north coast. In August, they landed another force at Milne Bay.

Just 1,000 Australian militiamen—'Maroubra' force—were

sent to hold Kokoda and its airfield. By the end of July this contingent was in retreat and fighting well against the odds. It held out a month before reinforcements from the 7th Division reached them. The 7th's diggers had been trained to fight in the desert. Jungle warfare was a far more fearful experience.

The arrival of the 7th Division was the last that Chitty and the POWs at Changi knew about the conflict. They hoped that the diggers with North Africa and Middle East experience had been appraised of the way the Japanese would fight.

They would try to outflank the Australians on the lesser tracks.

29

Incident at Barracks Square

Good feeling developed among the POWs by sport was shattered on 30 August 1942 when the Japanese demanded that Changi inmates sign a document that pledged they would not try to escape. It would have seemed ludicrous if it had not been taken so seriously by the Japanese. This was compounded by the 8th Division and British reaction; no-one wanted to sign. In turn, the captors ordered 15,900 British and Australian prisoners into Selarang's barrack blocks and parade ground. The blocks catered for just 800 men. Only three taps were working. By the morning of 1 September prisoners from all over the Changi area hustled into the square.

'Peter Chitty took about twenty of us to dig latrine pits,' Lemke said, 'They had to be six feet deep and as long as we could make them. The asphalt and cement were rock hard. After all [the centre of Selarang] was a parade ground.'

No-one worked harder than Chitty. While the others took it turns to have breaks, he grunted on without a stop for several hours, swinging a sledge hammer and then wheeling the concrete pieces away.[1]

Kitchens and hospital beds were also squeezed into less than a square kilometre.

'We were only allowed two pints of water [one water bottle] each to drink and wash in,' Lemke noted. 'You can imagine how much we washed. Fortunately it rained every day and that was our wash . . . then the Japs turned all the water off except for half an hour a day. That was used for the cooking and the sick . . . the Barracks were a mass of people . . . and bits and pieces of little humpies to get under and out of the sun.'[2]

Japanese troops set up machine-guns and mortars around the fringe of the square. They all pointed in at the men huddled close.

The next day, 2 September was hot. Tempers frayed as men were forced to relieve themselves anywhere they could. Queues formed everywhere. The POWs didn't know if they were for food or latrines. Either would do. Many sought shade in the blocks and on the staircases. The stench was high. Some of the sick died.

The stand-off continued as the British and Australian prisoners stood firm. They were not signing. It was their right to attempt escape, whatever the consequences. Officially the punishment was death.

The Japanese decided to make their point. They ordered that the four April escapees, including Breavington and Gale, and several commanders of the POW force should be rounded up.

Breavington, a former Victorian police sergeant, had been confined to bed for several ailments caused by his flight to Malaya and the canoe experience in the Indian Ocean. He had malaria. He was suffering from 'drop feet', where the person's feet would drop from their normal walking alignment. A rubber strap had to be attached to his knees and linked to the toes of his boots to keep his feet up. It allowed him to walk with difficulty.

Late afternoon on 2 September, a Japanese officer flanked by six soldiers with fixed bayonets burst into Breavington's ward. Surgeons argued with the officer, explaining that the patient was extremely ill. Matters became heated: the Japanese officer was under orders to retrieve Breavington; the doctor was acting professionally and courageously by insisting that the former escapee was in no state to go anywhere. The officer could only gain a minor concession. Breavington was to be taken away by stretcher.

He was removed to Changi beach, where the other three escapees, and the Australian and British officers were assembled. The Japanese then announced that the four escapees were to be shot. Breavington pleaded with the captors not to shoot Gale.

'He was under my orders,' he said. 'I am a corporal. I ordered him, a private, to escape with me. Therefore he was not responsible. He should not be executed!'[3]

Breavington's unselfish attempt to get a reprieve for his mate Gale was ignored. The four condemned men were forced, with their officers watching on, to dig their own graves. When this dreadful task was completed, a Japanese soldier began to put a blindfold on Breavington. He refused it. This encouraged the other escapees to brush them aside also. He stalled proceedings again, by offering the other condemned men a cigarette. Then he asked for a New Testament Bible, which he read from to his condemned comrades. He kept his manner measured, offering solace as if he were a padre. That done, he pledged his allegiance to Australia and the King. Turning to his commanding officer, he wished him 'all the best'.

Six Sikhs, seen as 'renegades and traitors' by POWs, were ordered in to do firing squad duties for the Japanese. They took up positions. Breavington took from his pocket a photograph of his wife Margaret. He looked at it for a moment. Then he held it to his heart.

The Sikhs were ordered to fire. They seemed to kill the other three outright. But Breavington was struck by a bullet in the leg and another in the groin. Two more struck him high on the body. He fell forward. A second later, he lifted himself up and cried:

'Shoot me in the head! In the head! Finish it off, please!'[4]

Nervous as well as being poor shots, the Sikhs pumped another round into him. But he was still not dead. A Sikh officer moved forward, knelt down and fired a revolver at Breavington's temple from a few centimetres away.

The execution ordeal, to be used as an example for the British and Australian officers, was over.

The Japanese added another 'incentive' to sign the 'no escape' clause. If it were not done, all hospital wards would be emptied. Medical staff and patients would be forced to 'march' the more than 5 kilometres to the square. There were about 1,000 patients ill with dysentery and diphtheria. There was no medical equipment. Several POWs had already died since the Japanese had begun the mass punishment in the barracks and the square.

It was enough for Black Jack Galleghan. He ordered all POWs to sign papers. But he also directed that they add the words 'under duress' to their declarations. The Japanese, also at the end of their tether, acceded to that demand, which rendered the order ineffective and illegal.

By 5 September, the stand-off was over. Australian officers collected all the signatories. They were alert to the enormous number of POWs who seemed to have the same names. There were more called 'Ned Kelly' than any other. Plenty of others were named 'Don Bradman', 'Phar Lap', 'Dame Nellie Melba', 'Captain Cook' and 'Roy Cazaly'.

Japanese concern about escapees impacted on A Force, which was at first split into two groups: 1,000 men were engaged in fixing the (British) damaged airport at Victoria Point, located at Burma's southernmost coastal tip. The other 2,000 were taken to the Burma end of the proposed railway.

Eight members of the Victorian 4th Anti-Tank Regiment escaped in the valley near Victoria Point airport and made it into the hills and jungle. But they were only free for four days before being rounded up. They were tortured and interrogated to find out if any locals had assisted them. After a week of brutality, which was made known to all the POWs, these men too were executed by firing squad. Their bodies were piled in an uncovered pit that the men had to file past to work. It was a reminder of what awaited any others attempting to break away.

The sensitivity to the issue caused overreaction. Private Robert Goulden, suffering from malaria and malnutrition, wandered outside the camp in a delirious state. He was rounded up. The camp of 1,000 POWs was ordered on parade. Goulden was placed in front of them. A Japanese officer read the charges and verdict. He pulled out his sword. The assembled POWs thought he planned to decapitate Goulden. But the prisoner was taken out of the camp by a Japanese officer and a three-man firing squad.

'He winked at one of our men on duty at the gate,' medico Major Hobbs recalled. Ten minutes later he was shot. 'He was taken past us [the POWs] again, dead, wrapped in a bag shroud.'[5]

The POWs reacted angrily. But they could do nothing. A machine-gun was in position overlooking the parade ground.

The Japanese were making their point, yet the conditions for POWs were causing some to commit desperate acts.

Hard labour, malnutrition and disease increased at the Burma end of the railway to Rangoon at Thanbyuzayat on the coast, the first camp site, 152 kilometres from the Thai border (at Three Pagodas Pass). This caused more men to take the risk of making a break. Some figured they were going to die anyway, and that it was worth the gamble. Others felt experienced enough in the surrounding terrain to depart and live rough until they reached a 'safe' destination.

A trio of such Australian soldiers, Major Mull, Sapper Bell and Private Dickerson broke out. Mull had served with the British Army attached to the Indian forces on the Burma border. He knew the terrain and the people and how to survive in the jungle.

Dickerson came down with malaria and had to stop a few kilometres from the camp. While the others pushed on, he was caught and shot. Mull and Bell reached a point 320 kilometres north of their camp, but were rounded up by local police, now controlled by the Japanese. Bell was also given summary execution, but Mull, the officer, was tortured. His arm was shot and bashed before he was taken back to Thanbyuzayat. Aware of his fate, he refused to have his injured arm dressed.

'Save it for someone who'll need it,' he said.

He was tried, found guilty and sentenced to be executed in front of his own grave. Mull asked the camp commandant, Colonel Nagatomo, not to blindfold him or tie him to a stake. Nagatomo shook hands with him.

'You are a very brave man, Major,' he said.

Mull replied:

'There's plenty more where I come from.'[6]

Then he was shot.

Japanese officers were impressed with his bravery. They brought an Australian officer to the site and ordered guards to 'present arms' in a little ceremony in memory of Major Mull.

The Japanese had gone to extremes at Changi, Victoria Point and on the new railway site in Burma to deter the men from breaking out. But Mull's parting remark and attitude demonstrated that efforts would continue, especially as the treatment of POWs and conditions worsened.

30

End Games

T he POWs in Changi had no idea of the atrocities perpetrated against their comrades at Victoria Point and in Burma. The Japanese would keep the work parties such as A Force out of Singapore. No-one had come back to report on the slave labour conditions, which were in complete contrast to the promises made before they left Changi. The food was far worse and the medical supplies were kept to a bare minimum. They were inadequate to deal with starvation and epidemics in the jungle, such as malaria, dysentery (both bacillary and amoebic), tropical skin ulcers, diphtheria, typhus, smallpox and pneumonia. Malaria and dysentery affected just about everyone. But the most dreaded of all diseases was cholera, an acute intestinal infection usually caused by faeces contaminating water and food. (This in turn was due to the lack of hygiene.)

No POW expected paradise or an easy time. Yet no-one expected the woeful, inhumane conditions encountered.

The Japanese camp commander in Burma told A Force members everything they needed to know in one sentence. After verbal abuse about being 'sons of convicts' and 'rabble of a defeated army' he said: 'We are going to build this railway in one year, and if necessary we will do it over your dead bodies.'[1]

It may have sounded like an exaggeration, or even a cliché to the POWs. But when the food rations were poor and limited, men began to starve. Diseases set in. It became clear that the commander meant what he said. The prisoners realised that they were being given enough food to barely survive while being forced to do long shifts of back-breaking work running sometimes more than 24 hours. The Japanese had done their sums. They had worked out how much had to be done and they would enforce a regimen to reach their goal. This meant a certain number of men filling quotas of earth shifted or rocks removed every day. Sick men had to turn out on parade each morning to make sure the numbers of workers were maintained. This led to a continual battle between the medical staff holding men back and the Japanese commanders demanding they turn out. Men were dying but that did not matter; the jungle had to be cleared; railway sleepers and tracks had to be laid; bridges had to be constructed.

Someone did a calculation. For every sleeper laid, a POW died.

The Japanese had a deadline and they would stick to it; even over the POWs' 'dead bodies' as the commandant had so graphically told them.

After the Selarang incident, sport resumed through September and the Rules competition proved a big hit in Changi. Chitty was having a fine season. Many observers and those he played against reckoned he was the outstanding player in the competition. The only flaw in his performances was his kicking for goal, which still tended to let him down. Mid-season he had as many goals as behinds. But his possession gathering and passing with hand or foot into the forward line was a dominant feature. He rarely went back to take his kick, unless on the forward line and the goals were in range. Chitty liked to move the ball on to catch the opposition back men off balance. His roving commission put him in the umpire's eye every match.

Les Green was also having a good season with Carlton.

'A mate playing for Melbourne [out of the hospital area] persuaded me to transfer,' he said.[2]

Green received his three bowls of rice and made the move.

The football aficionados did a good job at creating a football league replica, but they were outdone in creativity when racing fans in the camp staged a fictional Melbourne Cup call near enough to the actual first Tuesday in November 1942. Captain Alan Bush, quartermaster for the 13th Australian General Hospital, had been 'chief announcer' for Victorian radio station 3AR. He was deputised to produce the call of the big race. He was supported by technicians, who rigged up a broadcast in the POW mess.

Typical digger humour emerged as a list of acceptances for the race was produced. Each horse had a pertinent name, some referencing their enemies such as Fruit Fly (Australia's biggest pest) ridden by A. Dolf.

Bush wrote an entertaining script. He described the entire Melbourne Cup scene, lingering on the fashions ('plenty of ankle being shown and not just by the horses'), the mounting yard ('there are an amazing number of flighty fillies today'), the grandstand ('packed to the rafters with punters in smart attire rooting for their favourite jockey and horse') and the course ('hard, fast and fantastically green with the recent rains').

The call was superb. Bush tweaked his rounded vowels to sound like a nasally race broadcaster. The cup was won by 'King' with 'Poitrel' second, and 'The Tramp' third. (The latter may have been in deference to Charlie Chaplin, whose film sketches in the 1930s had been most disrespectful to Adolf Hitler.)

The sound system was taken through all the hospital wards for the benefit of the sick and wounded. The program was so authentic that many asked if it was the real Cup.

Less than a week later, the camp held a parade at the cemetery to commemorate Armistice Day, 11 November. Every section of all services was represented in a march past, where British generals took the salute.

As the year dragged on in Changi, the men and officers were inventive in their attempts to keep up morale.

*

They were helped by titbits of news from radios hidden around Changi. Reports had been positive about Australia's counteroffensive against the Japanese in Papua's Owen Stanley Range. By mid-September, the diggers had entrenched at Imata Ridge, 50 kilometres from Port Morseby. They had been ordered to hold that position. The Japanese, stretched and held up for months, were out of supplies. They also feared an attack by the US at their (Japanese) Buna base on the north coast.

They began to withdraw. It had been a victory for the stubborn, undermanned Australian force. The diggers began pursuing them back through the rain-drenched jungle, mud and slippery Kokoda Track.

On 13 November, a radio broadcast picked up at Changi said that the Australians had recaptured Kokoda. It was 11 days after the event, but the report rippled like a small earthquake through the 8th Division camp as the word was passed around.

Every Australian was lifted. A sense of hope pervaded the barracks.

Christmas 1942 became a focus at Changi. It took on more meaning for most POWs than ever before in their lives. The men who had lost most, such as the amputees in the convalescent depot, did most to make others feel some joy. They made toys for the children detained in another prison on the island, and decorations and flower arrangements for all hospital wards to cheer up the wounded and ill. 'The Nelsons' as the inmates of the depot were nicknamed (after Lord Nelson, who was missing three body parts), also managed to scrabble together a Father Christmas figurine. Somehow the hospital cooks managed to conjure 800 pounds of pudding and cake, even slicing rations off everyone in the previous month to make sure they could do something special for 25 December.

Church services were arranged for the day followed by a mega sports event, featuring Australian Rules, cricket, rugby, baseball and athletics. The men were noticeably underweight, having endured poor nutrition for 10 months. But they maintained their mental spirits with competition on a special occasion.

By the end of December the smooth-running football competition was under threat because of injuries, but not so much in the Australian Rules games. Rugby matches were seeing one or two broken bones a match, and this worried the medicos. Collarbones were snapping, ankles were tearing and knees were being wrenched. The lack of nutrition was depleting muscle strength, and bones were less protected and more brittle. There were more 'hits' in rugby where the battering ram impact was central to the game. Bulk was the common denominator. In Australian Rules, a player could be any size. Stamina was more important than bulk. Courage was the common denominator, especially if you were on the lighter side.

Doctors conferred with officers, and they conferred with the Japanese. The captors became aware of the worrisome number of injuries. They had secret plans for these POWs on the Thai–Burma railway. The numbers of fit men had to be kept high.

'We were informed by the Japanese that a new commander was to take over Changi,' Les Green noted, 'and we would be working seven days a week. There would be no time for sport.'[3]

'I blame it [the end of the football competition] on the pathetic rice diet,' Barnett remarked. 'Players were gradually getting weaker. They were losing weight. Injuries were far more prevalent towards the end of the year [1942].'[4]

Hedley Hatch at the hospital also thought the food was the problem. He estimated that all codes were sustaining 50 injuries a week.

'Cricket is still played,' he noted at the time, 'each unit having about one match a week. But only a few enjoy that as material is so short.'[5]

Chitty was one of the few players who did not sustain injury or lose weight. His physical make-up was rare. He thought differently.

'I don't want to argue the toss about the matter,' he said later, 'but that [the excuses that a new Japanese commander had been against sport, or injuries] wasn't why we were asked to wind up the season. Our officers made us do it. There was too much ill feeling about the competition, and the fellas were betting everything they had on the matches.'[6]

Whatever the reason, the games had to end. The Australian officers discussed the issue with all football codes. Rugby and soccer stopped. Australian Rules went on but finished by the end of 1942, long before the planned finish of the season.

Geelong was undefeated and on top with one more win than Richmond, but there would be no final deciding games. Geelong also had the best 'percentage' (worked out on the formula of points 'for' divided by points 'against'. The number arrived at would be multiplied by 100). It was announced as the premiership winner in an anticlimax.

The Football Association had an emergency meeting. It had no choice but to acknowledge the competition was over and unresolved. But they emerged with a proposal to play two 'representative' games in January 1943 to end Australian Rules at Changi forever.

After much deliberation, Australian officers agreed to the proposal. There would be a 15-man-a-side game between Australian General Hospital staff and Selarang POWs on Friday 22 January. Two days later the biggest game of the season would be played between Victoria and The Rest of Australia—players from every other state and territory.

There had been disappointment that a grand final between Geelong and Richmond could not be played, but the new concept was soon appreciated for what it would present: the best players of the entire season performing in the representative game.

Another ripple of good feeling passed through the 8th Division in early January 1943. The BBC radio broadcast was brief, but it was enough. The Australians had continued to push the Japanese back along the Kokoda Track. The US 32nd Division had taken Gona on 9 December and Buna on 2 January.

The enemy resistance was being broken in Papua.

Australian Lieutenant-Colonel E. E. 'Weary' Dunlop arrived at Changi on 9 January 1943 with some of his command of 878 POWs from the 7th Division. The Japanese were taking them from Java to Singapore, where they would stay about two weeks. Then they would be taken by train somewhere else.

Dunlop and his men had been with the 7th Division, which had been deployed back to Australia after serving in the Middle East and Syria for a year. A contingent, including Dunlop and other medicos, known as 'Black Force', had been dropped off in Java earlier in 1942 in an attempt to shore up local Dutch troops, who were expecting a Japanese attack. 'Black Force' consisted of the 2nd Pioneers and 3rd Machine Gun Battalion. Dunlop supplied the medical support with the 7th Division's 2nd Casualty Clearing Station. The Australians and the Dutch were defeated by the Japanese and taken prisoner. Dunlop, a non-combatant doctor, found himself in the unusual position of being in charge of combatants.

There was immediate tension at Changi between 'Dunlop Force' (as 'Black Force' became known), and the British officers he at first encountered. Dunlop and Co. were not impressed with the British training camp atmosphere and smart appearance. 'Diggers on guard controlling traffic at points,' astonished Dunlop, and 'officers with sticks and ever so much saluting.'

On arrival, he was surrounded by British officers of the former Malayan Command . . . 'neatly dressed . . . carrying canes, blowing out puffy moustaches and talking in an "old chappy" way.'[7]

The new arrivals looked scruffy to the Changi POWs and officers. They had either poor footwear or none at all. Their clothes were rags, and their general condition poor because of their ill-treatment by their captors on Java. 'Dunlop Force' was branded a 'rabble'.

'Black Jack' Galleghan, steeped as he was in military rigour and protocol, wanted to know why Dunlop was in charge and not a combatant. Dunlop had to explain in writing that the Japanese had not recognised combatant POWs. They had chosen him to command the contingent. His number two was a combatant, Major Wearne.

There was a formal AIF 8th Division officers' dinner that night. Someone callously referred to the 'Java rabble'. It was meant in jest, but underestimated the sensitivity to what Dunlop's force had been through. Dunlop jumped to his feet and in his firm, articulate way defended his men. He listed battles of all military arms and the places they had fought: the Battle of Britain, the Atlantic, the Mediterranean, the Western Desert, Greece, Crete and Syria. His tone was angry and cutting, as he referred to 'this rabble' and ended by mentioning the Battle for Java. He was out to embarrass his thoughtless hosts, who were very conscious of their relatively limited and failed war in comparison to the other Australian divisions, including the 7th.

'And now we, the Java rabble,' Dunlop concluded, keeping up a level of sarcasm, 'salute you, the 8th Division, who have fought so gallantly here in Malaya.'[8]

Dunlop received far more respect from the 9th Field Ambulance. Doctors Glyn White and Bennett promised medical supplies for the onward march, wherever it might be. But Galleghan continued to frustrate Dunlop concerning boots for his men and money for the onward trip. They had a frosty, sharp relationship.

The volatile Dunlop, an Australian Rugby Union international player, helped get rid of his frustration in two short rugby matches, interrupted by bouts of diarrhoea, which saw him diving into the nearby sea.

A few days later he and his proud 'rabble' were waiting on the long Singapore train station in 22 metal freight trucks.

Their stay had been brief at Changi. They would increasingly see it as a fortunate holiday camp by comparison to what they had experienced. Their next stop would do nothing to change that view.

It was Bangkok en route to the slave labour camps at the Thai end of the railway to Burma.

31

Brownlow Winner

Every fit player registered with the Changi Australian Football Association, and some who had not, wanted to play in the last match at Changi. Two selection panels sat down all day on 15 January 1943 to select two teams—Victoria and The Rest of Australia.

Chitty was selected captain of Victoria. Lou Daley, who played for Geelong in the real VFL competition and Subiaco in Western Australia, was made skipper of The Rest. They had both had outstanding seasons.

Super-fit Chitty was one of the few players to perform in both final games. He paced himself well in the hospital match played in front of about 5,000 spectators. Chitty played full-forward for Selarang, which ensured he would not exhaust himself for the big one on Sunday 24 January. Hospital won

9 goals 5 behinds (59 points) to Selarang 8 goals 8 behinds (56 points).[1]

For the first time in 12 games in Changi, he was not mentioned among the best four players for his team.

On the evening of 23 January, umpires Smallhorn and Fox counted the Brownlow votes for the disrupted season. The 'count' was held in a barracks room behind closed doors. The votes for each game from the first to the last were opened at a card table. Smallhorn would call out the votes; Fox would keep tally for each player. The outstanding Lou Daley polled well and consistently. He came in second with 13 votes.

Chitty with 24 votes was the clear winner of the Changi Brownlow Medal.

Just after completing the count and sending the medal off to be engraved, Smallhorn felt ill and went to hospital with stomach pains. It was thought to be food poisoning.

'Odd,' Smallhorn remarked. 'We just don't eat enough to get poisoned, do we?'

He was to be kept overnight for observation. Nurses told Fox that Smallhorn was too ill to be running around in the heat. They advised he should not take part in the game. Fox, who had umpired Friday's match, was not feeling too fit himself after chasing the ball from one end of the ground to the other covering about half a marathon. But it seemed he was left with no choice. He would have to stand in for 'Chick'.

The crowd was expected to be big, given the line-up of players and the rivalry between Victoria and all other states.

*

A slight breeze picked up an hour before the game on Sunday 24 January 1943 but provided no relief from the humidity as thousands made their way to the padang. A band played as spectators took up positions all around the ground. Bookmakers weaved among the crowd picking up bets and shouting odds. Since the closing down of the competition, the punters had missed their gambling on the football. Plenty of bets were on the match's outcome and the winners of the two proposed medals for the day—the Best and Fairest for the match, the Little (Bore Hole) Trophy; and the Best and Fairest for Victoria, the Doug McQueen Trophy. There were also wagers on who would kick the first goal, and the last. But the big money was on the Brownlow. It had the bookies sweating.

Chicken Smallhorn defied the doctors in the morning, took painkillers and turned up at the padang to umpire. He walked out onto the hard surface, dressed in white again and flanked by the boundary and goal umpires. A terrific cheer went up. The diminutive, ever-upbeat Smallhorn was one of the most popular men in Changi. Most of the AIF camp had heard about his illness. It was a surprise to see him reach the centre of the padang and hold the ball aloft. A cow bell rang.

The trolley train, which ran from the hospital along one side of the padang, carried about 200 amputees who Chitty had organised to see the match. They were the happiest, most united group in Changi and he wanted them there as spectators. They, like many hundreds of others, were keen to put bets on with bookies, who scribbled extra details on little note pads. The gambling currency was not just money. Some bet clothes, others risked their daily rice ration. Many offered items such as watches and wallets. Every bet lifted the excitement. Every bookmaker's chit inserted the receiver into the contest.

The number that the game had attracted seemed to have caught the Japanese unaware. At first, only about a dozen guards with rifles could be seen at vantage points and towers. Minutes before the game began, there were about 50 armed guards doing their best to remain inconspicuous, but nevertheless there and ready for any possible disturbance.

The atmosphere was more intense than that most ever experienced. Smallhorn, a VFL star throughout the 1930s, ranked it with his first game for Fitzroy. It was special opportunity to perform in front of such an enthusiastic audience in such a weird predicament. It was the same for the spectators. They and the players in symbiosis had created an air of normality within the confines of captivity. This gave them all a sense of freedom. They were doing what they would do on any Saturday afternoon in Australia. It didn't matter that 1,000 guards with as many weapons could stop them doing anything else. The guards could not prevent this special moment. It was too late unless they themselves wished to precipitate a riot.

It was an empowerment the POWs knew would not last more than about three hours that eventful afternoon. But in that time they would enjoy passions that were important to all. They would bet, cheer, jeer and boo. They would clap, yell, abuse, praise, gasp and smile. Most would gape and utter 'oohhh' at the heavy hits: the fearsome shirt-fronts and hip bumps that could concuss and debilitate. Many would draw audible breath at the balletic high leaps for marks, and marvel at the tumbling beauty of the raking drop kicks and awesome nature of the spiralling, lifting torpedo. Others would utter guttural noises in appreciation of the rapier stab-passes, so aptly named as the ball spun like a drop kick but a metre above the ground, and with bullet-like pace. They would complain about and dispute the umpire's decisions or 'stacks on the mill' as five players grappled for the ball that could not be pushed free.

The spectators would take sides depending on their parochialism. But most of all they would enjoy the thrills. And there were hundreds of them. This home-grown brand of football, with its too many players, too big a ground and too many rules, was unlike rugby, its main rival contact sport in Australia. Rugby was derived from an English private school game. You could be at a match and talk to your companion and take your eye off the play for several minutes in the endless stoppages. The action was sometimes like being at a cricket Test match with lots of 'downtime'. In Australian Rules, you could not afford to look away for a split second. There was always something happening in the action, or even off the ball. In rugby, they tackled more expertly. In Rules, they had the sly, brutal act of the 'shirt-front'. In Rules, the skill level was more varied, kicking, passing and 'marking' (catching) the ball. Running with the ball was a more difficult skill than in rugby. A player had to bounce the ball every 10 yards, and baulk past opponents. It was also tougher in Australian Rules to pass the ball by hand. When the 'rules' were drawn up, the game's architects wanted it to be more challenging than throwing. Hence the ball had to held with one hand and hit with a clenched fist by the other. In rugby, baulking was important and scintillating to the eye, but it was much easier to run without bouncing the ball.

In 'neutral' territory such as Changi, the Rules games drew three or four times the spectators, which was partly due to the original organisers' fastidious planning.

Today fans expected nothing less than a classic thriller of the sport.

Chitty acknowledged his team was the underdog. The Rest boasted a powerful line-up of footballers, who had played top grade in South Australia and Western Australia. The experienced champion Daley led the way. Half of The Rest was made up of representatives of the 4th Machine Gun Battalion, one of toughest, best combined outfits in 8th Division. They carried their aggression and considerable skills onto the football field.

Yet Chitty's team was not short of talent and drive. He, Mullinger (South Melbourne) and Hallaran (St Kilda) had played in the VFL. There were others who had played with the VFA (Victorian Football Association). Some had come out of strong country leagues.

The teams' make-ups promised a willing affair.

Lieutenant-General Yamashita, Commander-in-Chief of Japanese 25th Army in Malaya.
(*AWM 127913*)

Japanese troops at the fall of Singapore.
(*AWM 127905*)

General view of Selarang Barracks, Changi.
(*AWM 132940*)

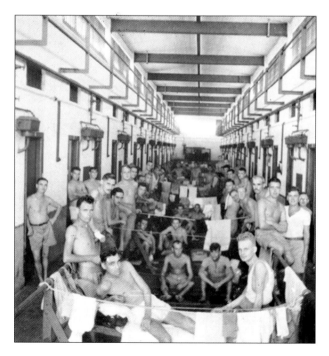

Conditions in Changi.
(*AWM 043131*)

Playing sport outside Selarang Barracks.
(*AWM P04197.041*)

Australian POWs, wearing artificial limbs made by a fellow Australian in Changi.
(*AWM 019327*)

Various utensils made by Australian POWs in Changi.
(*AWM 043135*)

A concert put on by Australians in the 'Command Theatre', Changi.
(*AWM P01433.010*)

Major-General Henry Gordon Bennett.
(*AWM P00266.001*)

Matron Olive Paschke (*front*), with other nurses in Singapore.
(*AWM P03315.007*)

Conditions at Tamarkan camp, Thailand.
(*AWM P01502.003*)

A trestle bridge built at Hintok, Thailand.
(*AWM 120511*)

Hellfire Pass – the cutting where so many Australian POWs worked under frightful conditions, and died. (*AWM 157859*)

The makeshift hospital, 'Cholera Block', at Konyu 2.
(*AWM P01087.002*)

Australian POWs building a bridge at Tamarkan, on the Thai-Burma Railway.
(*AWM 118879*)

At the end of the war: Australian POWs walking
through the open gates of Changi. (*AWM 019321*)

32

Match of the Century

The crowd was not disappointed in the spectacle as players ran at each other, trying to deliver early bumps that would give their team the psychological advantage. Chitty, rather than the goals, was the early target for The Rest. He took a head-high bump moments after delivering the ball and went down hard, but was on his feet just as quickly. He remonstrated with his attacker. Smallhorn stepped in and awarded Chitty a free kick. He passed nicely but the recipient kicked out of bounds.

The ball flew up and down the ground with both sides defending well. Daley was starring for The Rest, taking strong high marks and kicking long into his team's forward zone. But he did not have it all his way. The 29th Battalion's Haig was Victoria's high-flyer early.

'Haig [a former Coburg player] was working like a tiger in the ruck,' the official recorder of the match noted, 'and was brilliant in the air.'[1]

Chitty was active, picking up several possessions despite the constant close tagging by opposition players. But he missed two easy goals.

At quarter time, The Rest led 2.1 (13) points to Victoria 1.3 (9).

A fight broke out between spectators near one end as the two teams swapped ends. Four Sikh guards, who had joined their Japanese counterparts, were alerted. The fight stopped.

The second quarter began at speed.

'Straining every nerve, Haig leapt to drag down what seemed an impossible mark and shot directly to Chitty,' the observer noted. But his kick was intercepted.

'The standard of play brought the crowd to their toes and many times efforts were applauded to the echo.'[2]

The pace lifted in the second quarter, with drop kicks covering 55 metres, and some sensational marking. Half-time approached. The scores were close. Chitty weaved his way through a pack with two bounces and with players closing on him speared a 20 metre handpass to fellow rover Mullinger, who passed to McGrath for a goal. The kick put the Vics 9 points up as the half-time bell clanged.

The scores were Vic 6.4 (40); The Rest 5.1 (31).

The two teams gathered at opposite ends of the ground for the half-time break. Spectators swarmed around them. Players shed their jumpers. The sweat was pouring off them and most would lose even more weight than ever. All were dehydrated. The baring of chests showed the deterioration of many physiques over the past year. Some rib cages were evident. Smallhorn, who was struggling, removed his white shirt and lay flat on his back. He had suffered more than most from illnesses and was dangerously underweight. But he never complained. Emergency umpire Roy Fox, dressed in his whites, dropped to one knee and asked Smallhorn how he was feeling.

'I'm buggered,' Smallhorn sighed, 'but I'm going on.'[3]

Fox enquired about his stomach and was told the painkillers were working, just. Smallhorn had thrown up twice during play.

Players were sipping from their water bottles. Some smoked. Chitty, looking in perfect condition, was the only player to remain on his feet during the break. He moved easily among his men, talking quietly to one or two, encouraging others. He had a long chat with Haig. Chitty regarded him as the standout performer on his side and a match-winner.

The bell rang. Chitty clapped hands. Players pulled on their jumpers and gathered around the captain. Chitty spoke with inspirational calm, telling his team to keep working towards a win. He reckoned the Vics' speed would wear down the opposition. His words were telling. Everyone knew of his exceptional stamina. He expected every player to run hard until the final bell.

Daley addressed The Rest. He was more vocal, exhorting his men to give it everything. It would be the last game played at this 'hell-hole'. They had to 'knock the stuffing out of the Vics'.

During the half-time break, the Japanese commander appeared with an armed guard contingent on a knoll in a jungle clearing some distance from the wing area. He was accompanied by two Australian officers. They kept their distance as the players took up their position for the third quarter. It seemed that the new commander, who had shut down the original competition, wanted to learn a little about the game. An Australian officer appeared to be explaining things through an interpreter. But he and all the other Japanese never mingled with the POWs.

Both sides were defensive at the opening of the third quarter. Play became choked and tight in the first few minutes. Bodies were going in hard and there were some fiery clashes in close. Smallhorn kept control by giving plenty of frees and protecting the ball-players as much as possible.

Chitty upped his rating in an attempt to lift his team. He twice took strong marks in the centre from Haig passes but the moves fizzled out up forward for the Vics.

'At one stage the Coburg lad [Haig] beat four opponents when cornered,' the observer noted. 'The high standard of umpiring continued. There were no spiteful incidents. The play was kept open and fast.'

Haig took 'a finger tip mark' and began a chain of four foot passes that resulted in a goal that broke a 10-minute scoring hiatus.

'A very even quarter ended with pace still hot,' the observer concluded.

The scores were Vics 9.6 (60); The Rest 8.2 (50).

Big crowds again gathered around the two team huddles at three-quarter time. The Japanese commander left with his entourage. He had seen enough of this primitive, vigorous Australian sport. Smallhorn had kept strict control of the players, awarding frees when the clinches could not be broken, and letting play flow when it was open, which it was for the bulk of the third quarter. The commander would have gone away satisfied if not in the style of play, then at least in the orderly nature of it and the big, involved crowd.

There would be no uprising on the padang for the commander to worry about this Sunday afternoon.

Daley spent most of the break rearranging the players' positions. He fired up his charges, urging them to keep the play on the open flanks. Chitty told his men they would win if they kept up the running and pace. He claimed again the opposition would not be able to go with them. Perhaps he was talking about himself. He had had three different 'taggers', one in each quarter. No player could go more than 25 minutes with him.

The Rest were now desperate. They made six positional changes in an effort to lift.

Smallhorn bounced the ball high for the start of the final stanza. Haig was in superlative touch again. Chitty encouraged him to stay on the ball in a ruck-roving role.

'Haig marked magnificently over the pack and started a zig-zagging advance.' The ball ended up with McGrath (a Riverina player), who in a burst of brilliance kicked three goals for the Vics, adding to his three already on the board. This gave his team a grip on the game early in the last quarter.

The Rest fought back and goaled.

'The Rest threw themselves into the play,' the official recorder noted, 'with everything to gain and nothing to lose. Weight was used freely but fairly.'[4]

Chitty once more lifted his tempo as a player and a captain. When others grabbed their shorts, bent forward and caught their breaths when the ball was up the other end, Chitty was running, directing, talking, inspiring. He wanted to win this match very, very much.

Smallhorn was struggling to keep up with the play, stumbling here and there. He was in obvious pain, clutching his stomach. Sweat poured from him. He kept looking at his watch. He was feeling the strain.

With 10 minutes to play and the game to be won, Chitty burst out of the pack 15 metres into Victoria's back half. He bounced the ball twice as he baulked past two opponents in the centre. A third tried to run him down but could not catch him. Chitty launched into a mighty torpedo. It had the crowd roaring with it as it barrelled through for a goal.

This heroic solo effort was the play of the day to that moment. It all but secured the game.

Yet The Rest, especially with the 4th Machine Gun representatives firing, would not give up. Daley was now on the ball trying to quieten Haig. Daley took a mark and snapped a goal on the run. Despite this, Chitty ran to Haig and directed him to go deep into defence. The moved worked. Haig held up several thrusts.

The ball was bottled up in The Rest's half, but it spilled free and Mullinger for Victoria charged through the centre. He 'banged' away with an uneven punt. Chitty was near the goal square. He nudged his opponent off balance and then leapt high for a mark. The crowd cheered as one. Spectators knew that the resultant kick would seal the game.

Chitty's stroll back was measured. The crowd fell silent. He lined up the goals, ran in and put it straight through. At the critical moments of the final quarter, he had been the difference. His skill had been vital, but the team with the stamina, as he predicted, had taken control. Chitty, the running man, had led the way. He had the biggest 'engine' of either team and it told on his opponents in the last 15 minutes of the encounter.

The sustained crowd cheering in response to the umpire signalling a goal indicated there was no chance now for The Rest to come back. They were 28 points down. Paper and headgear were thrown skywards. Several players ran to shake hands with Chitty after he had capped off a good, sometimes sensational captain's game. He looked relieved. Was that a faint smile or a grimace?

Thirty seconds later, Smallhorn looked hard at his watch. The timekeeper on the boundary rang the bell. The crowd roared.

The game of the century for everyone in attendance was over.

The Vics won 14.9 (93) to The Rest 10.5 (65).[5]

It was a fitting finale to an innovative, dedicated season. Football had played a big part in maintaining the *esprit de corps* of a flagging division, which had been cooped up at Changi for the best part of a year.

The crowd spilled onto the arena again for the presentation of medals. Daley was awarded the Little Bore Trophy for best and fairest man on the field. Haig won the Doug McQueen Trophy for best Victorian. Both men were applauded generously.

Smallhorn, spent from his exhausting umpiring duties, congratulated the two and handed them their medals. Spectators clapped. The great Changi football show was over. Lieutenant Kearton, the sports officer, brought many present back to harsh realities with his standing order that 'Players and Spectators from this unit [Australian General Hospital] will be marched to No. 4 Gate immediately after the Cemetery Parade.'

The rest began filing back to their barracks and hospitals. The train carrying the amputees chugged off. Japanese guards stood well back, allowing the prisoners easy access to their barbed wire enclosures. There would be no trouble from the POWs that evening. They were more than satisfied with their surreal experience that had taken them back to a leisure mind-set so popular at home every winter.

The only apparent casualty was Smallhorn. He collapsed soon after the final ceremonies. Chitty rushed him to hospital, this time making sure doctors examined him properly. He had appendicitis. Chitty stayed with him until he was in bed and sedated. Doctors planned an operation for the next morning.

Chitty celebrated later that night. Outside his private life, this had been his greatest day. No matter what was to follow, he would remember this special afternoon for the rest of his life.

33

F Force to Hades

The Japanese propaganda sheet the *Syonan Times* did not appear at Changi in January, February and March of 1943. The POWs missed the 'fun' of sifting through items to find out what they could about the war. They had been coupling their hunches with the secret broadcast from BBC Radio New Delhi to work out what was happening and to judge if the US and Australia were making headway on the various battle fronts on sea and land.

One breakthrough pertinent to the Australians and picked

up in succinct radio news was news that the Japanese had capitulated on 22 January in Papua, 10 days after Sanananda on the north coast had been taken by the Americans.

The Changi POWs, learning this late in January, were buoyed. Perhaps a snide remark was picked up by the guards, or possibly the Japanese noticed a lift in spirits in the camp. Whatever the reason, guards and officers searched the camp looking for radios. But the transmitters, tucked in broom heads and false walls, were not discovered.

The non-appearance of the paper at first disappointed the men. Then they realised this might be a good sign. Was the war as a whole, and not just in battles on Papua, beginning to turn against the Japanese and their Axis partners? Speculation, whispered and in secret, was rife. At Changi, hunger for food was always first. But a close second was hunger for news. Any scrap off the radio, or even a strong rumour, circulating from a defensive remark by a guard, or an oblique comment from an Australian officer, was digested and mulled over.

The biggest recent breakthrough seemed to have been Emperor Hirohito's decision to allow 'his' troops to withdraw from Guadalcanal after five months of fighting against the US. This had happened on the last day of 1942. The US had won. The Japanese began an evacuation on 1 February 1943. A day later they ceased resistance. It was too big a lie to cover up in print.

A month later (2–4 March) the RAAF and US Air Force attacked a Japanese convoy of eight transports escorted by eight destroyers, which was attempting to reinforce its contingent at Lae, New Guinea. Lae, held by the Japanese, was being threatened by Allied troops. All eight transports and four of the destroyers were sunk in the Battle of the Bismarck Sea. Nearly 3,000 of the Japanese 51st Division coming from Rabaul were killed. Just 850 troops landed at Lae.

The *Syonan Times* propaganda had nowhere to go with these developments. The paper ceased temporarily.

These enemy setbacks on several fronts were exacerbated in Burma by the stepping up in March 1943 of British–Indian forces' guerilla operations. This made the building of the Burma–Thai railway ever more urgent for the Japanese. By April 1943 they had approaching 10 months' development of the railway. They had access to the track, rolling stock and locomotives. Yet progress seemed slow, especially after the inexperienced engineers discovered in January that construction parties working from opposite ends of the line would miss linking up by more than a kilometre. The consequence of the June 1942 air crash killing Lieutenant-General Nobuo and his senior engineers was apparent. Even without such a fundamental blunder, the project from an engineering perspective was tough, even near impossible, in the time allotted to complete it. But instead of extending the time from December 1943, the Japanese reduced it to August 1943.

Only 20 per cent of the railway had been completed. Track laying had been held up by the Wangpo viaducts at the 109 kilometre point and had only reached 30 kilometres south of Thanbyuzayat. To meet the new August 1943 deadline, the engineers calculated that each day they needed to remove 20,000 cubic metres of earth and build 10 metres of bridging.

April 1943 marked the beginning of a furious effort to make the final push a four-month project rather than one of eight months. It would become known as the 'Speedo' period, in reference to one form of an English word which both the Japanese masters and their 'slaves' comprehended.

The only factor that could make this frantic mission work was the deployment of massive numbers of human beings. The Japanese decided to step up their drawing on the Changi POWs and the indigenous population of the Asian countries they controlled.

The Japanese had been careful to keep A Force away from anyone involved with Changi. No-one could report the hideous conditions of slave labour at all sections of the track. This made 'recruitment' of other forces to work on the railway feasible. Had the rest of the POWs known of the horrific situation they would face, there may been a refusal to leave Changi. This would cause a confrontation that the Japanese would rather avoid.

The middle third of the 320 kilometre line from Hintok–Konyu (closer to the Bangkok end) to Neika (nearer to the Burma border) had yet to be constructed in the most inhospitable jungle area. This would be the new F Force's main job, although other parts of the line still needed much work.

Ignorance of what was happening on the project allowed the Japanese to deceive the POWs with enticements. On 8 April 1943, they told the British and Australian camp administrators they wanted to move 7,000 prisoners to 'an area where the food was more plentiful and the climate healthier than on Singapore Island . . . Bands could accompany each

1,000 men; gramophones, blankets, clothing and mosquito nets would be issued at the new camps . . . There would be no long marches . . . Transport would be provided for unfit men and baggage . . . There would be good canteens in each camp after three weeks . . .'[1]

The Japanese made the new destination seem like a holiday camp, just as they had to A Force. The Big Lie had worked then and it would again especially when making out that ill men could be taken. There would be more than adequate medical facilities there, it was claimed.

The POWs' commanders told the Japanese the quota of the required 7,000 could not be filled. There were not enough fit men in Changi. A 'concession' was offered. Thirty per cent of the quota could be ill men.

Chitty was among the 3,662 AIF men and 3,338 British in the F Force contingent. He was content enough with going. After the intensity of the football season, which consumed his interests and took away the boredom and concerns about internment, he was looking forward to a change of scenery. There were rumours about work labour camps, but even that did not put him off. Chitty had maintained his fitness since the last game of the season 10 weeks earlier, and his bush background gave him confidence he could meet any challenge.

He lined up at first light of dawn on 18 April in the barracks square carrying a shoulder bag of essentials, his Changi Brownlow tucked away out of sight for fear it would be confiscated. A convoy of Marmon-Harrington trucks driven by Japanese rumbled into the square just as it began to pour. It was a grim, grey start. Chitty's contingent arrived at Singapore station and 621 men were directed into 23 steel wagons of a rice train. It was the moment when he and everyone else had second thoughts about this journey into an alleged paradise.

'The loading was done with as much inconvenience to the Japs as we could manage,' Lemke said. 'Yelling, poking fun, jostling and anything else to cause a ruckus. We did not walk into our carriages like lambs.'

Twenty-seven POWs and their baggage were crammed into each wagon. They could not lie down. There was no toilet. The only ventilation was the door in the middle of each wagon.

'The [steel] wagons were sweat boxes by day and freezers at night,' Lemke said. 'At first they stank of sour rice that had leaked from bags.'[2] The train stopped twice a day for food—boiled rice and onions. A further stop came after a whistle blast, which signalled a toilet break. When the train stopped, all the men would leap to a specified spot by the track to do their business. Many could not wait. A man could either relieve himself in one designated corner of the carriage, which created a nauseating stench in the near airless conditions, or 'his mates hung him off the side of the moving train'.[3]

If the first 24 hours experience were anything to go by, most men were suspicious of the whole scheme put to them at Changi. After five days, most of the men were too stressed, hungry and nauseous to care.

They arrived at Bampong, 60 kilometres west of Bangkok. Most of the men had never seen vultures before. Hundreds of these large, black birds of prey sat on house tops and in trees along the route.

'The sight of Thai traders offering a hat full of ducks' eggs or a hat full of tomatoes for an army shirt was too much for me,' Corporal Lex Arthurton recalled. 'I wolfed down the ducks' eggs almost non-stop.'[4]

Thoughts about the Japanese-described 'happy tropical health resort in the hills of Siam' took another dive into stark realism. The area was filthy, a disease trap. There was excreta in many of the staging huts. The next directive made most realise they had been duped. The contingent of 1,000 (the balance coming from following trains) were ordered to march the 290 kilometres to Neika.

The troops, exhausted and angry, had no choice but to obey.

All heavy kit, stores, tools and most medical supplies were dumped and left unguarded against certain pilfering. Men could not afford to carry surplus clothes, which were left or traded to local Thais. Chitty volunteered to drive the transport to carry the ill. But there were no trucks, except for the Japanese. They had plenty of six-wheeled vehicles and one ambulance. The 'road' was in such disrepair that vehicles would be able to pass once. Torrential rain would be with them daily in a few weeks. There were already intermittent bursts, as if heaven was testing its pipes. There would be no return on the roads and tracks for many months. The only choice for the POWs was to make it on foot.

The fittest men including Chitty would be expected to aid the 125 ill POWs travelling with them (the number had been negotiated down from 300 by the medicos *before* they saw the poor conditions). Some of the sick would be carried on stretchers, but most would need assistance. Chitty selected one of the weakest men, private James (Jim) Downie of the 2/29th Battalion, placed his pack on his back with his own, put the man's arm over his shoulder, and began the long march.

Vultures followed them, looping high and then settling into trees along the way. They were an ominous sight, especially to the sick and wounded. But the tables were turned on some of them as the men made traps, caught them and then added their meat to the monotonous rice stew.

34

Good Doctor 'No'

It took two days by road and elephant tracks to reach Kanchanaburi 35 kilometres from Bampong. Chitty took the weight of his ill companion but was not stressed. They moved at night. During the day, Chitty and the others rested. He relaxed by watching the activity of the Thais in their rural habitat as they controlled hundreds of ducks by flicking long bamboo sticks as if they were giant conductor's batons. The water buffaloes again intrigued him as they had in Malaya. Most wallowed in paddy field bog.

Kanchanaburi village, no more than a collection of bamboo and attap huts and a few stores, had a base camp on its outskirts with a crude bamboo fence marking a perimeter. Sentries manned lookout towers. They seemed alert. A breakout would be folly. If the guards didn't shoot them, freedom would be brief. The town was in a jungle. The nearest allied force was in India about 1,500 kilometres away. Any escapees would be rounded up with the help of locals eager to earn money for acts they did not see as betrayal. Recaptured men would be executed. The Thais recognised and accepted their Japanese masters, although there was no love lost between them. The Thais had no reason for allegiance to the British and Australian POWs, but many of the Thais thieved from the Japanese at night and then sold the purloined food and drink to the POWs in the long line of 1,600. Other Thais followed the POWs and were generous in their exchanges of goods, usually food for clothes.

After Kanchanaburi, they continued to travel at night on jungle tracks and rest by day, which took any joy at all out of the trek. They were expected to cover around 20 kilometres a day for about 16 or 17 days. Marching began at 7 p.m. and ended at 7 a.m. the next morning. Torches were confiscated.

The tracks became steeper on the fourth day of the enforced march. Torrential rains did not abate, making the mountain climb a slog. Many men had dysentery. Their packs became a burden. Every few hundred metres tested their endurance. Lightning illuminated the jungle. Every now and again, drums could be heard above the storm. They were believed to be locals warning of the impeding 'train' of walking men. Thieves were ready to steal what they could.

Rather than fatigue themselves, some POWs decided to hire Thais to transport their packs in carts hauled by yaks. But this was an open invitation for theft. The flashing lights of torches coincided with points where packs would be tossed from the cart and hustled off into the jungle by waiting accomplices.

The drum beats brought an eeriness that gave the drenched POWs no comfort. When destination points were reached, the carts were much lighter than at the beginning of the night.

Chitty became concerned about his comrade Downie, who was weak from malaria and loss of bodyweight. They struggled on, Chitty swapping sides with his mate every few kilometres. The country was flat and open with sparse, low bush for the first few days of the trek to Wanlung, about 70 kilometres north-west of Bampong.

The test was harder from there. The jungle was thicker. They had to surmount hill tracks, and plough through clinging mud. At first, the downpours were welcome, but as they rotted shoes, increased the bogs and made the going even tougher, the men began to curse the black skies, aware that from May for three months in the rainy season it would be worse. Incessant rain at night developed acrid smells in the jungle. Mist enveloped the marchers. The dampness brought clouds of irritating midges and sand snails so small that they could hardly be seen. They found their way into eyes, ears, nose, hair and even into closed mouths.

There was less talk as the march progressed. The men were conserving energy. Noise was reduced to the steps taken, the jangle of tins carried, laboured breathing, the odd curse and the occasional groan.

'My whole body seemed to be on fire,' medico Lieutenant-Colonel S. W. Harris noted. 'My head like a drum, seemed to be rolling about uncontrollably. My eyes seemed raw and were kept open with the utmost difficulty. My shoulders were skinned raw from the chafing of shoulder straps of my pack, which was worsened by the loss of flesh.'

Each day brought more protrusion of bones, a gnawing pain in his stomach, and knees ready to give way at any moment. His feet were 'like lumps of raw beef'.

But when Harris looked along the line, he realised he was in relatively good shape.

'Most of the men had skin disease, which gave hellish irritation when perspiring. Or perhaps they had rashes or eruptions in the arm pits or crotch. These became raw through continuous chafing. In some cases, they turned septic with running sores, making every step more agonising. Others had malaria, dengue or some other form of mysterious jungle fever.'[1]

Chitty and Downie had to move gingerly on the narrow tracks and roads, which were 'corduroyed' (where logs are laid across swampy or miry ground). Snags and potholes made movement precarious in parts. Most men moved in single file, touching the gear of the man in front of them as they stumbled over rocks, through creeks or into bush with dangerous spikes of bamboo clumps, their bases as thick as men's thighs and running 20 metres high.

Further up country, the hills were steeper. At Wampo, another 40 kilometres north-west, a rocky hillside fell sharply into the River Kwai. British, Dutch, Australians, Javanese, Tamils, Chinese, Malays and other indigenous workers had constructed a 200 metre, triple-tier viaduct.

There was ambivalence about swimming in the river and drinking the water. Some naively believed if it were 'running water', then it was somehow fine to consume. But Chitty would not take a dip. He boiled any drinking water for him and his sick companion. It was always an extra chore but he did not think twice about it.

Despite Chitty's diligent nursing, Downie was struggling. He was finding it hard to eat, and his lethargy was alarming. Chitty talked to him as much as possible to keep him awake. The aim was to reach the first camp, where he might be able to have prolonged rest and medical attention.

They staggered on. The ill man collapsed. Chitty was worried about slipping back to the rear. Thai bandits and thieves were harassing stragglers. There were also warnings against tigers prowling close. Their low growls were heard but none was seen at night. The Japanese guards would not have cared if an ill man was left behind. They often belted those finding the going tough, using rifle butts or bamboo sticks, which had the same impact as a baseball bat. The guards fired off the occasional volley if bandits were close, but then marched on.

Chitty had no choice. His mission, come flood, famine, thieves, tigers or thrashings, was to deliver Downie to a camp with a medical facility. He could not drag him; it might cause the man's death. He decided to carry him and the two packs, which would add up to more than his own bodyweight. Chitty adjusted the packs, one over each shoulder. Then he asked another marcher to hoist Downie across his back. This done, he took tentative steps and then walked on. The others called forward to let Chitty reach the middle of the line where the ill were safer.

This was 'the Australian spirit', Bob Owen, medical orderly with the 9th Field Ambulance, noted. 'It was the unbreakable bond between the men. They helped and urged each other to keep going. No-one was left behind. Nobody was left by the side of the track. They were helped, carried, stretchered.'

When they stopped in the morning, the line would be spread out. 'Some of the men had been injured during the night, falling down gullies and breaking legs, that sort of thing. They were given the most protection. We would put them in the middle of the train [line of men] along with the sick and wounded.'[2]

Again, as at Kanchanaburi, no-one tried to escape. One look at the jungle, which was becoming thicker and more hilly as they moved north-west, made the POWs realise there was no chance of getting anywhere. Even if an escapee made it a kilometre or two, they knew they would be turned in anywhere for as little as a packet of cigarettes. The Thais were poor. Money, food and little 'luxuries' were more important to most of them than the lives of POWs.

They reached the dusty, large Tarsau base camp, 10 kilometres north-west of Wampo and a kilometre from the river. It was typically primitive with a handful of huts and stores for the camp administration and guards. One or two flimsy constructions would be designated 'hospital huts'. Chitty surveyed the country beyond. It was steeper. Hills merged into small mountains. The terrain was wild, rugged and covered in dense jungle.

Downie lay on the ground at the Tarsau camp. He was close to unconscious. Chitty informed Major Bruce Hunt, the 44-year-old Western Australian doctor travelling with them. Hunt examined Downie and agreed with Chitty. He should not go on.

Medical command in effect had taken over from combat command (just as it had with Weary Dunlop and D Force).

The official Australian commander, Lieutenant-Colonel Kappe, remained away from the labour areas and in seclusion from 'F Force', which did not endear him or his staff to the men. However, officers swore by his actions on behalf of the POWs. On several occasions, he covered for misdemeanours by his men and refused to turn them over to the Japanese who wanted to punish, even execute those who had 'transgressed against the Imperial Japanese Army'. Captain James Hardacre told of an incident when one pick went missing. The then Commandant, Lieutenant Fukuda, insisted that until the pick was 'found', no one in the camp, including the sick, would be fed. Soon the pick (or a pick) turned up. Then Fukuda wanted the culprit presented to him. Kappe insisted that the man could not be found and took full responsibility for the 'theft'. He was ordered to kneel in front of the pick before the entire assembled camp of POWs. Kappe told Hardacre that he just imagined the pick was a cross, and this eased the moment of humiliation. He was reproached by F Force's Commander, British Lieutenant-Colonel Harris, for this 'Un-British conduct'. (Later, back at Changi, Harris had to apologise to Kappe in front of the entire AIF POW contingent for his repudiation of Kappe.)

Natural leaders came to the fore among the doctors with the prime responsibility for the POWs. Hunt and Lieutenant-Colonel F. J. (Andy) Dillon were assisted by Major C. Wild, the force interpreter. (Wild's linguistic skills became vital on the railway.) Several other doctors with grit and character, such as Captain Frank Cahill, emerged as the going became tougher along the march and later in the camps, and on the railway.

Bruce Hunt stood out as the natural, dominant commander. A World War I veteran of a field artillery battery on the Western Front, he had seen plenty of action, death and blood before he qualified as a doctor. This toughened him up. He developed a reputation before World War II as a very direct practitioner while a resident surgeon at the Royal Perth Hospital. His bedside manner was non-existent. Yet many swore he was the best doctor they ever had. He would prod midriff and chest harder than any medico, causing the patient to wince, gasp or complain. But this went some way to him being regarded as an exceptional diagnostician. Another factor in this assessment was less tangible. Hunt was widely read, well beyond medical books. He claimed that this increased his capacity to cogitate and use his imagination about an illness from different angles. His fertile mind was kept active, learning, questioning, searching, refining. Hunt's recall was powerful. He reckoned he never forgot a patient or their illness.

All this was relevant to his work at Changi and on the railway. But it despite being quietly spoken most of the time, he had bursts of verbal aggression that were nothing short of bullying. He explained himself by reminding everyone of those artillery years on the Somme. Although he had come out unscathed of body and mind, there were scars of sorts. Apart from a little deafness in one ear, the experience gave him the occasional adrenaline rush. He was pumped up for challenges.

Everyone experienced his wrath. He could be tough on the patients. When POWs had trouble keeping down their meagre rations, and did not want to eat, Hunt ordered them to be force-fed. Prisoner Gordon Nicholl noted that when sick men vomited up food, Hunt said: 'Well catch it in the dixie and feed it back to them! That food is too valuable to waste. Make them eat it!'[3]

He would blast those who straggled in the march, even if they were ill with crippling foot injuries or diseases. Hunt would tell them they had to fight on, or rot in the jungle. Most of all, he was tough on himself, pushing as hard as the toughest men, such as Chitty.

He even took liberties with the Japanese, who received stinging rebukes or strong, articulate clear letters about what he wanted for his patients, and how far short he was of the list of promises from the Changi administrators. He pulled rank and weight, and had a considerable capacity to bluff. Only perhaps Weary Dunlop of all the medical staff or even the combatants had the same kind of daring and bold attitude to the enemy guards, doctors and commanders if he had a grievance. But where Dunlop was more of a forceful presence than a bully, Hunt was a fearsome intimidator of everyone with whom he clashed.

Some of the Japanese accepted his demands, aware that in the jungle they might need him for their own ailment. They did not always trust their own doctors. Others ignored him, but few confronted him. Hunt was used to demanding supplies from senior Japanese commanders. He was not so used to the little Hitlers among the guards, who were not intelligent or perspicacious enough to bend to his will. Some would back off from his blasts, find out who he was and deal with him more respectfully. The intellectually challenged reacted differently. After being bullied by their superiors they did not take kindly to a 'dishonoured' POW attempting the same.

One such Japanese guard was in charge at Tarsau.

35

Through Hellfire Pass

Bruce Hunt asked Chitty to place his ill charge with another 36 men also considered not up to any more marching. Hunt consulted Japanese doctors, who agreed with his assessment. Later in the day, a Japanese corporal insisted that only 10 of the men could remain at the camp. Hunt disagreed. The corporal said they should recover by the evening. Hunt said they would not. He reminded the corporal that he (the corporal) was not a doctor. Hunt would decide who was well enough to march and who wasn't. The corporal backed off, disagreeing.

At 7 p.m. when the prisoners were asked to fall in on parade before setting off again, Hunt ordered the 37 ill men to fall in away from the main parade. He and interpreter Wild stood in front of them. The corporal was agitated. He looked at his watch, yelled something and then moved towards Hunt and Wild, waving a thick bamboo cane. He sidled close to Wild, and spat words at him:

'I ordered you to only leave 10 men! You have many more. Many more!'

Wild remained calm. He tried to placate the irate corporal, who was feverish about all the men marching off on time. It was past 7 p.m. He grimaced. His face turned puce. The corporal smashed Wild in the face with his cane. Another guard moved close and menacingly. He also hit Wild, who reeled

back. The corporal whacked Wild in the genitals. The interpreter went down hard.

The corporal shifted his attention to Hunt. They were
joined by a third Japanese. The three men set upon the doctor,
crashing their bamboo weapons into his skull, back, hands
and arms. He was left lying on the parade ground, bruised
and bleeding.

'I took him and Wild down to the river to clean them up,'
Bob Owen recalled. 'Hunt was worried about his little finger.
It was broken. He was concerned it would impede his work
as a surgeon.'

'You shouldn't have put your hand up [to defend your-
self] like a boxer,' Owen told him. Hunt said he had to do it.
Otherwise he would have been bashed more in the head.[1]

The rest of the POWs stirred. They looked ready to rebel. A
dozen other armed guards stood watching them in case there
was a reaction to this senseless brutality. Twenty-seven of the
sick men were then ordered to join the rest of the parade. The
furious corporal had his way but there was angry resentment
among the POWs. Hunt restrained them.

'Keep out of this, you blokes,' he said. 'This is my fight!'[2]

If he had not spoken out, there was no doubt in Chitty's
mind that there would have been a rebellion. He watched this
episode with horror and disgust. The man he had assisted and
carried 125 kilometres was among those forced to carry on.
As soon as the men marched off, Chitty hustled to Downie.
With words of encouragement, he took his bags and placed
his arm over his shoulder again. Chitty knew he would soon
have to carry him once more. They had another 20 kilometre
battle against the terrain in the pitch-black of night.

It was suggested that Hunt go forward in a truck but he

retorted that his duty was to protect the men. Before long he was moving up and down the line where he could, inspiring them with comments and exhorting them like a football coach to keep going.

Chitty, the natural leader by example, appreciated the gesture, as did all the men. Hunt may have been an intimidator, but unlike the stereotype of this breed, he had outstanding character and courage to spare.

The ultra-fit bushie for the first time was feeling the strain in the harder country, especially when he had to have his companion again hoisted across his shoulder. Yet Chitty took it as a challenge, like the last quarter of a football match. The saving grace for him was the recovery time in daylight hours. After attending tedious parades and doing camp duties, he could stretch his body, eat the meagre rations, and tend to Downie and the other ill members of the party. There was not much time for rest, but he and the others managed about three, sometimes even four hours.

There was a stop where other Australians in the 2,242-strong D Force had aided in the construction of two bridges over the River Maeklaung (later named Kwai). One was a temporary wooden trestle span built to allow construction traffic to cross the river. This facilitated a second bridge of steel and concrete to be put up in just three months, using manpower again, a few pulleys, derricks and cement mixers.[3]

The Japanese were celebrating the end of the project when Chitty, with his human load, arrived. The line of POWs rested at Tamarkan Camp on the Maeklaung (Kwai) River's east bank about 150 metres from the bridge. Mango and tamarind trees covered the river bank to the south. Coconut groves and a banana plantation could be seen to the east.

He was able to mingle for a short time with D Force workers. It was a fleeting moment of reunion for several POWs from both groups. Chitty found his comrades in D Force in no joyous mood like their captors. The POWs passed on horrific tales of death on the project.

It gave him insights into what might lie ahead.

They reached Hintok, another camp, two days later, ending in a 5 kilometre stretch through 'Hellfire Pass'. The Australians noted that the prisoners working by candlelight in the rock cutting looked from above as if they were in the jaws of hell. Hence the name. The flat section through the fresh cutting itself was less difficult for Chitty with his human load and baggage, but the steep climbs up and down mountains either end of the pass were gruelling.

At Hintok, doctors gave Chitty the option of leaving Downie there or of battling on to Lower Neike, where his deteriorating companion could receive some basic medical treatment. Despite the hardship, Chitty was reluctant to part from Downie after having come 155 kilometres.

He decided to carry on.[4]

Moving north through the staging camps, Chitty began to understand the conditions the POWs could expect. They were all working areas featuring dilapidated or unfinished, leaking huts. Some men had to use worn-out tents if they carried them. Most moved into the huts and packed in, up to 30 POWs in places fit for just eight. Sleeping platforms made of split bamboo fixed to frames aggravated the conditions. They were torture for emaciated bodies and made worse by infestations of bloodsucking insects and lice. Mosquitoes buzzed overhead and competed for men's blood. At night, if a POW had dysentery, he would have to crawl or stumble over his mates to reach a latrine.

Japanese guards exacerbated problems. They had been brainwashed into believing they should die for their emperor rather than be captured, and they were urged to have contempt for the POWs. The guards too were far from the elite of the enemy force. Usually they were the dullest, and inferior to their comrades doing the fighting elsewhere. They were inconsistent, unpredictable and often brutal. They lacked initiative and common sense, and seemed void of imagination or sympathy. Food and medical supplies were often left unpacked and unused because no-one gave them orders to open and distribute their contents. The remoteness of the camps made matters worse. Camp commandants were too far away from higher authorities to care about anything, especially not POWs.

The food was worse than at Changi, and there was never enough of it. The rice had even fewer vegetables in it than in Changi, and it was no better than a watery stew. Minute quantities of dried fish, pork or buffalo meat were sometimes added. Meat and fish were often maggot-riddled. On occasions, the camp administrators judged it too bad for consumption and buried it. The prisoners were often desperate for extra nutrition. They would dig it up and cook it. The maggots would rise to the top of the stew and were skimmed off before being served. Rations of rice, salt and tea were now and again augmented by Thai traders, who arrived by sampan with duck eggs, peanuts, palm sugar and pig oil. Protein was vital in avoiding blindness, which was not uncommon. This made the eggs a much-sought-after item. Extra food was paid for by the POWs combining their meagre wages.

There were only basic medical supplies.

Men were dying of starvation and malnutrition, the brutal tropical climate, exhaustion, accident, despair and physical assault. Hundreds of men at each camp had various diseases, including malaria (which had taken its toll leaving men as near skeletons) and bloated sufferers of beri-beri caused by a lack of thiamine (vitamin B1). This was found in whole grain bread, fresh meat, vegetables, fruit and milk. These foods were not available in most camps in enough quantities. Beri-beri caused pain and paralysis in the body's extremities. It was characterised by severe emaciation or swelling of the body, features prevalent when the diet was mainly polished rice.

Beri-beri also caused psychotic problems and affected the heart. Death could come quickly, but a cure, if treated with thiamine, could be just as fast. Yet drugs were scarce. The Japanese were slow to bother with victims, if at all.

Then there were workers with ugly, deadly tropical ulcers and plain starvation.

Hunt recorded that the most featured diseases and disorders on the march were 'Senility and cardiac weakness . . . dysentery . . . increasingly common as the march progressed.' He wrote of his own troubles an 'acute attack of bacillary dysentery'. He noted also 'septic abrasions of the feet' and the fact that most men were not used to marching.

Fever, he said, apart from a few malarial relapses, was of lesser frequency and importance until arrival in the working camps.[5]

Hunt and the other doctors had not experienced these diseases which were more prevalent in the tropics than at home. They had to learn fast about other infections such as encephalitis. Some had been just words in text books, dengue fever and blackwater fever among them. The results of their impact were clear.

The most depressing sight at each camp was the cemetery, a reminder for all that the very sick men would die and be buried there. As they continued their trek, no POW could now believe the proposed paradise ahead was other than a fast-fading mirage. Their captors had deceived them on every issue from the food and conditions to the length of marches and the medical supplies.

This was exacerbated by the fact that F Force was under the administration of the Japanese at Changi, who were too far from the railway to make sensible, quick decisions. This left the force more in the hands of the local Japanese engineers, who had no or little care for the wellbeing of the labour to build their mighty constructions. They had a deadline. It had to be met no matter how many died achieving it. There was a never-ending supply of forced labour from Japan's many recent conquests. So much for the 'liberation' of Asian nations from European colonial rule. Their populations were mere fuel for the Japanese war machine.

Chitty moved on with Downie to all the other staging camps and milestones: at Kinsayok (at 188 kilometres), Takanun,

Tamjoa, Krian Karai (252 kilometres), Konkoita and Lower Neike (300 kilometres). Reaching each point was increasingly a test of endurance. The rest periods were not aided by repeated parades. The Japanese seemed obsessed with counting and checking the POWs. They appeared fixated, even paranoid about anyone escaping. They usually ignored the sick, but anyone making a break was of major concern.

The doctors' worries multiplied. Lieutenant-Colonel Harris found that 32 of his patients, on average, were dying each night.

'We went round each morning at daybreak,' he said, 'examining anyone strangely quiet to see if he were dead.'

Many times he felt for the pulse of a 'strangely inert form'. The patient would rouse and say: 'Not this morning, Taffy [Harris]. Perhaps some other time.'

Harris always dreaded waking a man.

'He always knew what I was doing,' he said.

The dead would be taken out of the huts and laid in rows.

'We could not spare blankets,' he recalled, 'so they lay there looking an awful sight: emaciated, bones protruding, eyes open and staring glassily. They lay there with the rain beating down on them.'

Later the bodies would be taken away on stretchers made of two bamboo poles pushed through a sack.

'The sacks weren't long enough to support the whole body. The head and legs would hang loosely and swing to the movement of the carriers as they took the bodies over the road to the cemetery, or crematorium.'[6]

When the contingent staggered into Lower Neike, even the fittest men were suffering. Chitty came through unscathed but considered himself lucky. He took more precautions than most, fastidiously boiling water and keeping his hands clean. But he knew sooner or later he would be hit with something, probably dysentery. The mosquitoes probably meant he could not avoid malaria either. At last Chitty could let go of Downie, his job done.

He was distressed to learn that Downie had lasted only a few days more, dying on 16 May. A lot of mates were struggling. The closeness of the men was a unifying force. When they later succumbed to the horrors of the railway it caused grief. Some men, like Chitty, held it in. Others could not. Apart from tending to patients, medical orderlies found themselves as untrained counsellors. Priests and pastors were working round the clock.[7]

They were struck by the way the fit men, who had been out all day, would return to camp and make their first priority seeing their sick mates. The Japanese refused to feed the patients beyond the barest minimum. The fit men would bring them part of their rice rations.

It was this sort of perpetual selflessness, along with the drive of doctors such as Hunt and Cahill that kept the Australian camps together.

36

In the Time of Cholera

The main camps at the F Force destination did not have any proper preparation for housing or food. Cooks were drawn from the ranks. They prepared the ubiquitous watery rice stew, which did nothing for the men's morale or health. The huts had no covering. The men were left in the open with no shade. Any housing that did have a roof proved to be a cruel mirage. Inside were indigenous slaves—'coolies'—Chinese, Tamils, Javanese, Burmese and Thais—living in squalor and filth. Many were left dying outside.

Hunt, the de facto leader of F Force, would not let the men work until the camps were cleaned up.

'He had slit trenches built for toilets,' Bob Owen said, 'then he built a water point [for the men to use on returning from labouring all day], and [water] boiling point [for the men to drink].'[1]

This was one of Hunt's outstanding strengths. He was meticulous about hygiene and forceful in getting his way in achieving it wherever the Australians were camped.

Chitty and thousands of others were put to work on bridge and road construction. First, tracks had to be cleared using limited billhooks, axes, saws and rope. It might take a day for 20 men to remove a big clump of bamboo or a sizeable tree. Once tracks were opened up, cuttings had to be built or embankments built up. Soil and stone had to be loosened by pick and shovel. It was then shifted by hand in small baskets. The Japanese engineers had calculated that each man daily had to clear one cubic metre of earth, which would have been tough for someone in a more agreeable work climate, let alone the oppressive heat or heaving rain experienced along the entire route. Rock cutting was laborious and slow using chisels. One-metre drills were sometimes used by one man in tandem with another wielding an eight-pound sledge hammer. There were also a few compression-driven rock drills.

Men were not simply labourers in these conditions. They were reduced to nothing more than slaves; driven and bullied 11 to 16 hours a day.

There was always some form of defiance from the POWs, especially in acquiring food. Some took turns to 'raid' the Japanese cook house in the hope of finding a few scraps. At one point, they learnt that the Japanese, as usual, had confiscated a Red Cross consignment designated for the POWs. Soldier Fred Seiker 'secured' a tin of fruit. Hustling back to the hut to share it with his mates, he was confronted by guards. One threatened him with a bayonet. Another kicked him in the groin.

'I was terrified,' Seiker said. 'I was marched to the guard house with the bayonet in close attendance. The ritual beating began . . .'

Several guards bashed him until stopped by the sergeant in charge of the camp. He drew his sword and pointed it at Seiker's neck, grinning. In broken English, he reminded him that stealing from the Imperial Japanese Army was a serious crime. The sergeant indicated the punishment would be decapitation. Seiker complained that it was not theft. The Red Cross-supplied tin of fruit had been his in the first place. The sergeant did not appreciate the logic. He ordered that Seiker be taken to the 'punishment tree', 10 metres in front of the guard house.

Seiker knew what he was in for, having witnessed the sadistic sergeant in action before with other POWs. He was propped against the tree, his arms pulled back and tied at the wrists behind the tree trunk. His feet were tied with barbed wire and secured to the trunk. Seiker was punched in the face a few more times. Then he was left alone in great pain to suffer through the night.

At daybreak, Japanese guards put a full bucket of water in front of him.

'They left me to it,' Seiker said. 'A sophisticated torture if ever there was one.'

Parade was called. The POWs assembled and were told that he would be executed for stealing.

'The terror of it was that you never knew whether it was an idle threat,' Seiker recalled, 'or an official statement.'

Seiker was in pain and shock. He passed out.

'I came to in the "hospital" with an orderly trying to pour water into my mouth.'

Many suffered this kind of extreme indignity. On occasions, the torture was not bluff. POWs were decapitated. It was just one of many sadistic acts perpetrated, which added to the horrors on the building of the roads, bridges and railways.

Seiker remarked that after his experiences, he was never

afraid of finding himself in Hell. There was no purpose, he said. He had been there, and worse.[2]

It did not take the POWs any time to dislike the Japanese commander of the camps, Lieutenant Murayama.

'He was the biggest Jap we had seen since the campaign started,' Captain James Hardacre observed in his diary. 'He stood about 6 foot 7 inches (200 cm) and well built in proportion.' Before his army days Murayama had worked for the Tokyo police force as a judo and physical training instructor. He had contempt for almost all members of F Force, and gave a foretaste of his mentality when he would not even allow any singing in the camps, which fell silent and lowered the POWs' spirits. Men who broke into song even while shaving in the morning were summoned to him, abused and then belted across the back with that ever-present weapon, the bamboo cane. Murayama was a brutal intimidator, who bullied at a whim and did not spare his targets any beatings. He also held back Red Cross and other food supplies designated for the POWs, even when they were sick and dying.

In mid-May 1943 after only a few days in the area, Japanese doctors discovered that cholera had broken out among the Asian workers at Lower Songkurai, 7 kilometres west of Neike. It had poor latrines, no kitchen area and accommodation in disrepair. Coupled with this disease trap was the nearby river that ran by all the Thai railway camps. People and animals did everything in it. Upstream the Japanese bathed and washed their clothes; further down elephants were bathed by the Burmese mahouts (their trainers, drivers and carers); downstream, the workers—the slave labourers— were allowed to wash. Men with open cuts and abrasions took risks. POWs and medicos suspected the flowing waters might harbour anything that could be transmitted, including enemy number one: cholera.

When Thais, Tamils and Chinese labourers caught it, there was near panic among the captors, not on behalf of the POWs but themselves. They knew that cholera, once on the move, would not discriminate. It could strike anyone coming in contact with the area. The Japanese doctors refused to go near the Asian sufferers.

They would be left to die. Then their bodies, housing— everything—would be burnt.

One of the Australian POWs contracted this most insidious disease of the Thai jungle. Hunt called a conference of all prisoner officers at one end of a hut. No-one present would ever forget the moment. His face was lit by flickering firelight as he told them:

'Gentlemen, things are grim. I have diagnosed a disease of which I have had no experience. It does not occur in Australia. But I have read of it in text books. I am sure it is cholera.'[3]

Hunt ordered them to 'pass eating utensils through flames' and to see that their men did the same. 'Water must be boiled for at least seven minutes; no water is to be drunk direct from the creek.' He directed that the next day they would 'scrape the surface filth from the camp area' and that it would be burnt. Then he added a graphic comment that drove home the gravity of the situation, if it were not understood by any listener:

'If a fly alights on the rice you are about to eat, the grains it lands on must be spooned out and burnt.' He paused and added, 'For I assure you, if one contracts cholera, one dies in great distress.'

On 19 May, Captain Frank Cahill joined Major Hunt in the battle to defeat the disease. They inoculated 1,400 men with anti-cholera vaccine. But the Japanese failed to deliver supplies of a second backup vaccine.

'We suspected that the vaccines were useless,' Bob Owen said. 'The Japanese had just given us water, not the actual vaccine.'

This suspicion was well founded. Cholera flared a week later. Hunt and Cahill became extra vigilant, visiting all the POW camps for about 27 kilometres between Upper Song-kurai and Lower Neike. Hunt confronted the two camp commanders Hukudu and Toyama, telling them that if they did not clean up the camps the way he wanted, there would be no POWs to go on the work parties. Cholera, he told them, would wipe everyone out. No-one, not even the Japanese commanders, would be safe. It was not bluff. The outbreak had begun in earnest.

'At one big Australian camp, we had only a few cases of chol-era,' Hunt recalled. 'Suddenly one day the pestilence smote us: 35 men went down with the disease in 24 hours.'

The medical staff was too small to supply adequate nurs-ing to these men. The evening after cholera struck, Hunt met the Australians who had been working for 14 hours in the monsoon rain knee deep in mud, carrying earth on bags between poles for two kilometres. He explained the situation to them. He told them that the mortality rate from cholera was 50 per cent. Every second patient they nursed would die.

'I need volunteers to help,' he implored them, 'right now—straight away!'

More than 120 men volunteered, Peter Chitty among them. Hunt required just 75. He was overwhelmed.

'This reaction from F Force,' he said, 'made me very proud to be an Australian.'[4]

Lex Arthurton, who was not trained in medicine, worked in the medical facility at Upper Konkoita. He found himself a cholera carer. A POW was brought in and attended by medico Captain Roy Mills. The man had severe stomach cramps and had passed a rice stool. Mills told Arthurton not to mention it. Panic would not help the predicament. The doctor then asked him if he would look after this first cholera case among the Australians. Arthurton agreed, without knowing what he was letting himself in for.

He carried the man to an open hut on the outskirts of the camp. During the night the victim lost body fluids at an alarming rate. Arthurton kept a fire going and attempted to counter the loss by cajoling him to drink the boiled water.

'Through it all, an elephant wandered through the hut, uninvited,' Arthurton recalled, 'adding to the unreality of my position.'[5]

The patient lapsed into a coma. He had trouble breathing. Arthurton was shocked to realise the man's body had shrunk over six hours.

Then he died.

Arthurton rushed to tell Mills. Mills then informed him he was in 'isolation'. Would he be prepared to care for other cholera victims? Every instinct in Arthurton was to reject the offer. In one way, he had been trapped. In another, he felt obliged to do his duty in a camp where everyone had to take on distasteful tasks in the battle to beat the jungle, disease, and in a moral sense, the Japanese.

A 'cholera hill' was set up. It was in a small marquee established apart from the main camp. Each day more victims would be sent in until Arthurton, living a nightmare, had 15 men under his care.

One man offered him his Australian farm if he could cure him. Arthurton tried to explain that he was not a doctor, but a Field Ambulance worker. Another patient who had been an atheist all his life turned religious and prayed for help. But no deity seemed prepared to take on cholera.

Each day, Mills called out instructions to him from 30 metres away.

One directive was how to use a scalpel. He had to make an incision in the ankle and expose a large vein. Then, still under the distant doctor's guidance, he inserted a bamboo tube into the vein. Saline was pumped into the patient.[6] All had to be treated this way. Arthurton felt he was in a room with a monster. This cholera stalked, attacked and killed. He could not see it, but he could see the result of its handiwork: the cramps that doubled a man up in agony, the never-ending thirst, the cold blue-grey skin, the sunken eyeballs, the sudden shrinking of the body, the weakening pulse, the hoarse whispers, and death. The speed of the demise made it seem more like murder. One hour, a big man was acting as a stretcher-bearer. The next hour, he didn't feel well. In a few hours, he was attacked by this invisible reaper. Then he was gone.

Arthurton felt helpless when the men died, not from cholera, which had been treated to the point of minor recovery. What killed them more often than not was septicaemia. The patients would have to have both ankles cut and tubes inserted. There were no dressings. Infections set in fast, especially if torrential rain swept into the marquee.

Mills came to his place 30 metres away the morning after a young lieutenant was admitted.

'He has an abscess on his back the size of a dinner plate!' Arthurton called to the doctor. Mills asked for more details.

'You must sterilise a scalpel and push it into the abscess,' Mills instructed. The man was to be treated with sulphanilamide tablets.[7]

Arthurton, the raw 'surgeon', obeyed.

The man lived only a few days longer. Arthurton was distressed. Mills consoled him by saying that he could do no more than he had. But the ordeal did not stop with death. Arthurton had to cremate the dead patients. He had to construct a funeral pyre, load the bodies onto it and set fire to some combustible bamboo. As he watched his little inferno, he offered a prayer for every single man, some he had got to know a little in their last agonising days.

'Once dehydration set in [with cholera], your place on the pyre was assured,' Fred Seiker said. 'I was one of a team attending the funeral pyre for a while, depositing the bodies of friends into the flames. This was an around-the-clock operation. It was particularly macabre and frightening at first during the night. Bodies would suddenly sit up, or an arm or leg would extend jerkily. Captain Fred Stahl was walking past a pyre one day with surgeon Frank Cahill.

'My God!' Cahill exclaimed pointing to a body on the pyre, 'he's waving to us!'

Stahl saw that it was almost literally true. He had been involved in the cremation but was inexperienced. He and another POW had placed the bodies on the pyre face-up with the idea of victims gazing 'skywards towards their Creator instead of the flames of hell.' One of the bodies had sat up. Contractions of arm tendons had caused it to lift an arm slowly.[8]

Such horrific experiences stayed in the deep crevasses of the minds of those who witnessed them. Chitty, like all those who worked the pyres, would never forget. His experiences gave him nightmares then and for the rest of his life. But those contorting bodies were the worst.

The Japanese were very aware of the 'cholera hill' marquee. Standing further away than Mills, they shouted instructions through an interpreter for Arthurton to go to a hut 100 metres from the camp. There was a Japanese victim in it. The soldier was nearly dead. Transfusions would not help him. He was soon dead. Arthurton torched the hut, then bravely informed the Japanese, not knowing how they would react. As it turned out, they were most relieved that this unsavoury work had been done for them.

Arthurton was proud that six of his patients recovered. They stayed with him and helped care for others as an epidemic developed. It began to have a marked impact on the entire project at the Burma end. Road works ceased at Upper Konkoita. By late May, less than half of the 694 men under the command of Lieutenant-Colonel Pond were well enough for any labour at all. But the Japanese remained ruthless over the project. They were terrified of cholera, yet they insisted that if a man could walk, he could work.

The disease peaked in its impact at the end of the first week in June. Lex Arthurton and others including Chitty, whose job it was to transport victims (mainly by stretcher), wondered then and forever afterwards why they did not contract the disease. They had been active in helping their stricken comrades before being injected with inoculation serum, which may have been a placebo anyway.

Bob Owen, who also worked with hundreds of cholera victims, concluded that not falling to the disease was simply 'pot luck'.

(But was it more than this? Throughout history, there had been survivors of such things as the Great Plague of London (1665–1666) where 100,000 people died, which was then 20 per cent of the city's population. Yet some managed to survive when all around them died. A genetic mutation could have been the reason. Did it apply with people such as Owen and Chitty who were also survivors?)[9]

Owen was intrigued by what happened to some at the end. They would be very ill and close to death. Then they would have a sudden burst of energy. They would sit up and say they were 'going to see Mum', or 'they were going to Albury in a truck'. On one occasion, an ailing fellow orderly told him that a mate had come to visit him and they were going away together in his car. The 'mate' was already dead. In all cases, after this apparent recovery, they would die quickly.

Owen saw this phenomenon as 'the spirit closing the door'.

'Men were dying left, right and centre,' he said. 'There was no minister, no padre. All I could do was offer to say the Lord's Prayer. No-one ever knocked it back.'[10]

There was always a service led by officers for these men at the place of their 'cremation'. Thirty kilometres up the line at Songkurai camp, Len Lemke, who was a reluctant volunteer for cholera work, remembered scraping the ashes from the funeral pyre and putting them into bamboo urns.

'We gave them to the sergeant-at-arms,' he said. 'I don't know where he put them.'

It was all part of the continued respect for comrades.

One POW always played the Last Post. At Songkurai, there were often three trumpet calls a day.

'We all used to down tools and stand to attention,' Lemke said. 'Even the Japs stood to attention. The bugler put his heart into it.'

Lemke recalled his last day at the camp during the cholera outbreak there: 'The sun was coming out. The rain had stopped. You could see the hills [of Burma] in the distance.' He remembered the bugler, a mate of his, telling him: 'I can't finish up on the hill myself. There would be no-one to play the Last Post.'

He died a few days later. There was no-one to play a last note of respect for the bugler.

*

Lemke summed up the feelings of survivors as their comrades fell daily: 'Death was sort of nothing. If so and so wasn't dead, he was just hanging on. Death was with us all the way, a part of life, not something far away that you never thought of. You were expected to die. It was fate. It made life in the jungle very different . . .'[11]

All through this period, the doctors, led by Frank Cahill, handled the 'big' surgery with poor tools. They continued on as they had when bombs dropped around them in the cathedral in Singapore. Instead of blood, they were now ankle deep in mud and slush. It was often in near darkness with flickering, poor light. Again, the doctors were tired and hungry. Once more men were dying around them. But the medicos stopped for little.

Hunt protected everyone possible, even stretching diagnoses to fool the Japanese. He claimed dysentery sufferers or men with bad ulcers had 'incipient' cholera and put them in the huts set aside for it. This bought time for the very weak.

'His greatest success was the day when only 100 men were pronounced by him to be fit for work,' Lieutenant Kelsey noted. 'Hundreds of Australian prisoners owed their lives to him.'[12]

Through the depths of misery that the disease caused, the Australians kept their humour, the one underlying facet of their character that was indestructible. When Lemke was relieved of his cholera duties at Songkurai, he and one of his mates, big, raw-boned Allan 'Lofty' Sleeves, a Red Cross worker, stayed in the camp but well away from the hill where the victims were quarantined.

'No-one ever comes near us,' Lofty observed. 'They must think we have leprosy.'[13]

37

Engineering Madness

After the cholera epidemic subsided, the Japanese directed that most of the growing camp of sick men be shifted 20 kilometres north of Upper Konkoita to Neike. The rest were to be transported 60 kilometres south to Takanun. Chitty was among the ambulance men who volunteered to carry patients by stretcher to both new camps. The tracks each way were beside the newly constructed railway. He and the others would often finish work at 4 a.m., only to be roused again four hours later for the same exercise.

Chitty remained a little below peak fitness. He dropped very little, if anything, below his normal 76 kilograms. He was eating the same as those around him. The meagre supplement of whitebait had no elixir of good health in it. There was the occasional unauthorised slaughtering of a stray, emaciated yak found near a village. That allowed an extra feed of meat for a day or two. But apart from this he was surviving on the unappetising, monotonous watery rice stew. A handful of men were similar to him. The rest lost some weight. The great majority of the POWs lost considerable weight, some dropping alarmingly to half what they had been before Changi. Others, such as Chicken Smallhorn, were down to 30 kilograms. Normally muscular, strapping men had noticeable rib cages and the ugly protrusion of hip bones. Still others, lean men to start with, looked like nothing more than walking skeletons.

Yet Chitty kept his sinewy, muscular angularity. He reckoned that his strength was kept up by the continual lifting and carrying, whether it was patients on stretchers, or when detailed to work on the roads, bridges and railway. He knew nothing about his metabolism other than it was better than most. He had never put on weight, no matter how much he ate.[1]

Chitty may have been the beneficiary of the Japanese in the food stores, who responded sometimes to the requests made by those with the Red Cross brassard for extra salt and food for patients. There were bonuses in gaining food for the shrewd, the determined and the fortunate.[2] The Japanese in the stores were a different breed than the guards. Occasionally, one would react well to a request. It was never done with a kind smile or knowing gesture. That might see a man beheaded by his masters. The manner would remain gruff and detached; the foods asked for would be slapped on the counter in the amounts requested.

Chitty was highly regarded not only by every member the POW contingent who came in contact with him, but even some of the Japanese guards. There was never going to be sympathy for his plight, but there would have been respect for him. On one occasion, a Japanese got himself fall-down drunk while on duty guarding Chitty and a group of mates. This was not unusual. The 'watching' job was depressing and monotonous. The guards knew that the POWs had nowhere to run even if they tried to escape. Some of the captors became slack. In the godforsaken conditions many found solace through alcohol. Instead of leaving the guard where he lay, which would have meant he would be punished severely by his own superiors, Chitty hoisted the man over his shoulders, and carried him and his rifle the 15 kilometres back to camp.[3]

Not long after this, the same guard made Chitty wait outside a place called 'the Brewery', the Thai–Burma railway's equivalent to a Japanese pub. It was a hut where crude beer was brewed, situated between the camp and the railway. The guard was soon intoxicated. Remembering Chitty's 'Good Samaritan' act a few days earlier, he invited him to drink with him. Chitty obliged. Some days they could get a lift back on a truck to the camp, and the guard indicated that they would not have to walk. They could both hitch a ride on a vehicle. But in the convivial drink-for-drink atmosphere, the truck was forgotten. They missed it.

The Japanese was very worried.

'You no tell we at brewery?' he said urgently eyeballing Chitty. 'You no tell huh? I in big trouble. *Big* trouble!'

'Don't worry,' Chitty said, 'I won't tell.'

The guard took one more hard look at him, trying to sense if he could trust this prisoner.

'Then he shot through,' Chitty said, 'running as hard as he could.'[4]

Chitty kept the incident to himself. The guard said nothing

but did acknowledge him always with a certain respect. There was a strange trust between the two men. Chitty had twice now saved him from a heavy penalty, which could range from imprisonment to even execution. In a strange way, the two men were inextricably linked. If Chitty ever reported the guard for his misdemeanours, the guard would face severe punishment at the very least. But such an act would certainly see Chitty brutalised, even murdered, by the man and the other guards.

During this time, there was another guard, a sergeant, who kept challenging the Australian POWs to a fight.

'The gunso [sergeant] was a real bully,' fellow POW Charles Edwards said. 'He was a wrestler, who used to throw his weight around.' The sergeant also boasted he was skilled at martial arts.

The sergeant was always confronting Chitty, who had the reputation as one of the strongest, most durable men on the railway. Beating him in a fight would give the sergeant a certain prestige. He would shape up in front of Chitty.

'No, mate,' Chitty would say, politely dismissing his overtures. 'We don't fight that way in Australia. We fight with these [indicating his large fists].'

The sergeant became more and more insistent. He showed off his wrestling and martial arts movements in front of Chitty, a couple of times demonstrating his chopping ability on pieces of wood or kicking as high as his head. Chitty ignored him with his usual nonchalance. When the sergeant's antics did not work, he taunted Chitty, asking if he was afraid. Still Chitty just smiled and showed him his fists. After several weeks of this goading, Chitty had a quiet word to his guard. He was given the 'nod' to take up the challenge. It would be literally a 'no holds barred, anything goes' fight with straight boxing, kicking, wrestling and karate moves allowed. There would be no consequences, whichever way the fight finished up.

'Once told this,' Edwards recalled, 'Chitty agreed to fight the gunso.'

The men went down to a clearing near the railway. About 20 POWs were allowed to be spectators with the guards. The two men shaped up. The sergeant went through his preparatory movements, including a few throaty, threatening cries and some ritualistic stances and contortions.

Then he sidled up to Chitty. The Australian had stood stock still while this foreplay went on. Now he shaped up, fists high, elbows in, feet positioned. The sergeant moved close, grappling Chitty, trying to get him in a headlock. Chitty fended him off, then in a lightning movement, feigned a left to the solar plexus and then threw a perfect right cross to the jaw. The sergeant's head snapped back, his eyes rolled. He fell back, unconscious before he hit the ground. The POWs cheered as much from surprise as elation.

Chitty took two paces forward and hovered over him. There was no fist in the air, or wave of victory. Chitty motioned to a Japanese guard to throw a bucket of water over his stricken opponent. The sergeant groaned, tried to raise his head but could not. Chitty examined him, and mumbled that his stricken opponent would be fine, but for a sore head.

The Australian onlookers, who seemed nearly as stunned as the Japanese, walked to the railway with Chitty, some congratulating him. There would be no gloating or further remonstration after the initial POW reaction. But the incident and that KO would be discussed for a long time.

The sergeant did not recover for several hours. In his semi-concussed state he was furious and ranted about beheading Chitty. But he was strongly disabused of this by the other guards. Instead he had to wear a swollen jaw and a damaged ego for some time.

For weeks after the incident the sergeant and Chitty stayed out of each other's way.[5]

Another whose courage and demeanour gained respect from the Japanese was Adjutant Ben Barnett.

'He stood head and shoulders above the rest of the (POW) administrators,' Captain Hardacre observed. (Hardacre himself had taken beatings for protecting his men, particularly over their killing of local farm animals for much-needed food.) 'Barnett was absolutely fearless in dealing with the Japs. Like savage dogs, they seemed to sense when a man was afraid and it had dire consequences. Ben showed no such fear and was often on the end of a bashing when intervening in incidents when men (POWs) were being punished. He was the [almost the] only person Murayama would talk to on rare occasions, and he referred to him as 'Captain Barnetto.'[6]

Only one thing bothered Chitty concerning his physical condition. Every now and again, he experienced a back twinge. As yet, he had never missed a day's labour because of it. Doctors shrugged and told him that he was doing the work of an elephant. Something had to give. He was advised to stretch every morning when he got up and every night before he slept. This seemed to work.

As the weeks turned into months on the railway, his back played up more. Yet he never complained. Chitty looked around him at the dying and the ill, and believed he was most fortunate. He saw his job as helping those with a lesser constitution, which was just about everyone.

Conditions worsened during late June. At Songkurai, 20 kilometres short of Three Pagodas Pass on the Burma border, the rain turned the road into one long mud bath. Even six-wheeled vehicles struggled to slide and slip through it. Bridges were collapsing and had to be rebuilt. Supplies from Burma, where the Japanese faced increasing hostility from British and Indian army guerillas, were unreliable. The clothes that the POWs had left were useless. Boots were discarded; so were pants and shirts; loincloths predominated. Hunt and the other medicos screamed, begged and cajoled in person and in writing for more blankets for the very ill.

The Japanese refused to concede precious hours for the workers as their task became nearly impossible. Those on the road never finished before 9 p.m. Then they faced a two-hour slog through mud and rain back to the camp in darkness.

On one occasion, too many POWs were ill. A work party was impossible to muster. Murayama compromised. He proclaimed that if the sick were sent out, they would only have to do 'light work.' The doctors managed to put together a group. But the ill men were still forced to labour at the rate of the others. Late in the afternoon, a fit POW bravely challenged the Japanese guard in charge, saying:

'How about the promise of light work for the sick men?'

The guard did not respond immediately. Instead he ordered some of the ill POWs to collect some dry bamboo and pile it on an embankment. Night was closing in. The Japanese guard directed that the pile be lit. Once there was a fire going, he smiled.

'Light work!' he said sarcastically, 'you know, sick men, light work.'[7]

Food became scarcer than ever and medical suppliers dried up. Ben Barnett and Roy Mills repeatedly protested the situation. But Murayama ignored them. Mills was taking his turn to gain an audience with the sadistic giant one evening when a guard told him to wait outside Murayama's hut. Mills waited while the Japanese Commander finished his meal. Then Mills was ushered in.

'He was sitting at a table sucking on his numerous gold-filled teeth,' Mills recalled, 'and continued to drink sake.'

'Captain doctor,' Murayama, on his way to being drunk, said, 'I challenge you to a fight to the death by judo. If you win I will have your request granted.'

Mills knew of the huge man's background in judo. But instead of backing down, he replied:

'I don't know anything about Judo, but I will box you to the death.'

This response was even more courageous given that Mills would have had no hope of winning. But instead of taking up the offer, Murayama rejected it and the pleas for food and medicine.

Mills, like many of the gutsy medicos such as Hunt, was prepared to take beatings on several occasions to prevent sick men from working.[8]

In the midst of this ordeal, there was the odd occasion when the Australians risked much for a tiny 'victory' against their increasingly inhumane captors. Lemke met up with Lemin and Chitty at Songkurai late in June. The three plotted a little scheme.

'It was raining,' Lemke recalled, 'and so quick thinking me worked out if two of our blokes put up a sort of fight, I could pinch vitamins out of their [Japanese] pockets.'

The Australians noted that all their captors munched on vitamins to supplement their meagre rations. The ruse, if detected, could have seen the three men executed. Chitty and Lemin put on a realistic brawl in the rain. POWs surrounded them. The Japanese guards moved in. In the chaos, Lemke relieved one of the guards of his bottle of pills.

'When the Nips left us after the fight,' Lemke said, 'the three of us sat down and ate the whole bottle, and they worked. We peed flat out for three days and our bodies came back to normal for the time being.'[9]

The Japanese at Songkurai kept a herd of yaks in the jungle.

'One day they wanted one killed,' Lemin recalled, 'but they didn't know how. They got one of our blokes to butcher it and cut it up. Another time one was hit by a train. Because it wasn't bled properly they gave it to us. It wasn't much but it gave a bit of flavour to the rice.'

Then Lemin, Chitty and their mates had an idea. They spread out along the train line in the jungle.

'Jack "Swanee" Smerdon—one of Peter Chitty's mob—was the yak herder,' Lemin said. 'He would be ready with a yak. When we saw a train coming, we'd yell down the line. A bloke with a wedge hammer would hit the yak on the head. It would be dragged close to the line and the bloke would call out to the Japs that a yak had been hit by the train. The Japs said we could have it. The butcher cut its throat and we had some meat flavoured stew.'

The ruse worked well on several occasions until one Japanese train driver swore that he had not hit a yak.

'We were in trouble,' Lemin said. The punishment was uniquely Japanese. They would line up the prisoners in two lines and make them belt each other. The guards would walk up and down the line 'yelling and screaming' for the POWs to hit each other harder.

'If you weren't hitting your hardest,' he added, 'they would call a stop and get stuck into you.'

Lemin and his mates hated having to hurt each other this way. The punishment put an end to the yak ruse, although it gave the men a sense of putting one over their captors for a short time.[10]

The POWs stole food from the Japanese whenever possible to stave off hunger. One of the 2/2nd Motor Ambulance Convoy contingent was a 'professional' bank robber. He had a theory about theft. You stole just enough—a little at a time—from the 'owners' to confuse them. They might not be sure if anything had been taken at all. The 'pro' never explained how this worked in a bank, but his mates were willing to take his advice when it came to purloining food.

Thailand was hilly, especially in the upper reaches of the north-west near the Burmese border, and there were abundant sweet potato farms. The Japanese used to bring bags of them down in trucks for their own consumption. The POWs would spread along a steep hill above the road. When the trucks drove by, three of them would jump onto the vehicles, remove six potatoes from each bag and toss them onto the road for collection by their mates. If a complete bag-full were ever stolen, then the other bags would be shifted to fill the space so that the Japanese would not notice the theft. This was successful until the Japanese had enough potatoes in store and the trucks stopped coming.

Little 'wins' such as these demonstrated the undying spirit of the men, but they were too few to have any impact on the breakdown of F Force.

By 31 July, and after 100 days of slave labour, 1,265 men at Lower Songkurai—two thirds of the workforce—were in hospital. Of the remaining third, only 375 men were working. These were typical numbers along the railway. Yet the Japanese engineers, perhaps now insanely, pushed on. They threatened that the sick men would be 'let loose' in the jungle and replaced by fit Malayans, Indonesians, Tamils and Chinese.

Major A. E. Saggers wrote in his diary:

'Men taken from hospital were lined up with the others. Many would break down and cry. Others would vomit. Others would defecate from nervousness and/or illness. Others sat in the mud in the ranks, awaiting the orders to move, pitifully preserving their strength. The faces of all appeared haggard and drawn. It was perfectly apparent that all were suffering from extreme exhaustion, lack of sleep and undernourishment.'[11]

In August, the madness of the drive to build the bridges and railway peaked. More than 800 Australians were sent to Songkurai camp number 2 to help 1,000 British POWs. This area of the line was the last link that had to be built. Destroyed bridges had to be reconstructed. It was the worst site on the entire railway. More than 600 British troops had died there. The guards used wire whips as much as bamboo canes to drive the men. Those too ill to stand were forced to drag huge logs and beams from a sitting position.

The Australian officers and medicos continued to stand up to the captors, insisting that hygiene had to be improved before men worked. Cookhouses were built; latrines were dug; wood was cut and stacked.

The Japanese still responded to the cholera threat. It was the one word in English that petrified them. The Australian doctors warned that another outbreak was certain if camp conditions were not improved. Along with this, there was the perpetual battle by the doctors to hold back men who were not fit to work. The Japanese always wanted many more than the doctors believed advisable. Once more, the Japanese had done their sums. Months ago, an engineer had worked out the number of men needed to remove 'X' amount of rock and dirt, or carry 'Y' amount of logs for a bridge construction.

This had to be adhered to by the fanatical engineers, who went into rages if their equations were not met. When the doctors refused to supply the quantity required, the engineer commander at Songkurai, Lieutenant Abe, sent guards through the hospital. They rounded up the first 200 patients they came across and forced them to work on a bridge.

Some of these ill men collapsed, fell 10 metres into the river, and drowned.[12]

38

End of the Line

By mid-August 1943, nearly 70 per cent of the POWs in all camps were hospital patients. This caused more tensions between the captors and the Australian and British doctors, who, in effect, were in control of F Force. The military commanders had to bow to the medicos' comprehension of the problems.

Although the Japanese never revealed their dates or plans, there was a feverish drive in July and August 1943 to finish the railway. The completion date had to be approaching. The Australians were forced to march and concentrate most of the POWs at Upper Songkurai; the British had to move to Songkurai. Both camps were close to the Burma border.

The last push to complete the project, it seemed, would be in these two locations. The rains flooded the Australian camp. Latrines overflowed and washed under the hospital hut floors. Some huts collapsed. Cholera broke out for the second time as the doctors predicted. Hundreds caught it. Fifty died before it was contained.

The Japanese engineers, fixated with their railway, remained callous to the suffering. They again informed the doctors that if the numbers of fit as well as ill patients presented for work were not doubled, then all the POWs would be turned out into the jungle and replaced by other slave labour from among the Asian groups. This had never been a bluff, but this time the captors meant to carry out the threat. British Colonel Harris, commander of F Force, had to negotiate hurriedly with the Japanese. F Force would make one-third of the accommodation area available for fresh labour. This was agreed.

In effect, Harris was giving away nothing. He had made a grim calculation: the number of deaths in F Force over the next few weeks would make space for a new batch of slaves anyway.

On 18 September 1943, three weeks over the secret deadline, the completion of work on the railway was official for F Force. The POWs were granted a day's 'holiday'—their first for the entire time of the project.[1]

The Japanese engineers celebrated with even more gusto than they had in completing the bridge over the River Kwai earlier in May. A week later on 25 September, Hunt wrote to the Japanese medical officers in charge of F Force about conditions in Thanbaya hospital camp, where 1,900 men had been transferred in early August. He referred to the chief diseases in the camp: 'Malaria 573 cases . . . very virulent and resistant to Quinine. High relapse rate; Beri-Beri, 492 . . . Increasing daily in working staff. More than half of the cases contracted in this camp. Much heart involvement— many recent deaths; Dysentery, 521 . . . All cases getting steadily worse in the complete absence of drugs for treatment; Tropical ulcers . . . Most getting worse in the absence of Vitamins (A, B & C), drugs and dressings.'

Hunt warned that the camp's health was on the decline. He predicted 500 deaths from beri-beri in the next six weeks and pointed out that the F Force of 7,000 had already had 2,000 deaths.

'The real tragedy lies in the fact that much of the disease is really curable,' he wrote, 'if proper vitamin-containing foodstuffs, such as beans and towgay and proper drugs were made available . . . Men are dying in hundreds and will continue to die until help comes.'[2]

Hunt's pleas and warning went unheeded.

The Japanese philosophy about 'honour' floundered at these moments. The belief that a prisoner's life was to be forfeited, or was not worth anything, meant unspeakable brutality in the name of the emperor. If the deaths of thousands of Allied POWs were not bad enough, 10 times as many Asian slaves came from countries that had not been fighting the Japanese. Allegedly, they had been 'liberated'. Where did the Samurai warrior philosophy fit with their deaths in huge numbers? There was no war 'honour' involved. Inhumanity, insanity and barbarism were exhibited in the construction of the Burma–Thai railway.

It was a symbol of an ancient Japanese tradition that had been corrupted and used as an excuse and propaganda tool for excesses in a bid for subjugation of all other races and nations in the Asian–Pacific region.

Lilian Chitty's father George received word from the army that her brother Horace had been killed in action fighting the Japanese in Lae on 6 September 1943. After a stint in the Middle East, his 2/23rd Battalion had been transferred back to Australia. He had been sent to Milne Bay on the extreme eastern tip of Papua early in August 1943, then into battle once more. Horace was a bandsman, who doubled as a stretcher-bearer. He had a reputation similar to Simpson (of 'Simpson and his Donkey' fame) on Gallipoli as a brave operator who saved many lives. Had his commanding officer not been killed, according to the family, he would have been recommended for the Military Cross.

His death was sad enough for Lilian, coming 14 months after her brother-in-law Toxa (in the same outfit) was killed.

It increased her fears for Peter, whom she had not had word from for some time. The messages, official and otherwise, had been mixed and disturbing. In April 1942, the army reported that it did not know where he was. In July 1942, she had a letter saying that he was officially posted as 'missing'. In May 1943, the army informed her that 'VX48247 Chitty LA' was now 'reported missing believed prisoner of war interned Malaya camp'.

*

The bulk of F Force had to be moved to Neike by early November. Mid-month, the transfer of the men began back to Kanchanaburi and Bampong at the other end of the line. This would be followed by the return to Singapore. Nearly 1,000 Australians had died. The British lost twice that many. Approaching half the entire F Force never left the railway. Dysentery and diarrhoea accounted for 832 men. Cholera killed 637.

The higher attrition rate among the British was partly due to the greater number of unfit men that left Changi in the first place. The Australian commander's Colonel Kappe put his men's higher survival rate down to their better discipline and sanitation. They adapted better to the conditions. Many like Chitty were bushmen who handled the harsh circumstances well. They knew how to live rough. They had never before encountered the conditions imposed by the Japanese, which were as dreadful as anything perpetrated in history. But the men from outback and bush backgrounds had far more adaptability. The Australians from the city were disadvantaged, but they learnt from their country cousins.

On top of that, Kappe believed the better survival rate was also due to the exceptional work of the medical personnel. When hostilities ceased in February 1942, the medicos became more important than the military commanders. On the Thai railway, all the medical officers and workers were in charge. Health and survival were their territories. Doctors such as Bruce Hunt, Frank Cahill, Lloyd Cahill, Rowley Richards, Albert Coates, John Taylor, Weary Dunlop and others made the difference in the greater numbers who survived in POW camps, including those in the Dutch East Indies (Indonesia), Thailand, Singapore, Burma and Japan. They were backed up by the medical orderlies such as Chitty, Bob Owen, Lex Arthurton, Joe Jameson, Frank Lemin, Len Lemke and scores of others.

British commander Harris agreed with his Australian counterpart and went further. He believed the far lower Australian death rate was due to their unity. They were all members of one volunteer force 'with a common emblem and outlook'. Other troops were 'a heterogeneous collection of men of all races and units, many of whom found themselves together for the first time'.

Harris added that the 'average physical standard' of the Australians 'was incomparably higher than that of the mixed force of regular soldiers, territorials, militia-men, conscripts and local volunteers,' who made up the British half of F-Force.[3]

There was a POW exchange between Australia and Germany in October 1943. Phil and Ron Chitty were taken from their detention in Austria and Germany, arriving at Alexandria on 3 November, for the swap. On release, the brothers visited Toxa's grave at El Alamein.

They wondered about Peter. They only knew via mail from home that he may also have been a POW. The war in the Pacific was still raging. Would he survive?

On 25 January 1944, Ron and Phil left by ship for Australia.[4]

The only groups to stay on the Burma–Thai railway in late 1943 were small rear parties and men too sick to move. Volunteers were needed to look after them.

Chitty was among those who opted to stay until the last patients were well enough to leave the purgatory of the Burma–Thai railway. Bob Owen was another. They were taken by open truck to the Burmese border at Three Pagodas Pass and then on into Burma along a bad road parallel to the railway extending more than 100 kilometres. Thanbaya hospital was 60 kilometres north-west of the border. It had been a work camp and hospital for A Force and the Dutch. Now the sickest of F Force—those the Japanese thought unlikely to make it back to Changi—were being placed there. The Australian volunteers worked closely with the British in looking after the ill prisoners. Usually this worked well. But on occasions, difference in approaches caused clashes. One day, Owen arrived at the main hospital tent. Hunt and a British medical orderly were on the ground, fighting.

Owen broke it up. Later, the orderly spluttered an account of what had happened. He had been upbraided by the tough, direct-speaking Hunt and did not appreciate it.

'He [the British officer] didn't know the major's manner,' Owen said. 'We were all used to his direct style. The argument was about hygiene. Hunt was much stricter than the British. It's one reason that we lost half as many men as them on the railway.'[5]

Differences were settled in the interests of the main goal: to save the worst-case patients. Chitty, Owen and many others such as Gordon Nichol helped with everything. Nichol recalled assisting Frank Cahill in amputations, mainly of legs.

'The arteries and blood vessels would be tied off but they would slough away,' Nichol said. The poor nutrition would not allow wounds to heal. The arteries would 'spurt blood everywhere'. Cahill and the other doctor would be forced to cut more leg off and retie and dress them, but that often did not work. Other patients would have tourniquets ready to aid patients who needed fast treatment. Nichol remembered one patient whose leg had been amputated so far up that the only way to stop the bleeding was to put digital pressure on the femoral artery found high up on the base of the stomach. Nichol did this while Cahill tried to tie off the blood vessels.

'It was of course hopeless,' Nichol said. 'It was one of the most terrible things I've ever seen.'

The desperate patient asked Cahill if he was going to die.

'I think so,' the quietly spoken doctor said.

The patient looked at Cahill and Nichol and began reciting the Lord's Prayer.[6]

Cahill often faced a dreadful dilemma. Should he amputate while there was still a chance of recovery for the limb? Or should he wait until he was forced to amputate? The decision to delay often reduced the chance of a patient's survival. He and the other surgeons, praised by Hunt for their skills, faced this type of question every day at Thanbaya. Cahill, a Catholic, would find a clearing away from the huts and pray for guidance. It helped him through the perpetual ordeal of being a surgeon in a camp that promised more death than life.

He and all the volunteers in this camp of last resort literally had 'a never say die' mentality. That's why they were there. They never gave up hope for their friends and mates. Strong bonds were built.

*

Owen had a mate in the last camp, Phillip Baulton, who was extremely ill.

'He won't make it,' Hunt told Owen.

'Yes he will,' Owen said. They both knew that the Japanese would not let men onto the trains (taking them back to Bangkok and Singapore) if they were not well enough to walk to the carriages themselves.

The weakest would be left to die.

Owen was determined to get Baulton onto the train. Each day, out of sight of the guards, he would help his mate walk around the camp. At first, it seemed hopeless. Owen persevered.

'[Each day] I would bow and scrape past the guards to work on Phil,' he said. 'I paced out the distance to the train [100 metres] and made that the distance Phil had to build up to in our walks around the camp.'

The day came where Baulton would have to walk past the guards to the train. Owen was next to him. He couldn't prop him up. He just had a quiet few words every now and again as they stepped to the train. As they passed each guard they bowed low, making sure not to make eye contact.

'They were a very tense few minutes,' Owen said. 'Phil made it, just.'[7]

Baulton was a most fortunate beneficiary of the remarkable spirit and character of the POWs. Bruce Hunt, who endured the hardships of both world wars, observed after coming off the completed Burma–Thai railway with the last of F Force:

'I have on many occasions seen men tried up to and beyond the limits of reasonable human endurance. I would say that

"F Force" was [put through] the most searching test of fundamental character and guts that I have ever known. That so many men—British and Australian—came through this test with their heads held high and their records unblemished was something of which we may not be unreasonably proud.'[8]

39

Postcards from Thailand

Lilian Chitty received a small card containing 25 words from her husband in October 1943. It was the first news she had had since the fall of Singapore in February 1942 and was at least a year out of date.

It read:

IMPERIAL JAPANESE ARMY

Then followed standard, typed lines:

I am interned at the Prisoner of War Camp at Changi, Singapore.

My health is good [the words 'usual' and 'poor' were crossed out].

I have not had any illness.

The words, 'I am (have been) in hospital' had been crossed out.

'I am with friends . . .' Chitty then wrote references to several colleagues, and told Lilian he loved her. He signed the card.

The army had earlier informed her that he may have been heard in a Japanese propaganda radio broadcast picked up on short wave in Australia. She was told by the AIF to 'take it with a grain of salt'.

'Whether he ever sent that [radio] message,' Lilian said, 'I don't know.'

This new card was more credible. Yet it said very little. The words had been vetted by the Japanese, who would never allow the horrific facts about the rail construction to be public in the West.

Lilian still had reservations about Peter's wellbeing.

'We were warned [by the AIF] that the Japs were putting through propaganda,' she said. 'I received three cards [all from later 1943]. He would always mention names of friends [also serving and POWs]. We could then pass on [these references] to different wives and mothers. And his friends did the same thing [for us].'

This happened with Chitty's cousin Charles Edwards, also a POW. He wrote a letter to his mother, which was broadcast by a Japanese announcer in Tokyo. Edwards had mentioned three names of three fellow POWs. One was read out as 'Petty Thitty'.

The Australian Government asked Mrs Edwards if she knew who this was. She went to bed that night tossing around that strange name. It clicked in the middle of the night. She rang Lilian Chitty to tell her that 'Petty Thitty' had to be her husband.

These references in Peter's cards, and similar comments by

his mates about him to their loved ones, made them seem authentic. Lilian felt some relief. He had, after all, been a POW, but he was alive and at least well enough to communicate. There was hope for him, especially if the war turned the way of the Allies.

'I never gave up hope,' Lilian said. 'I felt all the time that he was probably a POW. You see, Peter was a survivor. I always said that you couldn't kill him with an axe!'

Lilian had a busy time with her two children. Son Lindsay was now 3; daughter Dawn was approaching 5. Lilian tried working in Melbourne's Myer store to earn enough money for Christmas presents. But her father had trouble coping with the two kids. She raised money for the war effort, sometimes going door-to-door collecting. One man in her own street refused to donate.

'He was a pacifist,' she said. 'I wasn't very happy with him.'[1]

The Japanese ended their air raids on northern Australia on 12 November 1943. There had been nearly 93 since the first attack on Darwin on 19 February 1942. The scores of airfields built for the war had been the main target in and around Darwin, which took 64 hits.

Other towns and cities to be bombed and strafed were Queensland's Horn Island (10 strikes), Townsville (three) and Mossman (one). Western Australian targets included Exmouth (three strikes); Broome (three); Wyndham (five); Port Hedland (twice); Derby and Drysdale Mission (one strike each). Apart from these raids, Sydney, Newcastle and Port Gregory (near Geraldton, Western Australia) were either bombed by planes or torpedoed by Japanese submarines.

The silence in the skies over the nation's north in the second half of November, December and into the New Year of 1944 was another indicator that Japan was struggling. Attacks from the air and sea, and on land on many other nations had been going on since the first raid on Pearl Harbor two years earlier and this was beginning to stretch supply lines, exhaust their personnel and create doubts about their self-image of invincibility.

Richard (Dick) Chitty became the seventh in the family to enlist. He chose his 18th birthday in January 1944 to join up with the 13/33rd Australian Infantry Battalion, which would be stationed and trained at St Ives, Singleton, Canungra and Cowra in New South Wales. He was the fifth brother of nine in the family to serve. Frank, who had polio, was unfit. Bob, Carlton's 'enforcer' was in 'Essential Services', working in an explosives factory in Maribyrnong and continuing to play well in the VFL. (Ken and Pat remained too young to serve.) In 1943, Bob led his team into the finals and was one of the best in a losing first semi-final against Fitzroy.

After his ordeals on the Thai–Burma railway, Peter Chitty was sent to a camp at Kanchanaburi, north-west of Bampong, where F Force's journey had begun just over a year earlier. Even this return journey by train, which should have been of some relief, had him and everyone else on edge, especially at the Wampo viaduct and the River Kwai bridge. Chitty and the others knew of the faults that had been left in these constructions, some deliberately by the POW builders, in the hope that one day they would collapse into the waters far below. There was fear too that Allied planes might bomb the train. Only when the carriages had crawled uncertainly over the bridge did tensions among the passengers ease.

There was one more incident on the over-crowded train just after it crossed the River Kwai. The ill and wounded on board were struggling in the fetid, airless carriages, and a POW died. Japanese guards, nervous about the body, were ordered by a sergeant to toss the corpse from the train. Chitty was in the carriage. He pushed close to the body.

'This man will stay on the train,' he said, eyeballing the Japanese sergeant in charge. The sergeant bellowed the order to the guards again. Two of them made hesitant moves to pick up the body. Chitty stood in front of the dead digger, saying:

'No. He will be given a proper burial at the destination.'

Several other POWs, emboldened by Chitty's defiance, formed a phalanx around the body. The guards backed off. The sergeant muttered under his breath and pushed his way into the next carriage.[2]

After this last ordeal of many, Chitty received an unexpected surprise at Kanchanaburi when given two letters from Lilian. He was overjoyed. They meant so much. He had not seen her for nearly three years. It seemed an eternity. But those letters, in a familiar scrawl, brought him a certain tenderness and closed down the time considerably. They brought him close to her. They gave him hope. Without that, he and his mates had little.

Another surprise was the food. It was supplied by local Thais and the best experienced since before Changi. Eggs, bananas and other 'luxuries' were obtainable.

It allowed Chitty to say that he 'came off the railway a pound heavier' than normal.[3]

At Kanchanaburi, Chitty caught up again with Len Lemke, who was fatigued after the travails on the railway at Song-kurai to the point where he could not even prepare his own sleeping quarters.

'Tony [a friend of Lemke's from the railway] and I were exhausted,' Lemke recalled, 'and I asked Peter Chitty if he would clear a bit of ground for us to sleep on. Great man Peter.'[4]

Chitty took several hours digging and clearing land.

Kanchanaburi should have been a happier place, given that the hard labour was behind them. But it may have been the saddest of all. So many men who had survived the railway reached there and never left. (The massive 8,000-person cemetery dedicated to the POWs is solemn testimony to this.) Others struggled. Chitty, Lemke and others had as much work to do tending the sick as they had on the railway. They were still in for shocks and ways of dying that would stay with them as long as they lived.

'One man had an ulcer slap-bang on the front of his heart,' Lemke recalled. 'When you have malaria an ulcer runs wild. It actually ate the front of his chest away. You could see his heart beating. He used to walk around and show it to us. No-one could stop the ulcer from growing. It killed him.'

Lemke articulated the attitude that made him and Chitty, and scores of other selfless men in the Ambulance Corps, characters of exceptional quality: 'In the cholera ward and at Kanchanaburi I used to treat every bloke as if he were some mother's son,' Lemke said, 'and I did the best I could for him.'[5] There were some moments of relief not possible on the railway. Bartering with the Thais was a pleasure and the locals risked much to bring food goods to the POWs. The Japanese allowed concessions. One was to go swimming in the nearby River Kwai. The men loved it. The numbers requesting this luxury increased daily until 250 men went off under guard to the river. But there was an added attraction. Many Thais lived on 15 metre bamboo rafts crowded with people, animals, fruit, vegetables and other 'wonderful' food in the POWs' eyes. The Japanese warned the POWs not to go near the rafts, but the men found a circuitous way out of the guards' view to reach them. They bought the goods and secreted them back past the guards. After weeks of this, the Japanese even allowed the men to 'smuggle' their purchases back to the camp. The captors were capricious. The POWs could never be sure how they would react. Brutality was always an eye-blink away. But here and there at Kanchanaburi, some of the guards relented a fraction. There was not the pressure of the need to push men beyond humane limits as they had on the railway.

The respect for the Thais increased with more contact with them. The POWs realised how much more the Thais now hated the Japanese after another year of 'occupation' of Thailand The POWs were impressed with how the Thais defied or stood up to their official 'masters', sometimes at their peril.

After the less arduous but no less harrowing few weeks at Kanchanaburi, Chitty was sent back to Changi, arriving on

Saturday 29 April 1944. He had been away just over a year. His exceptional physical and mental fortitude had played a part but he was first to admit he had been fortunate. He had not yet contracted one of the more serious of the many diseases in the camps of death along the more than 400 kilometre rail and road route. Not getting cholera had been his biggest bit of luck, especially as he had been so close to so many who had died.

Back in Singapore, all POWs, except for 1,000 patients, were to be moved to the Changi jail. The jail's inmates were relocated in Singapore town. Extra huts were to be built around the jail for the increased numbers.

Chitty was thrilled to receive more letters from home, something he and all the other POWs craved. But the news was not all good. He learned that Toxa had been killed in action at El Alamein in July 1942. Phil and Ron were back in Australia after prison terms in Germany or Austria. Dick had just joined up.

Lilian spoke of their children. 'Dawn is an angel . . . Lindsay is a little devil, but adorable . . . everyone says to me you [Lilian] must have a great time with Lindsay, and I tell them "you didn't grow up with him." He is a comedian, I can tell you; a mischief! . . .'[6]

Chitty was more nostalgic for home than ever. He tried to glean in Changi every titbit on the progress of the war that he and all the other railway workers had been starved of for a year. There were a few secret radios in the Thai camps, but the news was harder to obtain.

Rumours abounded in Singapore. The BBC broadcast from

Delhi seemed to be indicating the war raging around them in the Pacific and South-East Asia was swinging the Allies' way. The US was the big hope. It was tackling the enemy everywhere, island by island. Australia was fighting hard in New Guinea, where reports suggested the Japanese had been thwarted. UK and Indian troops early in 1944 had recaptured parts of Burma. The desperate effort to build the Thai railway was now vital for Japanese ascendancy there.

But they appeared to be losing their grip. Tales spread about the railway supply line already being down because of Allied bombing. Perhaps it was wishful thinking. Chitty took solace from the fact that before he left for Thailand there seemed little hope of defeating the Japanese. Now the possibility seemed real.

The tide appeared to be turning for the Allies in Europe too. In June, a strong story spread through Changi that the Allies had invaded France.

Another useful sign was the camp conduit for Japanese propaganda—the *Syonan Times*. It was no longer published. The POWs took this to mean that there were too many lies to be told about Japanese setbacks to make publication plausible.

Changi was more a hospital than a POW camp. The survivors from the railway had all been returned and the majority had illnesses. Even Chitty, who had come back with a nagging back injury, had a bout of malaria, as did many in the camp. He recovered quickly, but the disease was something that took some time to dissipate. Relapses could plague sufferers for years.

The Japanese continued their pressure for forced labour projects. The worst on Singapore was the rebuilding of the aerodrome at Changi. Food was as ever a problem. It lacked nutrition. There was never enough; the rations were being cut.

In July 1944, there was an increase in instances of cruelty by the Japanese guards. Bashings of patients too ill to work and staff defending them were seen by the POWs as a sign of frustration from their captors. The enemy administrators monitoring the war would be upset by events. They in turn would take it out on the guards, who would respond in kind to the POWs. The prisoners were sensitive to the whims of the guards. If they were unhappy, something unpalatable for the Imperial Army was making them this way.

The POWs were two and a half years into their incarceration and looking for any signs that they would not be spending the rest of their lives in this state.

This had been settled already for more than 15,000 POWs who had died.

40

Cowra Break-Out

A shrill bugle call split the cool night air in the little country town of Cowra in western New South Wales. It was 2 a.m. on 5 August 1944. More than 1,100 Japanese, armed with sharpened cutlery and baseball bats, attempted to break out of a POW camp. Two of the four escapee gangs scaled three fences and then hit the barbed wire at two different points. First they threw blankets over the wire; then they climbed over 10 metres of it, their hands protected by baseball mitts.

The other two groups, shrieking as they went, headed for the bright lights of Broadway, the 700 metre thoroughfare running north–south in the huge 30 hectare camp. One gang would attempt to break into D Compound holding Japanese officers; the other would strike for outer gates of the Australian garrison.

They set fire to huts as they left. Soon their compound was ablaze.

The Australian guards of 22nd Garrison Battalion had a good view of events as light from six towers swept over Broadway and the other 'boulevard' known as 'no-man's-land', which ran at right angles to Broadway. Fixed lights were trained on the wire and roads. But these advantages to the guards were hampered by a stray bullet severing the main electricity line. The camp was plunged into darkness, making defence tougher.

Privates Benjamin Hardy and Ralph Jones manned a No. 2 Vickers machine-gun and commenced firing into the first wave of escapees. Realising they would be overwhelmed, Jones removed and concealed the gun's lock, rendering the weapon useless, before he and Hardy were killed.

The other three escapee gangs broke through the fences. The Australians at both ends of Broadway spotted them and opened fire, cutting down many of them. Prisoners were pinned down for hours. Thirty of them made a dash for one end of the long thoroughfare. Guard Private Shepherd tried to block their move. He was bludgeoned to death. Four other guards were injured.

The Japanese group trying to link with their officers was cut off. Its members were killed or rounded up. Many committed suicide, either in a planned move as soon as they escaped, or to avoid recapture.

The group of 330 breaking out of B Compound made it to freedom.

The sleepy rural town of Cowra (population 3,000), 330 kilometres south-west of Sydney, was in a living nightmare. The RAAF, the police, Australian Military Force trainees from the 13/33rd Battalion, including young Dick Chitty, and the Australian Women's Battalion, were mobilised. It was the nation's biggest mass manhunt. Some civic-minded local farmers, useful with rifles, joined in. They shot two escapees. Members of Chitty's battalion shot and killed 10.

Dick Chitty was also involved in rounding up several men, and in discovering the bodies of scores of others who had decided to slit their own throats.

Lieutenant Harry Doncaster became the fourth Australian to be killed when he was attacked and murdered by six escapees 11 kilometres north of Cowra. Others managed to reach points as far as Eugowra, 50 kilometres away.

The posse took nine days to round up all of them. There were 231 Japanese soldiers killed and 108 wounded.

No Australian civilians were killed or harmed, which had been planned by the leaders of the break-out. The escapees were pushed back into their Cowra jail, once more joining three other compounds full of Italians, Koreans and Indonesians.

Inquiries into the break-out searched for a reason for such a desperate move. They were not in the jungles of Thailand, but any real chance of escape was about as futile in Australia's wide open spaces. Apart from the impossibility of success, the conditions inside were good. The inmates improved in health, unlike their counterparts in Changi and on the Thai railway.

E. V. Timms, an officer of the 22nd Garrison Battalion, wrote:

'They did not understand the articles of the Geneva Convention . . . Our strict adherence to its terms merely amused them.'

Perhaps they chose to ignore them, in the manner of the Japanese POW camp commanders in Thailand, Singapore, Indonesia and elsewhere.

The humane approach by Australian commanders, Timms said, also 'further convinced them [the Japanese] of our moral and spiritual weakness. They read into our humane treatment a desire to placate them. This they felt sure sprang from our secret fear of them.'[1]

Dick Chitty had been stationed near Cowra but not in the prison. He never expected to see action. Instead, he became the fifth brother in the family to be in a life-and-death war situation.

41

The Wheel Turns

The Japanese officers and guards at Changi in September and October 1944 began to show signs of strain. They were tetchier, even more likely to deliver bashings, and never relaxed. The POWs noticed it when they looked around the camp. When they gazed up, they saw more activity in the skies. Japanese small planes were using the aerodrome with greater frequency.

Air raid sirens and drills came more often. Blackouts were common. There was a ban on all sports, music, entertainment and community singing. Gatherings of more than six of any kind were stopped. The Japanese now wore tin hats at all times.

11 November—Armistice Day—brought the greatest joy to the entire POW camp to that point. Forty US B-17 bombers rumbled overhead. Air alarms sounded. POWs stood, cheered and waved, much to the horror of the guards, who admonished them for looking up and not running to their jail cells.

Lemke was at one of the many lagoons outside the area, on a detail to spray it with kerosene in the daily effort to kill off malaria-carrying mosquitoes.

'Well stuff the mosquitoes,' he said. 'We stopped work and cheered and waved and yelled and hugged one another . . . those beautiful, big, four engine bombers. They flew over in a line for a month.'

The regular, daily drone in the skies was one of the most wonderful sounds the POWs ever heard.[1]

Japanese fighters took off after the B-17s, but they were too high to attack. This and other 'fly-overs' caused the commanders to order the increased digging and deepening of trenches. It indicated that an Allied invasion was feared. Australian hospital staff marked the area with a big red cross, hoping this would avoid attacks.

On 8 January 1945, at 1 p.m. a US air raid of B-29 Superfortress bombers loomed over Singapore and unloaded on the Seletar naval base on the north-east coast in full view of the POWs. This sophisticated plane, the biggest ever built by the US, had superseded the B-17. The B-29 was the single most complicated and expensive weapon produced during the war. Nearly 4,000 were rolling off the production line. The three-hour Singapore attack was one of the early raids by this model, which promised to play a huge part in the outcome of the Pacific war.

One of them was shot down. The POWs booed the Japanese success. Guards moved into the camp, bashing anyone watching the skies. On 14 January, there was another air raid, which was met by a powerful barrage from the ground. The naval base took another hammering. Rumours spread that the airfields on the island had been damaged.

The POWs believed it was now only a matter of time before they were liberated. Meanwhile, life went on in the camp. Rats became a problem. Australians officers demanded they be eliminated. The Japanese allowed them to let loose 75 cats, but within a week they had disappeared. The prisoners had killed them and added the meat to their meagre rice rations.

The rat infestation remained.

The cultural gap between the captors and the inmates was accentuated with an incident on 15 January. Chitty, an experienced sawmiller, was working in a mill outside the jail when another POW caught his hand in a planing machine. A deep cut needed immediate attention. Chitty rushed him to hospital. The hand was sutured and put in a splint. The mill was shut down. A few days later, tiny 'dolls houses' began appearing on ledges inside the sawmill and close to the offending machine. The Japanese had constructed them to accommodate 'evil spirits' they believed had invaded the machinery.

It was a quaint, almost genteel, yet still inexplicable side to the captors that kept their mentality an enigma to the Australians. Chitty had no time for such superstition, yet he was intrigued that his captors did.

He and the other POWs saw it as a weakness that they did not know how to exploit.[2]

1 February 1945 saw the biggest assault of B-29s. Ninety of them in 11 waves ranging from three to 20 bombers thundered overhead. They released their bombs as they passed over the camp, aiming again at the Seletar naval base but spreading them alarmingly more than before. Six big pieces of shrapnel, one weighing 14 kilograms, landed at the Kranji camp, close to Seletar. Some bombs did not explode.

On 3 February, a further raid by 17 B-29s bombed the civil aerodrome at Katong.

The attacks marked the end of the third year in captivity. In February 1942, the Japanese ruled the skies with hardly any competition. The B-29s had reversed the situation. They represented the new, massive technology and while there were plenty of Japanese fighters, they were hardly a match for the huge high-flying new machines.

On 13 February, the US 493 Squadron made its first major attack on the Kwai bridges using new guided weapons (Azon bomb systems). Two of 11 spans of steel bridge were demolished. A wooden bridge (rebuilt by the Japanese) was damaged. But the bridges were repaired quickly. Each air attack by the Allies led to POWs at Tamarkan camp (adjacent to the bridges) being killed. On 14 February the Japanese evacuated the remaining POWs to the Chungkai camp, two kilometres north of Kanchanaburi, on the bank of the River Kwai. (Two more spans of the steel bridge were destroyed during air raids between April and June 1945.)

During these weeks of uncertainty rumours were rife that the Americans were coming after the Japanese. Fly-overs of big bombers were frequent, but they were so high that no-one could be sure if they were Allied planes. The nervousness of the Japanese gave clues. The braver POWs such as Lemke gave cheek to some of the Japanese with comments such as:

'Americans bomb Japan! Boom, boom, boom!'

One of the POWs had been taught by Aborigines how to tell the time by the sun. (The Japanese had taken almost all watches.) He would chide the guards, telling them when the bombers would be flying overhead. After the bombers had thundered by, the Japanese wanted to know where his watch was hidden. They were angered when he insisted he did not have one.

The reminders seemed to play on Japanese minds. They became agitated in anticipation of the fly-overs at the same time each morning.

Chitty's 33rd birthday on 12 March came and went without celebration. He and most of his mates felt they could wait until there was something to get really excited about. In the meantime, the Japanese had projects. There was always work at the docks loading and unloading the godowns.

On one occasion, rice bags were unloaded on the Selarang parade ground and had to be carried to stores. One of

Chitty's companions was so weak from malnutrition that he could not lift a bag. A Korean guard punched him hard. A rifle butt crashed into his stomach. The POW went down. The guard kicked him. He was about to put another boot in when he stopped. Chitty stepped between the Korean and his mate. He stared straight into the guard's eyes, putting up a hand. The guard took a step back, unsure about attacking Chitty. Chitty then lifted his mate, who weighed under 34 kilograms, and hoisted him onto a shoulder. Then he picked up the rice bag and slung it over the other shoulder. Chitty moved off without looking back at the Korean guard.[3]

One major program was the building of massive trench systems (bunds) that surrounded the entire Changi camp. Chitty and his fellow workers were uneasy about this. The use of the words 'speedo-speedo' chilled many of them again. Some wondered if it was not a trench at all, but a mass grave for the POWs left in the camp. In three years, the Japanese had so far been responsible to a large degree for the deaths of more than 23,000 prisoners in the camp.

The Australians did not believe it was beyond their captors to carry out a big-scale slaughter. It had already been done in a disorganised way on the Thai railway. (Had they had access to a Japanese document—number 2701—found in a Taiwan camp's records, it would have confirmed their worst fears. This was clear and unequivocal. All POWs were to be liquidated.)[4]

The POWs were all concerned. What would happen to them if there were an Allied invasion?

*

When not working, the sameness of life in a fixed, large camp was becoming ever more boring for most men. Some kept themselves busy learning. There were still some small groups discussing books, history and mathematics. Vegetable gardens were vital to supplement the diminishing rations. They had to be fertilised, not in the traditional Australian way with cow, sheep or goat's manure, but with human sewage. Other enterprising types created a broom factory. Some made chalk from clay, or glue from fish scales. Still others made knitting needles or reconditioned shaving brushes.

The ingenuity of the prisoners knew no bounds. Every possible item was utilised, often far beyond its use-by date. Razor blades were rubbed against a piece of glass, which kept them sharp for shaving. Small pieces of wood were pared back at one end until they looked like a broom, and this was used as a toothbrush.

Despite all the activity, many had lost interest in everything except eating the rations (down to a woeful 8 ounces of rice and 4 ounces of vegetables a day in March 1945), and sleeping. Les Cody of the 4th Machine Gun Battalion summed it up:

'The deadly monotony of a daily round of doing bugger all, talking to the same blokes, saying the same things, lining up for the same tasteless meals—the repetition of heat, hunger and hopelessness—created a mental pressure that at times became unbearable.'[5]

The number of patients in the mental ward at Woodlands Hospital, Kranji, increased. It was run by 2/9th Field Ambulance medico, Major John Cade. Before the war, he had been a senior psychiatric specialist in Melbourne. During his Changi years he witnessed firsthand how mental health was affected by chemical imbalances and nutrition. (After the war, he pioneered work on the development of lithium, a naturally occurring salt, in the treatment of bipolar disorders and manic depression.)

Chitty's salvation from despair brought on by the conditions at Changi and his work on the Thai–Burma railway was in part due to his insistence on keeping fit. He would play 'kick to kick' with a few mates on the padang on most days, and he applied himself to physical work whenever he could, despite his back problems.

But even this kind of approach for many could not fend off the building boredom, frustration in the camp, malnutrition, and starvation for many.

The number of walking skeletons increased in March and April.

In April, Adolf Hitler's suicide in a bunker in Berlin was reported but not believed by all in the camp. Then, on 8 May 1945, Germany capitulated. But Japan had no intention of following its Axis partner in surrendering.

The US could now turn all its mighty resources to defeating Japan in the Pacific. One secret area had been the development of the atomic bomb—the Manhattan Project. It was complete by mid-1945. A test at a US site in Alamagordo, New Mexico was successful in mid-July. US President Truman was told by his military leaders that Japan would have to be invaded to end the war. This would cause an estimated

500,000 further American casualties, along with thousands of Allies, including Australians. Japanese casualties in the same numbers were anticipated.

These figures were predicated on the basis of a swift US victory. If it were prolonged, the casualties on both sides would grow. If the war continued, countless POWs in Asia in camps like Changi would also be starved to death, or liquidated as instructed in orders already circulated to Japanese commanders.

Truman weighed his options. He decided to drop one of these new, terrible weapons on a Japanese city to force the emperor to capitulate.

At 1.45 a.m. on 6 August 1945, the US B-29 bomber *Enola Gay* took off from Tinian Island in the Marianas. The plane carried one atomic bomb with an enriched uranium core. The bomb, like the B-29, was given an innocuous, user-friendly name: 'Little Boy'. It had an explosive force of 12,500 tons of TNT.

It was dropped at 8.15 a.m. on the city of Hiroshima, killing 80,000. Three days later on 9 August, another atomic weapon ('Fat Man'), this time with a plutonium core and an explosive force of 22,000 tons of TNT, was dropped on Nagasaki, killing 40,000.

On 15 August, Emperor Hirohito surrendered in a radio broadcast picked up in Changi. The Japanese officers and guards were stunned. Some cried. They had expected a 'fight to the death', but their emperor, appraised of the destructive power of the two atomic weapons, realised any 'battle' against such a force was futile.

*

After three and a half years of fighting hunger and disease, and often savage treatment, it was over for POWs on Singapore and everywhere. There was no immediate celebration in Changi, or outside for those on work assignments. Two radio operators in a hut outside the jail picked up the news from the BBC and were the first to know. But work programs did not cease until 17 August. When those involved came back to Changi, the only part of the camp that became even busier than before was the hospital. Since it had begun functioning in March 1942, 80,000 cases (many of them more than once) had been admitted. There would be no rest for doctors and orderlies just yet. More than 2,000 ill men still had to be attended to.

It was not until 23 August that the Japanese commander Saito called a conference with the senior POW officers and told them the war was nearly over, although it had officially finished eight days earlier. He asked if they wanted anything for the prisoners. Ship-loads of Red Cross food supplies from Australia, Britain, Canada, South Africa, the US and Holland were unlocked. Meat, butter, cheese and sugar were provided for the inmates. Nutrition improved. Some men responded and put on weight. Others, ill and emaciated, would take years to recover.

On 28 August, an Allied plane flew over Changi and dropped leaflets about help on the way. This was the first real contact with the outside world. POWs cheered, cried and hugged one another. It was almost complete acceptance that they were safe. Celebrations began.

Fred Seiker summed up the feelings of many POWs throughout South-East Asia:

'I had become a person again, as sudden as it had been ripped away from me all those years ago . . . I cannot begin to tell you how this news was received by us. Some sank to their knees and began to pray. Others just stood there, tears streaming down their haggard faces. A few were running around, wildly gesticulating and screaming. I could not grasp the enormity of what had happened. I remember the feeling of triumph that swept over me. I had done it! I had outlived all attempts by Hirohito and his murdering freaks to kill me. But above all else, I could say "NO" again to anyone and everyone. It is called democracy and freedom. Believe me, it's worth fighting for.'[6]

On 29 August, British ships entered Penang Harbour. Medical supplies were dropped on Changi aerodrome.

A few days into September, Australian troops arrived, followed by British occupation troops led by Lord Mountbatten.

On 7 September, Allied troops occupied Singapore. They had to take over little Japanese camps all over Singapore, and some were expected to put up resistance. Not all would have known that the war was over. POWs intent on roaming around the island looting were prevented from doing so.

The Japanese guards and soldiers were made to clean the streets, latrines and anything else that was considered in need of a polish. Several Australian St John nurses appeared and engaged the men, who had not seen a 'white' woman for four years. Photographs showed the men's emaciated condition. Their faces—all smiles—expressed another kind of hunger.

Lord and Lady Mountbatten lifted spirits by visiting the camp and hospitals.

Soon after this, Vivian Bullwinkel and the other women internees held on Sumatra were liberated by a platoon of British paratroopers and two Australian soldiers.

The women knew it was September. One of the questions they asked their countrymen was about the VFL football results. The finals were on. Who was in them?

One man knew the answer: South Melbourne (Swans); Collingwood; North Melbourne; and Carlton (led by Bob Chitty), which had scraped into the finals after beating Footscray in the last round of the season.

During all this time, Peter Chitty was helping keep the camp clean. He had picked a crew to assist him. Their work included much burning off in an incinerator that was remote from the camp.

He had no idea for three weeks that he was a free man again.

Chitty was able to communicate with his wife. He wrote on 6 September:

> 'Dearest Lilian,
> This is a great pleasure to be able to write to you, after such a long time, with very little news . . . I am in the pink of condition; in

fact I am much heavier now than when I joined up. Glad to know Carlton is in the [final] "four" . . . we now hear the news and get quite a few of the race and football results. I hope Phil and Ron are keeping well and have not suffered too much through their ordeal. Tell dad to put a couple of bottles on ice as it is a long time since I had any. You looked very well in the last snap of you I received; not a day older than when I left . . . I am looking forward to seeing you all, and no words can express the joy we felt when the war was over . . . I have made some very good friends and you will meet them all when I get back . . . all my love to you and the children and may we meet soon,

Fondest love and kisses,
Yours for ever,
Peter.'

Lilian wrote back and sent photos. Peter replied on 12 September:

'My dearest Lilian, Dawn and Lindsay,
Well darling, I had the greatest thrill in three and a half years yesterday when I received the letters and the snaps. Gee, don't the children look well and you yourself look wonderful; you look still as young as ever. I have kept in the very best of health and will come back to you a bit wider. I have been mostly around 12 stone [76 kilograms] and have suffered no ill effects at the hands of the japs . . . Darling, when I return I have plans for a trip for you and I. Every day of waiting to get away from here seems like a life time, but I suppose they [authorities] are doing their best . . . what a celebration you and I will have when we are together again. I have prayed for you and the children and that it would not be long before we were together. While we were at Selarang way back

in 1942 we started a football comp. I was captain of our side. We played under the name Geelong. Ben Barnett the cricketer and Heyne of St Kilda played for us. We finished the comp just before we went up North to build the railway. I was lucky enough to win the Changi Brownlow Medal for the best and fairest. It is a great souvenir, so you can see that I can still play the old game. It is a lovely medal and I intend to make it into a necklace for my lovely wife when I get home. I was very sorry to hear about Auber [Lilian's brother] but it is not under our control to stop. Thank the good 'Lord' that the world has come to a standstill at last . . . I have lost a bit more of my lovely mop of hair . . . but I hope you will love me just the same . . . everyone here admires the children and they say that young "Peter" [Lindsay] is a chip off the old block. They also asked how I married such a lovely girl as you, but they don't know me, do they? . . .

Goodnight sweetheart. God Bless you and the children. Lots of love to all the family especially you, Dawn and Lindsay . . . LOVE ever yours, Peter.'[7]

After the years of nothing, false information and worry, the sudden flood of letters filled Lilian with joy and hope. Her instincts had been right after all. Her man was coming back to her and, from his description, bigger and better than ever.

42

The Not So Grand Final

The *Largs Bay*, a converted passenger ship, left Singapore on Friday 21 September 1945 with a big contingent of the former POWs bound for Darwin, Brisbane, Sydney and Melbourne. The next day, Peter Chitty and 1,000 other men were listening to the ABC broadcast over the ship's tannoy system of the preliminary final between Carlton and Collingwood played at Princes Park, Carlton's home. (The MCG was used by the armed forces during the war.) They were all thrilled to be hearing the footy again. Many felt a sense of home from the atmosphere coming from the tannoy of a big, noisy crowd, and the excited voices of familiar radio football commentators.

Peter listened as keenly as anyone. Bets were laid. Most of the money went on Collingwood (the Magpies), but Peter put a little money on Carlton (the Blues). Brother Bob was captain. The commentators informed the listeners that he had led his team 'brilliantly' to victory over North Melbourne in the first semi-final. North was making its first finals appearance since entering the league in 1925. But Bob had sliced the top off a finger in an accident at work just before the North Melbourne semi-final. No-one could tell how such a handicap would affect his game. 'He has a special [leather] guard over the injury,' the audience was informed. It had held up in the semi-final but he had taken plenty of knocks on it. He would play with pain.

Carlton was on an amazing roll. They had been on the bottom after game 4 of the 18-round season; 9th after 11 rounds, but had charged home to win eight of the last nine games to make the finals.

Now they were fighting (the operative word) Collingwood in front of 41,305 fans. Collingwood had been beaten by the Swans in the second semi and had to overcome the Blues to have another crack at the Swans in the grand final.

Peter looked to have lost his money in the opening term when Collingwood burst away to lead 5.2 (32) to 1.0 (6). The Blues fought back with two goals early in the term. Bob Chitty was 'prominent' getting kicks and flattening opponents, which brought jeers and cheers—for Peter's benefit—from those on deck. Tempers flared in the game. Players hurled themselves in. Brawls broke out. The roar of the spectators drowned out the raised voices of the commentators. After deciphering the comments that could be heard, it was clear that several players were throwing punches and kicking.

The crowd could be heard screaming and booing as the broadcast whistled in and out with variable reception. The commentators' mention of 'sinking the slipper' (kicking) raised eyebrows. Kicking had been almost taboo in Australian Rules. Everyone listening realised the match had to be extremely 'willing' for the affrays to stoop that far.

Carlton was inaccurate in front of goal, allowing the Magpies to hold a lead at half-time: 6.4 (40) to 4.7 (31).

Carlton overdid the vigour, led by Bob Chitty, in the third term. The Magpies, with more eyes on the football, skipped away again to lead 11.7 (73) to 6.9 (45) at three-quarter time.

At this point, the *Largs Bay*'s captain decided to shut down the broadcast.

'It was a pommie ship,' Bob Owen said, 'and the [English] captain thought the violence was too much for the audience!'[1]

The passengers learned later that Bob Chitty fired up his team positively in the last quarter after a vicious third term. Carlton turned on scintillating football, slamming on 7 goals 3 behinds in 18 minutes to win the game: 13.12 (90) to 12.8 (80).

Bob was adjudged in the top three on the ground, despite his nagging injury.

Peter was excited, but disappointed that he would miss the VFL grand final in Melbourne.

The *Largs Bay* arrived at Darwin Harbour on Friday 28 September. All on board were struck by the look of Australia's most northern city. It was a devastated war zone with the navy in occupation. The ex-POWs were aware that Darwin had been bombed many times, but seeing the results was another thing. The harbour was dotted with sunken ships. The wharf where 22 wharfies died in the initial raid was a tangled mess. The post office, where 11 telephonists had died, was in rubble, as were the hotels and other buildings on the esplanade looking out on the Harbour. Chinatown had been bulldozed except for some stone houses. A string of military camps dotted the horizon.[2]

The ex-POWs were placed in camp and treated well. Some went on picnics; others were taken on tours of the destruction.

On Saturday 29 September, Peter settled down in a hut with several mates to listen to the VFL grand final between South Melbourne and Carlton. Again, Carlton, which had come from nowhere mid-season, was the underdog. The general consensus of commentators was that the Swans would be too strong and talented. They appeared to have more incentive. Each South Melbourne player had been offered £20 if they won.

A massive crowd of 62,986 squeezed into Princes Park, the biggest attendance ever at this famous old ground. The gates were shut at 2.45 p.m.

A group of four young Australian students watched from the terraces: Arthur Boyd and John Perceval (two outstanding future artists), Tim Burstall (future director, who began the Australian film renaissance), and Brian O'Shaughnessy (who would go to England and become the UK's best and most radical philosopher). They were all fervent, one-eyed Carlton supporters.

'I remember Bob Chitty very clearly,' O'Shaughnessy said, 'he had a sort of faintly florid "drawn" face—not too many jokes in him. And of course with all our total approval, he was reputed to be one of the dirtiest players in the league, along with [Carlton's] Ron Cooper of the bare, greased arms . . . Chitty was a good, but not dazzling player . . . tenacious . . . A bit grim looking and deadly serious. He played Ned Kelly in some rather amateurish film. It seemed a pretty odd choice—but no odder than Mick Jagger who Tony Richardson cast for the role. [Richmond's tough guy] Jack Dyer said that this was the first time Bob Chitty ever needed armour.'[3]

No radios were allowed in the Darwin camp where officious officers were still acting as if Darwin could be raided again at any moment. Peter turned the radio down to avoid detection and sipped a beer. His mates leaned close over a card table.

Bob Chitty won the toss and kicked with a strong wind. But Carlton, uncertain and nervous in front of such a rowdy, involved crowd could not take advantage of a four or five goal breeze. The commentators remarked that there had been plenty of 'push and shove' in a fiery encounter. It was scrambly as South Melbourne bottled the ball up in Carlton's forward line. Star Blues forward Lance Collins, who had kicked 4 goals against Collingwood, was limping around the flank.

Carlton led 2.4 (16) to 0.5 (5) at quarter time. But the Swans' solid defence had given them a moral victory for the first term. They opened sweetly with the wind, with two snap goals to hit the front. Bob Chitty, tearing off his half-back flank position, ran through the Swans' young Ron Clegg with a shirt-front. Clegg was out cold. The bump was deemed legitimate under a rule that had been rewritten during the war, which stated a player could bump another within four and a half metres of the ball. It led to more use of the shirt-front, where a player could charge another, who might have his eyes on the ball, as long as it was seen to be 'in play'— again, less than four and a half metres from the ball. Chitty was the leading exponent of this bump in the competition, even more proficient at it than Jack Dyer.

In this case, Chitty's intervention had the desired effect of slowing South down. It was a grand final. A lot was at stake.

A scrimmage ensued. The umpire (Spokes) did not resume play until the pushing and abuse stopped.

A minute later, Bob Chitty scored his second shirt-front victim: South's Billy Williams. He was unconscious for many seconds, but trainers revived him for his free kick at goal. He was groggy and missed. South supporters screamed that Chitty raised his elbow. Carlton supporters said it was a 'fair bump' under the rules. Whatever happened, the umpire turned Chitty around and took his number, indicating he had been reported.

Bob Chitty was being booed by South fans, who urged their players to 'even up'. But again, his tactical use of violence early in the game had real impact. The pattern of play changed. Players became heated, and the hot heads on South's strong forward line, such as the brilliant Laurie Nash, were put off their game and concerned about their opponents. They became conscious of Chitty's movements. Later, journalist and state footballer and cricketer Percy Beames said the Swans had the 'jittery Chittys'.

Peter in Darwin could hear the family name floating above the crowd noise. The commentators reported that Bob would face the tribunal during the week. Peter knew that his brother wouldn't care. Bob, 29, was nearing the end of his career after a decade at the top. He was desperate to be captain of a premiership side. Besides, there would be quite a lot of cash for him if the Blues won the flag.

Moments after the second Chitty incident, Carlton's Price goaled. South was rattled. As the ball was relayed back to the centre, Jack 'Basher' Williams knocked Carlton's Ken Hands unconscious. Williams, when asked about the incident, said Hands must have 'suffered sunstroke', an unusual if not inventive defence given the inclement weather. Umpire Spokes, trying to stop a melee, was informed by several Carlton players of Williams's guilt.

Now Carlton fans bayed for blood. The two teams started an all-in-brawl where fists and boots (again a surprise for listening Peter) were used.

The half-time bell rang. This helped stop the melee. The

umpire ran across to Basher Williams and spoke to him close up. Williams looked as if he might punch the umpire. His fellow players dragged him up the race and into the bowels of the stand.

A still unconscious Ken Hands was stretchered off the field. The booing by Carlton fans of the entire Swans team was so loud, that the commentators could not be heard even after the bell.

Peter Chitty poured a drink in the Darwin hut. His mates lit up cigarettes. None could remember such a fierce encounter. It sounded so hostile that there were fears the match could be called off.

Carlton 7.5 (47) held a 2 point lead over South 6.9 (45).

It was anybody's game, if it continued. A commentator wondered if the large number of ex-servicemen in the audience was a factor in the brutality. Were the players, most of whom had not served, showing how tough they were?

Rain fell during the interval. It was cold. Fights broke out in the closely packed crowd. The slippery surface and mud would increase the chance of more brawls on the field. It would also be better for Carlton. South was relying on its excellent foot short-passing game. The wet would slow them down.

Carlton trainers spent the entire half-time break reviving Ken Hands. He had severe concussion. The team's reserve was already on the field. Hands was expected to take his place on the field again for the start of the third quarter. He wandered on, trying to look alert. Inside a minute he took a strong overhead mark and goaled.

The weather helped Carlton a little but it was the Blues' longer kicking game that was a telling factor. Chitty was in the play, running hard off a back flank and marshalling his troops in the centre. He had turned the game. Now he was 'managing' it.

The match settled down in the third quarter. The continued fireworks did not transpire. Carlton seemed to have control at three-quarter time with the scores: Carlton 12.9 (81) to South 8.10 (58)—a lead for the Blues of 23 points.

South believed that Chitty's leadership was the key to Carlton's success. Hard-hitting Laurie Nash was designed to 'take Chitty out'. Nash delivered Chitty a 'king-hit' (an unsuspecting punch from behind) when not in the play early in the last quarter.[4] The incident caused an all-in brawl, which encompassed players, trainers, officials and ambulance men.

Chitty got to his feet with help. He was groggy. Trainers began moving him to the forward pocket, the 'graveyard position' where concussion victims were placed in the hope they would recover. Chitty brushed them off and moved slowly down the ground. He had just reached his new, unaccustomed place when the ball spun down field. Chitty grabbed it as it rebounded from a pack and kicked a goal.

It was an inspirational bit of play at a critical moment and seemed to break the Swans' spirit. Now its players were playing the man as if resigned to the fact they could not win.

Rain was bucketing down. Carlton's Jim Mooring was hit by South's Don Grossman. Clegg, probably still concussed from the previous quarter, again went down hard, this time when Ken Hands made a late tackle from behind. It was doubtful too if Hands knew what he was doing.

Wines of Carlton kicked a 60 metre punt that sailed

through as the rain sheeted in. The Blues had a handy lead of six goals. With half the final term gone, the game was all but over.

Another big fight developed. This time some spectators followed the police onto the field. Carlton's suspended player Fred Fitzgibbon, wearing an overcoat, could not help himself. He jumped the fence and joined the fracas. Police escorted him off the field. The Swans' Whitfield, who later boasted he had his 'normal quota' of six beers before the game, pulled the back of his jersey over his head and hid his number. It drew a few laughs among the thrills and spills. Whitfield had thrown more punches than anyone. Some connected. But his lack of discipline was a factor in South's decline.

Bottles were hurled over the fence. They were cleared from the field. The game resumed.

At that moment, an officer entered Peter Chitty's hut and confiscated the radio. Much to his chagrin, and the groans from the other ex-POWs, they were left without knowing who won.[5]

He discovered later that Carlton had in fact been victorious in the grand final, 15.13 (103) to South 10.15 (75).[6]

Devouring newspaper reports a few days later, Peter read that brother Bob, for the third final of the series, was among the top six in the game. He was the player of the series, although he drew many enemies from among the opposition fans for his rugged play, which sometimes stretched the rules.

Yet he was a Carlton hero and legend, having led them to an upset win in the 1945 grand final. It would be known forever as 'The Bloodbath'.

Ten reported players faced the tribunal on the following Tuesday. Whitfield received the biggest sentence—a year's suspension. Bob Chitty received eight weeks, which he would serve in the following season (1946). Chitty was confronted by Jack Williams (who also received eight weeks) at the tribunal. In the time honoured way, he challenged Chitty to 'come outside' for a fist fight. Chitty ignored him. His aggression had been timed to precision in the second quarter of the football match. Observers such as Tim Burstall said that Chitty's toughness, within the rules, had turned the game.[7]

The afternoon of listening to the football, even in the bleak Darwin surrounds and humidity, brought Peter to the full realisation that he was truly on home soil again.

His brother's performance, whether overly rugged or not, lifted his spirits as he sailed on to Melbourne and a family he had not seen for four years.

43

Homecoming

Lilian Chitty had heard nothing about Peter in Changi apart from his letters and it was well into October 1945. She knew of scores of other POWs and servicemen and women returning home. It was almost two months since the Japanese had surrendered and the POWs had been released. Lilian had heard stories of men dying since being liberated but refused to believe Peter would not survive. But still, there had been no word of or from him. What was happening?

One day in mid-October, she was in her local butcher shop. Her brother Stewart rushed in and handed her a telegram.

'It said he would be home that day,' she said. 'He was coming down from Sydney [by train],' and added with a laugh, 'I don't know to this day whether I paid for that meat!'

She hurried home, removed Dawn (now six, nearly seven) from school and got Lindsay (four, nearly five) ready. They caught a train to the Melbourne Showgrounds and waited.

A train full of servicemen arrived. The family looked for Peter. He wasn't on it. But Reg Lemke, a friend of his, was. He waited with the family for about eight hours. Lindsay was excited. It wasn't his dad, but he could have been. According to Lilian, the toddler had always thought every man in uniform he met was 'Dad'.

'Lindsay followed him [Lemke] around like a little dog,' Lilian recalled.[1]

A second train arrived. The family and the friend stood at the end of the platform watching everyone who wandered by. Lilian wondered what he would look like after four years. After all the horror stories, mostly true, about the emaciated and haggard look of POW survivors, she did not know what to expect. Then she spotted him. He was tanned, straight-backed and in good condition, apparently.

'He had not altered,' she said, 'not really. He appeared to be the same weight [as when he left].'[2]

The family embraced and rejoiced in the moment, as did hundreds of families around them.

After less than a week at home Chitty and all the other Changi POWs had to report to the Heidelberg Repatriation Hospital (near Melbourne) for a variety of tests for diseases such as malaria, hookworm, tapeworm and others. They were given atabrine for malaria, which made the skin go yellow. He met up again with many mates, including Len Lemke and Frank Lemin. Observation went on for a month before they were released, but all had to report back on and off until early December 1945.

Chitty then had to settle in at home. One of the first meals he was served by Lilian was a rice pudding. It amused Lilian's brother Stewart, who waited for Peter to react. But he devoured the pudding without complaint, unaware that all members at the table, including the children, waited in silence for his reaction.

'He didn't bat an eyelid,' Lindsay recalled. 'He never flinched when it came to nutrition of any kind. Rice, in any form was never a problem for him. He enjoyed it [post-war].'[3]

There was no rule book on how to adjust after three years of captivity, a third of it as a slave worker in the project from hell on the Thai railway. Nor was there a manual on how he should cope with two children he did not know.

He was peeved by Lindsay calling him 'Peter'. The little boy was simply repeating the name he had heard all the family referring to ever since he could remember. Dawn had the same problem. Both the children had no memory of their father. Peter was also irritated by his son always saying 'Mummy said . . .' Lilian had been the authority figure. Peter did not know how to deal with this (natural and inevitable) usurping of his role in the family.

'They [Peter and son Lindsay] didn't have the closeness that they should have until later on . . . They sorted it out themselves . . . It wasn't until Lindsay was about 14 or 15 [a decade later] that they started to get close. They began as strangers and became good friends.'

Lilian believed Peter fell into his role as father 'naturally'. He was 'so easy going'.[4]

He thanked her for running the household while he was away. Peter was sympathetic to her role, her situation and her concerns about him being away.

'He was good,' she said, 'when a lot of sympathy was for the men, and very little for the women [left at home during the war].'[5]

One problem among many that the former POWs had to deal with was the ignorance about their experiences. No reporters covered *their* war. There was a stigma attached to the capitulation by the British on Singapore. POWs were somehow shunned. They were not hailed or honoured in the manner of the soldiers who had fought in North Africa, the

Middle East, New Guinea or the Pacific. The lack of under-
standing about the ordeal at Changi and on the Thai railway
brought insensitive remarks, sometimes from surprising
quarters.

A doctor once remarked to Peter, 'You had it easy during
the war.'

'He came home angry,' Lilian said, 'and he was upset for
days.'[6]

Bob Owen had a similar experience. A doctor examined
him soon after the war and told him how well he was. No
questions were asked about how he had been treated and
how he was coping. Owen was annoyed.

'He had no idea of what we'd been through,' he said.[7]

Peter attempted labouring jobs in a Coburg timber yard in the
immediate post-war years, then later at Caltex, which meant
much lifting of 44 gallon drums. But his back could not cope.
The injury also finished his football playing days. But he did
find time to coach a local church team for a few years. Peter
couldn't keep away from the game he loved.

'Dad had strong hands,' Lindsay said. 'He acted as a mas-
seur at Coburg in the VFA. He supported Footscray in the
VFL because Lilian did.'[8]

He had another gentle 'hobby' that amused his daughter
Roslyn (Ros). On Saturday mornings, he would get out the
horseracing form and listen to vowel-crushing radio race
caller/tipsters, and decide on the day's winners.

'But he never put a bet on,' she said. 'He was no more than
an occasional small punter and he advised us not to gamble.'[9]

In the late 1940s, he found a job as clerk in an ordinance

office, which suited him better. He worked in that occupation until retirement at 65 in 1977.

Ben Barnett found himself in Singapore on business early in 1947. For whatever reason, he decided to visit Changi Gaol.

'We have an old friend of yours here,' the British Superintendent remarked, 'would you like to see him?'

Barnett had no idea who it was, but agreed to meet this mystery 'guest' in Changi. Soon afterwards the Superintendent led in a very tall figure. It was Lieutenant Murayama.

'Do you know me, Murayama?' Barnett asked.

The Japanese came to attention, clicked his heels, bowed and answered:

'Yes, Captain Barnetto.'

Barnett knew that at best, Murayama faced life in prison; at worst execution for war crimes. Any hatred Barnett had gave way to compassion.

'Is there anything I can do for you?' Barnett asked.

Murayama nodded, bowed again and handed him a letter to his family.

'Could you post this for me, please, Captain Barnetto?'

Barnett obliged.[10]

On 6 March 1947, Peter Chitty was awarded the British Empire Medal for his selfless deeds on the Thai railway. It had been recommended by British Colonel Lilley. Chitty was one of just 24 Australian POWs in Europe and Asia to receive an award for services rendered. Chitty was more than deserving of this recognition. But he was first to admit that he was representative of hundreds of men who showed exceptional endurance, courage and selflessness.

This silver, 3.5 centimetre circular award is called the 'Medal of the Most Excellent Order of the British Empire for Meritorious Service'. It was instituted by King George V (Queen Elizabeth II's grandfather) in 1922. Britannia is depicted sitting with the sun to her right. The legend around the edge reads: FOR MERITORIOUS SERVICE.

It came as a surprise for Peter, but a pleasant one.

The citation read:

L/Sgt [Lance Sergeant] CHITTY was a prisoner of war in Japanese hands from Feb 42 to Aug. 45. In 1943 he was a member of an AIF party engaged in construction of the Burma–Siam railway. During various long marches through the jungle under extremely difficult conditions L/Sgt Chitty set an outstanding example of unselfish conduct and courage continuously helping the sick by carrying their kits as well as his own and helping them along and constructing shelter for them when halted. By these means he undoubtedly saved lives. During the whole period that he was in Burma–Siam and subsequently in Malaya, L/Sgt Chitty was outstanding in conduct and devotion to duty under difficult circumstances.[11]

Two years later, on 15 March 1949, Peter, Lilian, Dawn (aged 10) and Lindsay (aged eight) attended an investiture in Queen's Hall at Parliament House, Melbourne. Afterwards guests mingled in the gardens of Parliament House. Vivian Bullwinkel, the sole survivor of the Banka Island massacre, was there to receive her award: Associate of the Order of the Royal Red Cross. Peter had known her from the war and had the highest regard for her and all the nurses for their selfless work in the hospitals. He had never forgotten taking some of them down to the ship in Singapore in the hope they would escape. The fate of all those with Bullwinkel caused him further grief, especially when he reflected in later decades on this cruel injustice.

Don Bradman and his wife Jessie also attended to receive his knighthood. He asked Peter and Bullwinkel about their war experiences and congratulated them.

'What a lovely man Don Bradman was,' Lilian remembered. 'He had genuine humility.'[12]

Lilian pinned the medal on Lindsay's chest. He was most annoyed when the press and photographers showed more interest snapping Bradman, Jessie and Bullwinkel.

Later, Peter always said that although 'greatly honoured' to receive the BEM, the Changi Brownlow meant much more to him. His near-superhuman efforts on the Burma–Thai railway were nothing special to him. He had the strength to help his mates, and always did. He expected it from them if the situation had been reversed. This attitude exemplified the true Anzac spirit as much as any battle action. But the 'Brownlow' was something else, especially as his career in top football had been cut so short. It appealed to his competitive instincts—a striving to win and be the best. His performances in the Changi games had been also his way of telling his captors that the 'Anzac' collective spirit could never be broken.

He kept the football medal close at all times as a good luck charm. It was his most prized possession, ahead of the BEM and Phar Lap's 1930 racing plate (given to him by the great horse's farrier during a race meeting in 1930).

*

Lilian did not see any marked change in Peter's personality after the war. He was the same relaxed character he had been when she first met him. But like most of the POWs who had experienced so much horror, he did have nightmares.

Lilian tried to induce him to talk about Changi, but in the early post-war period, he would only tell her about the amusing moments. Peter reserved conversations about the less palatable incidents, especially on the railway, for the army mates that had been with him at his unit's reunions, or on Anzac Day.

'They'd talk about it,' Lilian recalled, 'and then that night he would have nightmares.' She would wake him up and talk with him until he calmed down.[13]

Other events that triggered exhausting and bad memories were the war crimes trials from 30 November until 9 April 1951. There were 924 enemy nationals—mostly Japanese— tried in 296 trials conducted by Australian military courts at eight venues: Labuan, Wewak, Morotai, Rabaul, Darwin, Singapore, Hong Kong and Manus Island. Of these, 146 were sentenced to death and executed. A further 496 were given prison sentences.

The media covered them. They were reported in the papers. Peter and all the POWs wanted to know what happened to the nastier Japanese of all ranks whom they had endured. The experience brought back horrific memories they would otherwise attempt to forget or block out.

Peter and Lilian had two more children after a long gap, who they jokingly called their 'second family'. Roslyn (Ros), born in 1952, went on to be a senior AFL administrator. Roger, born in 1956, has spent 30 years with the Melbourne Metropolitan Fire Brigade and is outstandingly fit, running brigade fitness training. He and Lindsay were very much their father's sons when it came to sports, hobbies and vocations that served the community. Lindsay (born in 1940) retired in 2008. He began his working life as a farmer. He next worked with St John Ambulance as a patient transport officer driving ambulances. Later Lindsay spent more than a decade working in aged care. His last three years was as a trainer at St John Ambulance. His life-long love was rodeo-riding of wild horses and bulls, a 'sport' at which he excelled and won many competitions.

(Peter and Lilian had 10 grandchildren and six great-grandchildren.)

The decision in the early 1950s to extend the family was in part to give Peter a renewed and complete sense of fatherhood after missing out on the early childhoods of Dawn and Lindsay. It also gave him peace of mind after what he perceived as the lost and wasteful years of a POW.

44

Of Memories and Medals

Nearly three decades after the war, Peter opened up a fraction to Lilian about what he and his fellow POWs had been through on the Thai railway.

Many images disturbed him. One was of the funeral pyres he had to make in the cholera camps for his fellow Australians, who had fallen victim to the disease.

'The bodies would squeak, sit up, crack and explode,' he recalled. These memories were among many that haunted him from the moment they happened to the end of his life.[1]

Lilian encouraged him to be with the men who had experienced similar events. She thought, despite the nightmares, it was 'good' for her husband; a form of catharsis. Yet it wasn't enough. In 1974, he was admitted to Rockingham Hospital in Kew, Melbourne for psychiatric care. It was about the time of the death of his mother, Hannah, which may have triggered emotions, for he had always been sympathetic to her pain over having seven children in service in World War II. He considered that she would have suffered more than anyone else in the family, especially over Toxa's death.

'It was the only time I saw him cry,' Ros Taylor (Chitty's daughter) said. 'He was stoic as most [of that generation] were. I remember it because it was so rare, despite him being a very compassionate man.'

While in the Kew hospital, Peter carved a wooden rocking

horse for Ros's daughter Kellie, who was two at the time. The family was touched by his generosity even in a time of such stress.[2]

Peter stayed two months at Rockingham and recovered, but was still haunted by events at Changi and on the Thai–Burma railway. In 1991, at age 79, he had open-heart surgery, in which a valve was replaced. Peter 'kept the whole [hospital] ward awake,' Lilian said. 'He reckoned the Japs were going through the ward.'[3]

Fred Seiker, who also managed well after some early post-war psychiatric care, said nightmares were the one 'incredible point' that he had in common with other POWs alive after half a century and more 'of civilised living'.

'It would seem that the brain does not forget,' he said, 'however hard one tries to wipe out certain events. I can't make up my mind if this is a good or a bad thing.'[4]

An analysis by the Department of Veterans' Affairs of ex-POWs indicated that many experienced one or more episodes of psychiatric problems.

'POWs often suffered nightmares about war experiences and avoided activities that might arouse recollection of those experiences,' the report found. It was put down to post-traumatic stress disorder (PTSD), a condition that was not recognised until about 1980—more than 35 years after the events that caused them for Changi POWs. Until then it was categorised as 'shell shock' or 'combat fatigue'.

PTSD has since been associated with 'psychologically distressing events outside the range of usual human experience'. This included 'rape or assault, earthquakes, plane crashes, bombing, torture and internment in death camps'. The Changi POWs fell into the last three categories, increasing their chances of experiencing such trauma long after the events that caused it.

The DVA report said that 'sufficient trauma will induce PTSD in almost anyone'. It also suggested that POWs experienced chronic depression and anxiety more than non-POWs. Experts suggested that the difference between the two groups was caused by 'catastrophic stress' experienced by ex-POWs.

The 1990 report—45 years after the POWs returned to Australia—said that 'because of the coping mechanism of the POWs, and their generally stoic approach, psychiatric and psychological problems tended to go undetected, undiagnosed and untreated'. This fitted well with Chitty and his mates. 'Suppression and denial', the report added, were what was expected from tough-minded men of their generation and background. One POW interviewed by the DVA said:

'If you admitted you were sick, then you were dead.'

In many cases, the report concluded, 'that ethos has persisted throughout civilian life'.[5]

Many wives of POWs spoke to Lilian about how bitter and moody their men became in their later years, three or four decades after the events at Changi and on the Thai railway. Peter had limited bad periods. There was also the occasional moodiness in front of his family and friends. But those close to him rolled with the 'grumpy' moments. Lilian felt they were more related to his deteriorating health, especially his poor back, than anything psychological.

The aftermath of Changi and the Thai–Burma railway experience affected many POWs in different ways. A small percentage committed suicide. Many sought psychiatric and other mental health specialists. Some were mentally crippled for the rest of their lives. Others spent the rest of their days in hospital. Character changes were enough to destroy marriages and families. Others appeared to cope with the mental side, but suffered physically forever. Intermittent malaria attacks, beriberi, tropical ulcers and other diseases left 'scars'. For instance, those with years of dysentery often ended up with enlarged spleens and livers, and permanent digestive system disorders.

Despite all he had been through, and all he had seen, Chitty seemed to hold few if any grudges against the Japanese. He felt that the guards were under orders to behave the way they did.

'He drove a Toyota,' daughter Ros noted, 'and never spoke ill of his captors. He hated the Japanese officers and the emperor, but not most of the guards, who he said at times were treated just as badly as the POWs.'[6]

Both Lindsay and Roger—a generation apart—found Peter to be a strict but fair father.

'He was the toughest man I ever knew,' Roger said, 'and I don't just mean in the physical sense.'[7]

Peter's selfless manner influenced them into work in community service. Peter's example and self-discipline influenced their approaches to life, as did their mother.

'Dad like many great men went over to fight for their country,' Roger said, 'and mostly received the accolades that they deserved. But lesser known is how the women of that era rolled up their sleeves and became the backbone of this

country, without complaint, with dignity and without thinking about themselves. It's just what that generation did and
my mother wasn't any different.'[8]

The bond between the POWs remained strong. The Chittys
would often visit the upper Murray region including Albury
and Yarrawonga and see fellow POWs and their families.
They attended a service in Weary Dunlop's honour in the
early 1990s. He congratulated Peter on his BEM and said
these kinds of awards (which he too received) were 'for all the
men and women who endured'.

Peter agreed. He had little to do with Dunlop, who only
crossed paths with him briefly at Changi. But he had 'enormous' regard for all the doctors, including Bruce Hunt, Roy
Mills, Frank Cahill, Lloyd Cahill, Rowley Richards, John
Cade and Albert Coates.[9]

Peter marched with his unit on Anzac Day until the latter
years of his life when the distance walked from the city to the
Melbourne shrine on St Kilda Road became too much. After
each march, he did not spend much time with his mates. Perhaps there would be one beer at a pub. But he never indulged
in the time-honoured several-hour binge of a happy reunion.
He preferred to return to Lilian, and the family home.

Peter's granddaughter Kellie was killed in a car accident, aged
22 in 1994. He had been close to her, as he had his other
grandchildren, and this hit him hard. He had seen enough
death and misery during the war to last several lifetimes.
This was a tragedy for him and the family. He had suffered

from 'survivor's guilt' often enough during his years as POW, and afterwards, seeing close mates about Kellie's age struck down in their prime. To have it happen again in his maturity touched him deeply.

Lilian had urged Peter to travel with her back to Thailand to face the past, thinking it might appease any lingering demons and put his mind to rest. He had made up his mind to do it just before he became too ill to travel such a distance. Peter died on 27 March 1996 aged 84, his valve replacement having failed after giving him 17 years more of reasonably healthy living. He had survived for more than half a century after his ordeal at Changi and in Thailand ended. Peter was buried at Melbourne's Fawkner Cemetery after a chapel service. About two hundred friends and family members attended. Lilian, determined to comprehend more of what he had been through, visited Thailand with Ros, Roger and his wife Tracy, six years later in 2002.

'We went to Hellfire Pass,' Ros recalled, 'and it was a terrific experience. We attended an Anzac Day service there on my 50th birthday.'[10]

On 20 August 2004, the Changi Brownlow was donated by the Chitty family to the Australian War Memorial, Canberra. On hand for the presentation were Lilian and son Roger. Australian Rules football legend Ron Barassi spoke at the ceremony. He felt a connection to Changi and World War II. Barassi's father, Ron Sr, like Toxa Chitty, was a Rat of Tobruk who was killed in Libya. Barassi's uncle by marriage was one of Weary Dunlop's first successful amputation patients in the POW camps. Barassi paid tribute to Peter Chitty and the Australian POWs who created and ran the prison competition.

'Given our [Australian] reputation in war, which is strong,' Barassi noted, 'and our reputation in sport, which is also strong, this [Changi Brownlow story] is a fascinating combination.'[11]

Accepting the medal from the family, the director of the Australian War Memorial Major-General Steve Gower said it 'symbolised the Australian tradition of turning to sport to maintain morale'.

'It emphasises the importance of supporting those in your team,' General Gower added. 'Given its unique history and significance, the Changi Brownlow will be a valuable addition to the memorial's national collection.'[12]

In 2005, the medal was shown to the nation as part of the memorial's Sport and War collection, in a travelling exhibition. Its significance was perpetuated in Singapore too. The Singapore AFC (Australian Football Club) decided to dedicate a replica of the medal to honour Chitty and the Australian armed forces. It is awarded to the best player for the visiting naval ship teams in games by the Wombats (the Singapore AFC) against the navy in Singapore.

The Changi Brownlow, symbolic of a unique Australian spirit at a time of crisis, will always be associated with an exceptional human being. Peter Chitty's physical and mental strength, his selfless acts and his compassion for others were demonstrated in the most testing of times in Australia's history.

He was an inspiration to all who came in contact with him.

Notes

Chapter 1: Changi Rules

1 Interview, Lilian Chitty, 8 February 2009; Interview, Len Lemke, 6 September 2004; Interview, Joe Jameson, 8 January 2009.
2 Chicken Smallhorn to Jack Dyer, *The Footy Show*, Channel 7, 2 September 1962.
3 Interview, Lilian Chitty, 8 February 2009; Interview, Len Lemke, 6 September 2004; Interview, Joe Jameson, 8 January 2009.
4 John Frew was later knighted and became a well-known figure in Melbourne medical circles.
5 Barnett, Ben, speech to Scotch College students, *Argus*, 22 October 1945. Barnett (AM—for services to cricket and tennis), was appointed President of the International Lawn Tennis Association in 1969 and was Australia's representative on the London-based International Cricket Council. His cricket achievements included wicket-keeping for Australia, Victoria and Buckinghamshire. In four Tests, he made 195 runs at an average of 27.85 and had five dismissals. He scored 5,531 first class runs at 27.51, including four centuries and made 357 dismissals, including a remarkable 142 stumpings. Barnett was a good Australian Rules footballer at school, playing for Scotch College, Melbourne's First XVIII in 1924 and 1925. He was a fine amateur player for Old Scotch Collegians in the 1920s and 1930s.
6 ibid.
7 Interview with Lilian Chitty, 8 March 2009.

Chapter 2: The Long-Distance Runner

1 Interview, Lindsay Chitty, 29 January 2009.
2 Interview, Roger Chitty, 28 January 2009; Notes from Roger Chitty 7 July 2009; Further information from Chitty family members: Lindsay Chitty, Nancy Pattison (nee Chitty) (Peter's sister), Ken Chitty (Peter's brother); and historian Carl Johnson.
3 Interview, Peter Chitty, Radio 3AW, 25 April 1992.
4 Information supplied by Colin Hutchinson at the AFL; *Sporting Globe*, 18 July and 1 August 1936; *Football Record*.
5 Interview, Lilian Chitty, 12 February 2009.

Chapter 4: Fire-Storm

1 Peter Chitty, Radio 3AW, 25 April 1992.
2 Interview, Nancy Pattison, 19 January 2009.
3 Interview, Lilian Chitty, 20 December 2008.
4 The author's great-grandfather.

Chapter 5: Fights Big and Small
1 Interview, Lindsay Chitty, 30 January 2009.
2 Interview, Ken Chitty (aged 79 and living at Wodonga, the last living brother of Peter), 4 August 2009.
3 Michael Davis, *Sun*, (undated), article in Chitty family archive.
4 ibid.

Chapter 6: On Again
1 Interview, Lindsay Chitty, 27 January 2009; Interview, Ken Chitty, 4 August 2009.
2 ibid.
3 Beattie, Rod, *The Death Railway*, Image Makers, Bangkok, 2006, p. 9.

Chapter 7: Destination Unknown
1 Lemke, Len, *Letters to Wendy: Recollections of a Prisoner of War*, Walla Walla, c. 2003, p. 3.
2 ibid.
3 Interview, Joe Jameson, 8 January 2009.
4 Veitch, Gerard H., Diary entry, 16 February 1941, from 'War Diaries and Recollections of Lt Gerard Harvey Veitch', AWM.
5 ibid., p. 4.
6 *Sydney Morning Herald*, 14 February 1938.
7 Interview, Joe Jameson, 8 January 2009.
8 Penicillin was first used to treat wounded Allied soldiers of the D Day invasion of Normandy, France, 6 June 1944.

Chapter 8: Mad Dogs and Englishmen
1 Interview, Lilian Chitty, 13 January 2009.
2 Ibid. Corporal Stewart Harvey Prowse (11757) served in the RAAF as an aircraft mechanic in 77th Squadron; Corporal Horace Auber Prowse VX48775 served in the Australian Army—2/23rd Australian Infantry Battalion—as a stretcher bearer. He also played in the band.
3 Lemke, Len, *Letters to Wendy: Recollections of a Prisoner of War*, Walla Walla, c. 2003, pp. 4–5.

Chapter 9: Confusion at the Top
1 *Telegraph*, UK, 18 July 1942.
2 Legg, Frank, *The Gordon Bennett Story*, Angus & Robertson, Sydney, 1965, p. 224.
3 ibid., p. 179.
4 National Archives Australia, File VX11669 on Ronald Henry Chitty.
5 The Brownlow Medal award was suspended from 1942 to 1945. The VFL believed that the competition had been weakened by the absence of top players who had enlisted to serve either in the regular or militia forces. It would be restored after WW2 in 1946.

Chapter 10: Japan Attacks

1 Johnson, Carl, *Carrying On Under Fire and in Captivity*, History House, Melbourne, 2009, p. 35.
2 ibid., p. 36.
3 Aspinall, George & Bowden, Tim, *Changi Photographer: George Aspinall's Record of Captivity*, ABC Enterprises and William Collins, 1984.
4 Bennett, H. Gordon, *Why Singapore Fell*, Angus & Robertson, Sydney, 1944, pp. 64–5.

Chapter 11: Wanted: One Digger Division

1 Lemke, Len, *Letters to Wendy: Recollections of a Prisoner of War*, Walla Walla, c. 2003, p. 9.
2 Bennett, H. Gordon, *Why Singapore Fell*, Angus & Robertson, Sydney, 1944, p. 74.
3 Morrison, James, 'Tiger's bluff led to a quick capitulation', *Weekend Australian*, 15 February 1983.
4 Johnson, Carl, *Carrying On Under Fire and in Captivity*, p. 42.
5 Interview, Frank Lemin, 13 January 2009.

Chapter 12: Ambush at Gemas

1 Legg, Frank, *The Gordon Bennett Story*, Angus & Robertson, p. 88.
2 Kappe, Charles, The Malayan Campaign, AWM <www.awm.gov.au/Mica_documents_catalogue/research_centre/RC00789_1.pdf.>
3 Legg, Frank, *The Gordon Bennett Story*, p. 198.

Chapter 13: The Hunter and the Hunted

1 Chitty family archive.
2 Kappe, Charles, The Malayan Campaign, Chapters 11 & 12: <www.230battalion.org.au.History>;AWM<www.awm.gov.au/Mica_documents_catalogue/research_centre/RC00789_1.pdf.>
3 Johnson, Carl, *Carrying On Under Fire and in Captivity*, p. 58. Croft was later killed by the Japanese when making a raid on them with the communists.

Chapter 14: Singapore Siege

1 Johnson, Carl, *Carrying On Under Fire and in Captivity*, p. 45.
2 Interview, Bob Owen, 8 April 2009.
3 Legg, Frank, *The Gordon Bennett Story*, Angus & Robertson, Sydney, 1965, p. 237.

Chapter 15: Softening Up

1 2/4th Casualty Clearing Station, Hobbs, Alan, diary entry, 3 February 1942 (*Carrying On Under Fire and in Captivity*, p. 74).
2 Coates, Albert, & Rosenthal, Newman, *The Albert Coates Story*, Hyland House, Melbourne, 1977, p. 62.

3 Bennett, H. Gordon, *Why Singapore Fell*, Angus & Robertson, Sydney, 1944, p. 163.

Chapter 16: Falling Fortress

1 Charlton, X., 'Humiliating fall of an impregnable fortress', *Australian*, 15 February 1992.
2 Interview, Frank Lemin, 13 January 2009.
3 Lemke, Len, *Letters to Wendy: Recollections of a Prisoner of War*, Walla Walla, c. 2003, p. 11.
4 Johnson, Carl, *Carrying On Under Fire and in Captivity*, p. 84.
5 Interview, Lindsay and Peter Chitty, 23 July 2009.

Chapter 17: End-Battles

1 Lemke, Len, *Letters to Wendy: Recollections of a Prisoner of War*, Walla Walla, c. 2003, pp. 11–13, p. 85.
2 Legg, Frank, *The Gordon Bennett Story*, Angus & Robertson, Sydney, 1965, pp. 241–2.
3 ibid., pp. 186–7.

Chapter 18: Capitulation

1 Lemke, Len, *Letters to Wendy: Recollections of a Prisoner of War*, Walla Walla, c. 2003, pp. 11–13; Interview, Len Lemke, 14 August 2004; Interview, Frank Lemin, 13 January 2009; Interview, Joe Jameson, 8 January 2009; Chitty family archive; Aspinall, George & Bowden, Tim, *Changi Photographer: George Aspinall's Record of Captivity*, ABC Enterprises and William Collins, 1984, p. 37; Cody, Les, *Ghosts in Khaki*, Hesperian Press, Carlisle, Western Australia, 1997, pp. 191–2.
2 ibid.
3 ibid.
4 ibid.
5 Sources: Angell, Barbara, *A Woman's War: The Exceptional Life of Wilma Oram Young, AM*, New Holland, Australia, 2003; Manners, Norman G., *Bullwinkel*, Hesperian Press, Carlisle, Western Australia, 2000; de Vries, Suzanna, *Heroic Australian Women in War*, HarperCollins, Sydney, 2004; Best, John, *Portraits in Australian Health*, MacLennan & Petty, Sydney, 1988; Camilleri, Jenny, *Some Outstanding Women of Broken Hill and District*, Broken Hill Historical Society/Broken Hill Council, Broken Hill, 2002; 'Nurses four years ordeal', *Australasian Post*, 1 February 1962; 'She looked for a warm place to die', *Barrier Daily Truth*, 1 May 1972; 'Butchery on Bangka', *Daily Mirror*, Sydney, July 1977; 'Bullwinkel honoured as WWII hero', *Barrier Daily Truth*, 17 December 2001; 'Heroic wartime nurse Vivian Bullwinkel dies in hospital', *Canberra Times*, 17 December 2001.

Chapter 19: Day of Infamy: 15 February 1942

1 Johnson, Carl, *Carrying On Under Fire and in Captivity*, p. 133 (Report written while POW).

2 Aspinall, George & Bowden, Tim, *Changi Photographer: George Aspinall's Record of Captivity*, ABC Enterprises and William Collins, 1984, p. 36.

3 Lemke, Len, *Letters to Wendy: Recollections of a Prisoner of War*, Walla Walla, c. 2003.

4 ibid.

5 Information supplied by Charles Edwards. Chitty was true to his word. After the war, he donated the plaque to the 'Man from Snowy River' museum at Corryong, where it is today.

Chapter 20: Plight of the Sisters

1 Sources: Angell, Barbara, *A Woman's War: The Exceptional Life of Wilma Oram Young, AM*, New Holland, Australia, 2003; Manners, Norman G., *Bullwinkel*, Hesperian Press, Carlisle, Western Australia, 2000; de Vries, Suzanna, *Heroic Australian Women in War*, HarperCollins, Sydney, 2004; Best, John, *Portraits in Australian Health*, MacLennan & Petty, Sydney, 1988; Camilleri, Jenny, *Some Outstanding Women of Broken Hill and District*, Broken Hill Historical Society/Broken Hill Council, Broken Hill, 2002; 'Nurses four years ordeal', *Australasian Post*, 1 February 1962; 'She looked for a warm place to die', *Barrier Daily Truth*, 1 May 1972; 'Butchery on Bangka', *Daily Mirror*, Sydney, July 1977; 'Bullwinkel honoured as WWII hero,' *Barrier Daily Truth*, 17 December 2001; 'Heroic wartime nurse Vivian Bullwinkel dies in hospital', *Canberra Times*, 17 December 2001.

Chapter 21: Changi

1 Nelson, Hank, *Prisoners of War*, ABC Enterprises, Sydney, 1985, p. 22.

2 Wall, Don, *Heroes of F Force*, D. Wall, Mona Vale, 1993, p. v.

3 ibid.

4 As related by Len Lemke, interview, Joe Jameson, 11 December 2008.

5 Interview, Joe Jameson, 11 December 2008.

6 Lemke, Len, *Letters to Wendy: Recollections of a Prisoner of War*, Walla Walla, c. 2003, p. 16.

Chapter 22: There Goes Bullamakanka

1 Aspinall, George & Bowden, Tim, *Changi Photographer: George Aspinall's Record of Captivity*, ABC Enterprises and William Collins, 1984, p. 79: Interview, Joe Jameson, 11 December 2008.

2 Common description by POWs.

3 Interview, Lindsay Chitty, 23 July 2009.

4 Sources: Angell, Barbara, *A Woman's War: The Exceptional Life of Wilma Oram Young, AM*, New Holland, Australia, 2003; Manners, Norman G., *Bullwinkel*, Hesperian Press, Carlisle, Western Australia, 2000; de Vries, Suzanna, *Heroic Australian Women in War*, Harper-Collins, Sydney, 2004; Best, John, *Portraits in Australian Health*, MacLennan & Petty, Sydney, 1988; Camilleri, Jenny, *Some Outstanding Women of Broken Hill and District*, Broken Hill Historical Society/Broken Hill Council, Broken Hill, 2002.
5 Interview, Joe Jameson, 15 January 2009.

Chapter 23: Mind Games
1 Barnett, Ben, speech to Scotch College students, *Argus*, 22 October 1945.
2 Nelson, Hank, *Prisoners of War*, ABC Enterprises, Australia, 1985, p. 26; Braddon, Russell, *The Naked Island*, Pan Books, London, 1963, p. 258.
3 A similar story is told about a Japanese officer bursting into a Catholic meeting, indicating that there was probably more than a grain of truth in the anecdote/story.
4 Lemke, Len, *Letters to Wendy: Recollections of a Prisoner of War*, Walla Walla, c. 2003, p. 62.
5 Hatch, Hedley, Letter home, 1942.
6 From *The Changi Song Book*, Sound recording, Sydney, Larrikin, 1993.

Chapter 24: The Force's Forced Labour
1 Aspinall, George & Bowden, Tim, *Changi Photographer: George Aspinall's Record of Captivity*, ABC Enterprises and William Collins, 1984, p. 27.
2 Main, Jim & Allen, David, *Fallen: The Ultimate Heroes*, Crown Content, Melbourne, 2002, p. 213.
3 Johnson, Carl, *Carrying On Under Fire and in Captivity*, p. 217. Dr Park was never awarded the VC.
4 Hall, Leslie, *The Blue Haze*, Kangaroo Press, Kenthurst, 1996, p. 17.

Chapter 25: Subs in the Harbour and Headway at Midway
1 In November 2006, divers discovered the wreck of the midget off Sydney's northern beaches.

Chapter 26: Good Sports in Changi
1 Lemke, Len, *Letters to Wendy: Recollections of a Prisoner of War*, Walla Walla, c. 2003, p. 20.
2 Johnson, Carl, *Carrying On Under Fire and in Captivity*, p. 257.
3 Perry, R., *Sailing to the Moon*, Pennon, 2008, p. 53.
4 Interview on 3AW Radio Melbourne, 25 April 1992 with Ron Barassi, Rex Hunt and Shane Healy.

5   *Football Life*, September 1969, p. 3.
6   Interview with Maria Capela, Supervisor of Sherrin manufacture, Spalding Melbourne, 27 November 2009.
7   Barnett, Ben, speech to Scotch Collegians, Melbourne, 20 October 1945.
8   ibid.

Chapter 27: End at El Alamein
1   According to Lilian Chitty, Toxa left everything in his will except his car to a mystery woman named 'Erica'. (Videotape of Lilian Chitty, interviewed by son Roger Chitty, 2006. Chitty family archive.)
2   After action at El Alamein in the Middle East and New Guinea, 'Auber' Prowse, as he was known, was killed in action by mortar fire in New Guinea on 6 September 1943. Fearless and selfless to the last, he was shot when he ran to assist a wounded officer.
3   Interview, Lilian Chitty, 9 March 2009.

Chapter 28: An Offer He Couldn't Refuse
1   *Football Life*, September 1969, p 3; Interview, Joe Jameson, 8 January 2009; Chicken Smallhorn to Jack Dyer, *World of Sport*, Channel 7, 2 September 1962.
2   Johnson, Carl, *Carrying On Under Fire and in Captivity*, p. 219.
3   *Football Life*, September 1969, p. 3.
4   ibid.
5   Barnett, Ben, speech to Scotch College students, Saturday 20 October 1945.

Chapter 29: Incident at Barracks Square
1   Lemke, Len, *Letters to Wendy: Recollections of a Prisoner of War*, Walla Walla, c. 2003, p. 18.
2   ibid.
3   www. Australian War Memorial 'Stolen Years'; www.det.nsw.au/ media 'Barracks Square Incident'.
4   ibid.
5   Johnson, Carl, *Carrying On Under Fire and in Captivity*, p. 169.
6   ibid.

Chapter 30: End Games
1   AWM file on A Force, AWM54.554/2/1A + B.
2   *Football Life*, September 1969, p. 5.
3   ibid.
4   Barnett, Ben, speech to Scotch College students, Saturday 20 October 1945, *Argus*, 22 October 1945.
5   Johnson, Carl, *Carrying On Under Fire and in Captivity*, p. 257.
6   ibid.

7 Ebury, Sue, *Weary: The Life of Sir Edward Dunlop*, Penguin, Ringwood, 1995, p. 369.
8 ibid., p. 371.

Chapter 31: Brownlow Winner
1 Special report for Les Green by a reporter who covered the game, p. 11;
   Additional information from Bob Owen, interview 8 April 2009.

Chapter 32: Match of the Century
1 Chitty family archive; official record of the game; Chitty family interviews; Peter Chitty interview, Radio 3AW, Melbourne, 25 April 1992.
2 Official record: 'Victoria v The Rest', Chitty family archive, p. 2.
3 Interview, Joe Jameson, 8 January 2009; Chicken Smallhorn to Jack
   Dyer, *World of Sport*, Channel 7, 2 September 1962.
4 Report based on the official record of the match and interviews with
   witnesses, including Len Lemke, Joe Jameson, Bob Owen.
5 The official record had the seven best Victorians in order as Haig,
   McGrath, Small, Chitty, Green (9th Field Ambulance, Mentone), Joyce
   (9th Field Ambulance, Melbourne Eastern Suburbs) and Mullinger.
   The best in order for The Rest of Australia were Daley, Broadbent
   (Glenelg, South Australia), White (4th Machine Gun, Swan Districts),
   Sparkman (4th MG, Western Australian Goldfields), Williams (4th
   MG, Wembley, South Australia), White (4th MG, Swan Districts) and
   Kenny (4th MG, East Fremantle).
      Victoria's goal kickers: McGrath 6, Joyce 3, Chitty 2, Robinson (of
   the 9th's Convalescence Depot, Geelong Seconds) 1, Byrne (13th Aus-
   tralian General Hospital, Abbotsford) 1, and Small (the 9th, Echuca) 1.
      The Rest: White 3, Pearsall (9th and Lefoy, Tasmania) 3, Pearce
   (4th MG, Swan Districts) 1, Curnow (Port Lincoln Association, South
   Australia) 1, Williams 1, and Daley (4th MG) 1.
      Analysis of play:
      Kicks: Vic 179 Rest 161
      Marks: Vic 59 Rest 59
      Frees: Vic 17 Rest 21
      Passes: Vic 17 Rest 11
      Hit-outs: Vic 20 Rest 6

Chapter 33: F Force to Hades
1 Cody, Les, *Ghosts in Khaki*, Hesperian Press, Carlisle, Western Australia, 1997, pp. 246–7.
2 Lemke, Len, *Letters to Wendy: Recollections of a Prisoner of War*,
   Walla Walla, c. 2003, p. 25.
3 Quote from Wilson, Philip C., Signals 8th Division in 'The peace
   generation', *Courier Mail*, Brisbane, <news.com.au/couriermail/extra-
   sCharles Wilson>.

4   Johnson, Carl, *Carrying On Under Fire and in Captivity*, p. 267 (Lex Arthurton diary/interview).

Chapter 34: Good Doctor 'No'
1   Pee, Kay, *The Death Railway & The Bridge on the River Kwai*, Kanchanaburi Publications, Kanchanaburi, 2006, p. 38.
2   Interview, Bob Owen, 8 April 2009.
3   Wall, Don, *Heroes of F Force*, D. Wall, Mona Vale, 1993, p. 26.

Chapter 35: Through Hellfire Pass
1   Interview, Bob Owen, 8 April 2009.
2   'The Story of F Force', <2-26bn.org/fforce.htm> p. 2; p 573, AWM report on F Force; Cody, Les, *Ghosts in Khaki*, Hesperian Press, Carlisle, Western Australia, 1997, p. 247.
3   These two bridges were the inspiration for the 1957 released film *Bridge over the River Kwai*, starring Alec Guinness, Jack Hawkins and William Holden. The movie won seven Oscars and inspired tourists to search for the River and the bridge. To meet tourists' needs, the Thai authorities changed the name of the Maekluang to 'Kwai' (which was the British POW made-up word) in 1960.
4   From interview with Chitty, *Herald Sun*, 26 April 2001; *Age*: 'The day a brave bush boy won Changi Brownlow', 23 April 1996.
5   Wall, Don, *Heroes of F Force*, D. Wall, Mona Vale, 1993, p. 9. Chitty's selfless efforts with many of his fellow diggers, including James Downie, helped him gain the British Empire Medal, bestowed in 1947.
6   Pee, Kay, *The Death Railway & The Bridge on the River Kwai*, Kanchanaburi Publications, Kanchanaburi, 2006.
7   The 2/29th Battalion's Private James Thomas Downie (VX56699), 28, of Shepparton, Victoria reported at Lower Neike. He enlisted on 26 May 1941.

Chapter 36: In the Time of Cholera
1   Johnson, Carl, *Carrying On Under Fire and in Captivity*, Note 406, p. 269.
2   From the text of a speech given by Fred Seiker at the Kwai Railway Memorial Annual General Meeting in Sydney, October 1997 (Reported in Pee, Kay, *The Death Railway & The Bridge on the River Kwai*, Kanchanaburi Publications, Kanchanaburi, 2006).
3   Wall, Don, *Heroes of F Force*, D. Wall, Mona Vale, 1993, p. 137 (Hunt's words reported by Lieutenant Kelsey, who served in the 2/26th Battalion).
4   Interview, Bob Owen, 8 April 2009.
5   Wall, Don, *Heroes of F Force*, p. ix.
6   Mills invented the use of a small bamboo tube, a funnel made from an old can and a piece of rubber tubing fashioned from his stethoscope

to give nearly 100 infusions of salt and water into veins of cholera patients. This saved many lives (see Wall, Don, *Heroes of F Force*, p. ix, comment by Bruce Hunt).

7   ibid., p. 268, Note 406.
8   *The Death Railway & The Bridge on the River Kwai*, p. 51; Hardacre, J.F., *Story of F Force*, unpublished, Carl Johnson Collection.
9   ibid.
10 ibid.
11 Lemke, Len, *Letters to Wendy: Recollections of a Prisoner of War*, Walla Walla, c. 2003, p. 48.
12 Wall, Don, *Heroes of F Force*, p. 139.
13 ibid., p. 43.

Chapter 37: Engineering Madness
1   Comments by Peter Chitty to family members: Lilian and Lindsay.
2   Chitty never spoke of this, but others such as Arthurton managed to get more supplies than others for the patients and medical workers.
3   Peter Chitty to daughter Roslyn Taylor; Roslyn Taylor interview, 14 July 2009.
4   Interview Lindsay and Roger Chitty, 23 July 2009; also family archive; interview Len Lemke.
5   Interview with Charles Edwards, 15 March 2010. Edwards was Peter Chitty's cousin.
6   Hardacre, J.F., *Story of F Force*, p. 44.
7   ibid., p. 63.
8   ibid., p. 66.
9   Lemke, Len, *Letters to Wendy: Recollections of a Prisoner of War*, Walla Walla, c. 2003, p. 32.
10 ibid., p. 36.
11 Beattie, Rod, *The Death Railway*, Image Makers, Bangkok, 2006, p. 48.
12 Wigmore, Lionel, *The Japanese Thrust: Australia in the War of 1939–1945, Volume IV*, AWM, 1957, p. 579.

Chapter 38: End of the Line
1   The railway was not quite completed. In late October 1943, the track-laying parties working from the north and south met near Konkoita. A Japanese general drove a golden spike to signify the joining of the lines. It was not until December (the original deadline) that the Thai–Burma railway was fully operational.
2   Beattie, Rod, *The Death Railway*, Image Makers, Bangkok, 2006, p. 33.
3   Wigmore, Lionel, *The Japanese Thrust: Australia in the War of 1939–1945, Volume IV*, AWM, 1957, p. 579.
4   NAA files for Ron and Phil Chitty.
5   Interview, Bob Owen, 8 April 2009.

6 Wall, Don, *Heroes of F Force*, D. Wall, Mona Vale, 1993, p. 95.
7 Interview with Bob Owen, 8 April 2009. Thanks to Owen's determination, Baulton made it back to Changi and Australia. He lived another 63 years after the incident.
8 Wall, Don, *Heroes of F Force*, p. ix; Lemke, Len, *Letters to Wendy: Recollections of a Prisoner of War*, Walla Walla, c. 2003. About 2,700 men of the 13,000 who worked on the railway died on the project.

Chapter 39: Postcards from Thailand
1 Interviews, Lilian Chitty; Transcript of 'The lived experience of partners of ex-prisoners of war of the Japanese—a phenomenological study', by Betty Peters, January 1994 (Chitty family archive).
2 Interview with Charles Edwards, 31 March 2010.
3 Peter Chitty to family members.
4 Lemke, Len, *Letters to Wendy: Recollections of a Prisoner of War*, Walla Walla, c. 2003, p. 49.
5 ibid.
6 ibid.

Chapter 40: Cowra Break-Out
1 E. V. Timms, 'The Bloodbath at Cowra', in *As You Were*, AWM, 1950. Timms, a novelist, had served in the AIF in 1914–17. He was a major in the 22nd Garrison Battalion.

Chapter 41: The Wheel Turns
1 Lemke, Len, *Letters to Wendy: Recollections of a Prisoner of War*, Walla Walla, c. 2003, p. 72.
2 Norman Fischer, Diary entries 19 and 31 January 1945.
3 Interview, Roslyn Taylor. Story as told to her by her father (Peter Chitty), 14 July 2009.
4 Johnson, Carl, *Carrying On Under Fire and in Captivity*, p. 383.
5 Cody, Les, *Ghosts in Khaki*, Hesperian Press, Carlisle, Western Australia, 1997, p. 323.
6 From the text of a speech given by Fred Seiker at the Kwai Railway Memorial Annual General Meeting in Sydney in October 1997. (Reported in Beattie, Rod, *The Death Railway*, Image Makers, Bangkok, 2006, p. 48.)
7 Letters in Chitty family archive.

Chapter 42: The Not So Grand Final
1 Interview, Bob Owen, 8 April 2009.
2 Interview Dr Michelle Dewar, member of the Advisory Council, National Archives of Australia; Freelance Historical Researcher and consultant, Darwin.
3 Interview, Brian O'Shaughnessy, 30 March 2009.

4 Interview with Ken Chitty, who saw the game, 4 August 2009; Discussion, Tim Burstall, 10 October 2001.
5 Interview, Lilian Chitty, 10 December 2008.
6 Carlton Football Club website; 'Blueseum'; Argus football publication 1956; Atkinson, Graeme, *The Complete Book of AFL Finals*, Five Mile Press, Melbourne, 2002; Shaw, Ian W., *The Bloodbath: The 1945 Grand Final*, Scribe, 2006; Review of this book by Martin Flanagan, *Age*, 16 September 2006; Author discussion about 1945 grand final with Tim Burstall, 10 October 2001.
7 Bob Chitty later told Peter Chitty the story about Williams' challenge at the tribunal and said: 'Jack didn't really get it. The game had been played four days earlier. It was over. Carlton won the flag.' Peter Chitty said that his money in any fisticuff would have been on brother Bob, although he was not altogether supportive of Bob's rough-house ways as a footballer. Peter said in his 3AW interview that he had taught his younger brother how to play the game, and dirty tactics were not in the Chitty instruction manual.

Carlton missed the finals in 1946. Bob Chitty left Carlton and took up a lucrative offer to captain–coach Benalla. He played 147 games with Carlton and kicked 32 goals in 10 seasons. He was captain in 1945 and 1946, and Best and Fairest in 1941 and 1944. He was suspended just four times despite his reputation, for a total of 16 games. He died in 1985 aged 70. Bob Chitty was elected to Carlton's Hall of Fame in 1991. In May 2000, he was named as one of the four emergencies in the Carlton team of the 20th century.

The Ned Kelly film referred to by Brian O'Shaughnessy was *The Glenrowan Affair* (1951).

Chapter 43: Homecoming
1 Interviews, Lilian Chitty, December 2008, January, February, March 2009 (Lilian Chitty died, aged 92, on 29 June 2009).
2 ibid.
3 Interview, Lindsay Chitty, 23 July 2009.
4 ibid.
5 ibid.
6 ibid.
7 Interview, Bob Owen, 8 April 2009.
8 Interview, Lindsay Chitty, 15 April 2009.
9 Interview, Roslyn Taylor, 14 July 2009.
10 Hardacre, J.F., *Story of F Force*, p. 44.
11 AWM, Series accession number 119, Control symbol, 173 Part 2.
12 Interview, Lilian Chitty, 15 May 2009.
13 ibid.

Chapter 44: Of Memories and Medals
1 Interviews, Lilian and Lindsay Chitty, 15 April 2009.
2 Interview, Ros Taylor, 14 July 2009.
3 Interview, Lilian Chitty, 13 January 2009.
4 Interview, Fred Seiker, January 1997.
5 1990 DVA report: 'Lifelong Captives: The Medical Legacy of POWs of the Japanese'.
6 Interview, Ros Taylor, 14 July 2009.
7 Interview, Roger Chitty, 15 April 2009.
8 Eulogy by Roger Chitty at his mother's funeral, 3 July 2009.
9 Interviews, Lilian and Lindsay Chitty, 15 April 2009.
10 Interview, Ros Taylor, 13 July 2009.
11 Interview, Ron Barassi, 30 March 2009.
12 *Canberra Times*, Saturday 21 August 2004; *Age*, Saturday 23 April 2005: Lyon, Karen, 'Changi champ won war within a war', Forbes, Mark, 'Symbol of men's unconquered spirit: Changi Brownlow joins our sacred relics', *Age*, 21 August 2004.

Bibliography

Aspinall, George & Bowden, Tim, *Changi Photographer: George Aspinall's Record of Captivity*, ABC Enterprises and William Collins, 1984.

Beattie, Rod, *The Death Railway*, Image Makers, Bangkok, 2006.

Beattie, Rod, *The Thai-Burma Railway*, TBRC, Kanchanaburi, Thailand, 2007.

Bennett, H. Gordon, *Why Singapore Fell*, Angus & Robertson, Sydney, 1944.

Braddon, Russell, *The Naked Island*, Pan Books, London, 1963.

Caulfield, Michael, *War Behind the Wire*, Hachette, Sydney, Australia, 2008.

Coates, Albert, & Rosenthal, Newman, *The Albert Coates Story*, Hyland House, Melbourne, 1977.

Cody, Les, *Ghosts in Khaki*, Hesperian Press, Carlisle, Western Australia, 1997.

Dunlop, E. E., *The War Diaries of Weary Dunlop*, Nelson, Melbourne, 1986.

Ebury, Sue, *Weary: The Life of Sir Edward Dunlop*, Penguin, Ringwood, 1995.

Geddes, Margaret, *Remembering Weary*, Penguin, Ringwood, 1997.

Hall, Leslie, *The Blue Haze*, Kangaroo Press, Kenthurst, 1996.

Harris, Richard, *All in My Stride*, Hesperian Press, Carlisle, Western Australia, 1999.

Hutchinson, Garrie, *Heroes: 150 Players 150 Years: Melbourne Football Club*, Hardie Grant, Prahran, 2008.

Johnson, Carl, *Carrying On Under Fire and Captivity*, History House, Melbourne, 2009.

Legg, Frank, *The Gordon Bennett Story*, Angus & Robertson, Sydney, 1965.

Lemke, Len, *Letters to Wendy: Recollections of a Prisoner of War*, Walla Walla, c. 2003.

Lindsay, Patrick, *The Spirit of the Digger*, Pan Macmillan, Australia, 2003.

Main, Jim & Allen, David, *Fallen: The Ultimate Heroes*, Crown Content, Melbourne, 2002.

Nelson, Hank, *Prisoners of War*, ABC Enterprises, Australia, 1985.

Paterson, A.B., *The Collected Verse of A.B. Paterson*, Angus & Robertson, Sydney, 1951.

Ramsay, Ian, *POW*, Macmillan, Australia, 1985.

Richards, Rowley, *A Doctor's War*, HarperCollins, Australia, 2002.

Savage, Russell, *A Guest of the Emperor*, Boolarong Press, 2004.

Share, Pat, (ed.), *Mud and Blood in the Field*, Heritage, Victoria, 1978.

Thompson, Peter, *Pacific Fury: How Australia and Her Allies Defeated the Japanese*, William Heinemann Australia, 2008.

Timms, E. V., *As You Were*, AWM Publications, Canberra, 1950.

Wall, Don, *Heroes of F Force*, D. Wall, Mona Vale, 1993.

Wilson, Keith, *You'll Never Get Off the Island*, Allen & Unwin, Australia, 1989.

Wigmore, Lionel, *The Japanese Thrust: Australia in the War of 1939–1945, Volume IV*, AWM, 1957.

Documents

National Archives of Australia, WWII files on serving Chitty family members and other POWs.

Australian War Memorial, Sport and War Collection; Sport and War exhibition 2006; REL 32808 Brownlow Medal: Corporal L A 'Peter' Chitty, 2/2nd Australian Motor Ambulance Convoy.

AFL Archive (Courtesy Colin Hutchinson, historian).

Two museums at Kanchanaburi (one in the town run by Rod Beattie and another nearby memorial to Dr E. E. 'Weary' Dunlop) and a third at Hellfire Pass, provided much information and perspective.

Articles/brochures/tapes

Burke, Graham, 'Peter Chitty—Brownlow Medal Winner . . .' Undated; *Melbourne Sun*.

Cassidy, Frank, 'Family gives Changi Brownlow to War Memorial,' *Canberra Times*, 21 April 2004.

Daffey, Paul 'The Ten' (10 examples of sport and war), *Age*, 24 April 2005.

Davis, Michael, 'Changi's Football hero,' *Sun*, 24 April 1984.

'The day a brave bush boy won Changi Brownlow,' *Herald-Sun* (undated).

Flanagan, Martin, 'The bloodbath: the 1945 VFL grand final,' 16 September 2006.

Forbes, Mark, 'Symbol of men's unconquered spirit, Brownlow joins our sacred relics,' *Age*, 21 August 2004.

Grant, Alan, 'Saints in World Wars. Legends of the Game—Peter Chitty'. Official Website of St Kilda Football Club.

Hobson, David, 'The Cowra Breakout', <anzacday.org.au/history. AWM>.

Lewis, Daniel, 'Sharman the showman is an official bloody legend,' *Sydney Morning Herald*, 18 April 2003.

Lyon, Karen, 'Changi champ won war within a war,' *Age*, 23 April 2005.

McGuinness, Marian, 'Prison Break in Changi,' *Sydney Morning Herald*, 9 November 2008.

Oliver, Pam, 'In peace and war: Japan and Australia before 1941', *Memento*, magazine of the National Archives of Australia, No. 1, 2009.

Probert, H. A., *Prison Industries*, New Zealand, 1988.

Richardson, Nick, 'Frontline footy mania,' *Herald Sun* Melbourne, 26 April 2001.

Soffer, Sam, 'Joining Army & Campaign in Malaya', Carl Johnson collection.

Wilson, Neil, 'War's footy legend', *Herald-Sun*, 21 August 2004.

Other

'Football Behind Bamboo'—*Football Life Magazine*, September 1969.

'The Fall of Singapore' supplement, *Weekend Australian*, 15–16 February 1992.

'Survival Japanese war horrors' (on nurse Phyllis Mary Erskin—obituary); *Telegraph*.–reproduced in the Elwood RSL magazine, December 2008.

'Victoria v The Rest', official Changi report of the final match 24 January 1943. (Chitty family archive.)

'Lifelong Captives: The Medical Legacy of POWs of the Japanese,' Dept of Veteran Affairs, 1990—Carl Johnson Archive.

'The lived experience of partners of ex-prisoners of war of the Japanese— a phenomenological study', by Betty Peters, January 1994 (Chitty family archive).

Pee, Kay, *The Death Railway & The Bridge on the River Kwai*, Kanchanaburi Publications, Kanchanaburi, 2006.

Trenoweth, John, 'Notes on Conditions in Thailand', Carl Johnson Collection.

'Wilfred (Chicken) Smallhorn: 1933 Brownlow Medallist', *Fitzroy-Brisbane Lions Historical Society Newsletter*, Vol. 1, 2006.

Acknowledgements

My thanks to the Chitty family, whose information, accessibility and encouragement were essential in researching and writing this book. Peter Chitty's wife Lilian was a valuable source. Her prodigious memory was an asset. Her sensitivity and humour gave depth and perspective to her husband's character and experiences. Son Lindsay and daughter Dawn from the early period of the 60-year Peter–Lilian marriage, and son Roger and daughter Ros from the latter period, gave their various perspectives on their parents. Peter's sister Nancy Pattison also demonstrated crystal clear recall from six decades ago. His last living brother Ken also provided stories and observations from the earlier family days which brought colour and humour.

Greg Thomas, the manager of Rolly Tasker's Australian Sailing Museum, was a thorough assistant and creative photographer on travels through Thailand, Burma, Singapore and Malaysia. His diligence and hard work were much appreciated, especially in trying conditions in the mountainous jungle areas of the Burma–Thai railway.

Staff at the Australian War Memorial and the National Archives in Canberra were as ever of more than helpful assistance, as were staff at museums at Kanchanaburi and Hellfire Pass in Thailand.

War historian Carl Johnson was of great help in directing me to many areas of research. Others to provide information and/or interviews were Lex Arthurton, Ron Barassi, Dr Geoffrey Barnett, John Barnett, Rod Beattie (who has a museum at Kanchanaburi), Tim Burstall, Helen Campbell, Dr Mickey Dewar, Charles Edwards, Paul Groenveld, Hedley Hatch, Neville Hendy, Colin Hutchinson, Kate Ingram, Joe Jameson, Frank Lemin, Len Lemke, Leon Levin, Dr. John Lynch, Paul Mishura, Jim Mitchell, Jim O'Farrel, Joe O'Farrel, Brian O'Shaughnessy, Bob Owen, Fred Seiker.

My thanks also to Hachette Australia publisher Matthew Kelly, who responded to the idea after hearing just the book's title. 'The Changi Brownlow' had a mystique and charm even before it was written.

Index

Prowse, Stewart Harvey 56, 336, 337
Pump, Sister Betty 73

Queen Mary 38, 42–5, 55

Radji Beach 144–7, 161
Rae, Vern 163
Raffles Hotel 58, 85
Raffles, Stamford 46
Rangoon 42, 68, 71, 79, 171, 188
Red Cross 83, 94, 115–16, 117, 128, 145, 266, 268, 279, 321
Regan, Frank 138–9
Richards, Rowley 294, 349
Richmond 55
River Kwai 179, 250, 258–9, 291, 302–3, 305, 315
Robertson, Lieutenant-Colonel J.C. 90
Rockingham Hospital 345–6
Roosevelt, President Franklin D. 65, 70
Royal Red Cross 137
rubber plantations 51, 110
Russia 65, 74
Russo-Japanese War 1904-05 22
Rutherglen FC 15

Saggers, Major A.E. 288–9
St Andrew's Cathedral 129, 138, 140, 142, 148
St Kilda 9, 15, 16–18, 53, 69, 202, 204
Saito, Commander 321
Sammons, Private Jack 101–2
Sanananda 241
Schneider, Major 181
Seiker, Fred 266–8, 273–4, 321–2, 346
Sekiguchi, Colonel 150, 151
Selarang barracks 1, 4, 148, 152, 154, 166, 180, 190, 195, 210–11, 224, 227, 316
sexually transmitted diseases 48
Shale, Captain Donald 114–15
Sharman, Jimmy 31–3

Shepherd, Private 310
Shimpei, Major-General Hattori 182
Singapore 41, 42, 44, 45–7, 50–1, 53, 57–8, 59, 63, 64, 65–6, 71–5, 99–134, 137–43, 150, 127, 138, 139, 294, 306, 313–14, 322, 326
Singapore AFC (Australian Football Club) 351
Singapore Herald 76
Sino-Japanese war 19
Sleeves, Allan 'Lofty' 277
Sloss, Bruce 191
Smallhorn, Wilfred 'Chicken' 5–6, 7, 8, 16–17, 53–5, 164, 191, 193–4, 198, 206, 228, 229, 230, 233, 234, 235, 236, 237, 239, 240, 279
Smerdon, Jack 'Swanee' 287
Snowy Mountain Range 11
Solomon Islands 176, 178, 209
Songkhram, Phibin 74
Songkurai 276, 277, 284, 286, 288, 289, 290
Soryu 187
South Melbourne FC (Swans) 17–18, 191, 327, 329–34
Sparks, Private Roy 114–15
Spokes, Umpire 331
Sporting Globe 58
Sri Lanka *see* Ceylon
Stahl, Captain Fred 274
Stalag VIIA 67
Stalag XVIIIA 59, 134
Stewart, Colonel Duncan 103
Straits of Malacca 42, 127, 135
Sultan of Johor 63, 108
Sutton, Judge Leonard E.B. 30
Sydney Harbour 184–6, 189
Syonan Times 157–8, 183, 240, 307

Takanun camp 262, 278
Tamarkan camp 259, 315
Tamjoa camp 263
Tarsau base camp 252, 255
Tasker, Rolly 192
Taylor, Brigadier H.B.114, 164
Taylor, John 294